Mr. Antiques'

Basic Book of

Antiques

4th Edition

George Michael

Published by

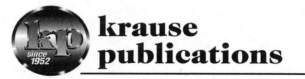

krause
publications

700 E. State Street • Iola, WI 54990-0001
Telephone: 715/445-2214
Web: www.krause.com

Please call or write for our free catalog of publications.
Our toll-free number to place an order or obtain a free catalog is 800-258-0929
or please use our regular business telephone 715-445-2214.

Library of Congress Catalog Number: 2001099536
ISBN: 0-87349-413-X

Printed in the United States of America

TABLE OF CONTENTS

CHAPTER TWO: GLASS 109

CHAPTER THREE: CERAMICS 145

CHAPTER FOUR: METALWORK 223

CHAPTER FIVE: DECORATIVE ART 265

PREFACE

Those of us who are World War II veterans have always held Winston Churchill in high regard. During the war, one of his aides noticed that the prime minister utilized every bathroom he passed. When asked about this, as to whether he had a kidney problem, he stated, "You should always go when you can; you might not be able to go when you want."

I transposed this into a very important tenet in my life; one should always take advantage of an opportunity; the opportunity may never again be presented.

Those involved in collecting can recall times when they have seen something in a shop, examined it and left, wanting more time to consider its purchase with the plan to return tomorrow, if needed, to pick it up. I recall a sign seen in a shop in Edmonds, Washington, several years ago— "The antique you are looking at now that you are planning to come back to buy tomorrow, will be sold today to a person who saw it yesterday." Many items are passed by at an auction, with the bidder later regretting not going higher on it. My old traveling partner, Frank Rowe, said, "When you're out traveling around, you should always buy something to pay for your gas." That was when gas sold for 25 cents a gallon. I recall his words very well when going to an auction or a show. Accept the challenge and see how well you do with your new courage.

It would be impossible to list my many teachers. I learned from scholars as well as scoundrels. In the early days, the latter would sell me items and after receiving the money would proceed to tell me all the things that were wrong with what I just bought. I think they liked me and wanted to help teach, but wanted to be paid for doing it. My PBS-TV programs taped from the 1960s into the 1980s brought me in contact with many scholars as well as a multitude of collectors who gave freely of their knowledge and experiences. Special thanks must go to the late Richard Carter Barret, the former director/curator of the Bennington (VT) Museum. He delighted in uncovering information that would destroy previously accepted "facts", much to the consternation of the "antiques" fraternity. Others who were of great help—some are still living—are Ray Barlow, Ken Wilson, former director of collections at the Henry Ford Museum, Dorothy Lee Jones, director of the Jones Museum of Glass and Ceramics at Douglas Hill, Maine; Robert Bryden of the Pairpoint Company, Carl U. Fauster, director of the Antique and Historic Glass Foundation; Dr. H.A. Crosby Forbes, director of the Museum of the America China Trade; Eric de Jonge, chief curator at the William Penn Museum in Harrisburg; Lowell Innes, Charles Montgomery, Philip Hammerslough, Sonia Paine, Marika; Tom Williams, Roger Bacon, Mary Earle Gould, and Ruth and Kenneth Wakefield, of Sandwich glass fame. Over 300 TV shows were made, which could preclude my listing all those who contributed the information contained in this writing.

Experience proves that the functional item is best to collect. Always, there is a ready market for chairs, tables, chests, china and silver services, oil paintings and prints for decoration; rugs, lighting devices, and the like. Many decorative objects have risen in value; more because of the maker and rarity than as a necessity in the home.

Dealers and auctioneers welcomed the acceptance of twentieth century collectibles. This provided the spark for the many flea and antiques markets, which appeared coast to coast. The former were created so anyone could exhibit, whereas the latter featured dealers who were invited by the promoter to create a balanced show. The 1960s witnessed the appearance of the group shops, which allowed more freedom for dealers to be out buying. Antiquing became a twelve-month business. More attention was given to encouraging the gift of antiques rather than new items for birthdays and Christmas—something unheard of but a few years before.

The rise in the number of auction galleries attests to this method of marketing. The major galleries proved that the majority of the larger estates are liquidated by auction. The estate and farm auctions, which have always been with us, were stimulated by this new interest in collecting on the part of young and old, alike. The treasures from these old places are dwindling, but somehow keep appearing, leading many to pursue the hidden rarity.

Many who collect eventually begin wheeling and dealing. They can upgrade in this manner and at the same time satisfy the gambling urge which is in most of us. In your travels, most likely information in this book will help you determine whether you should buy an item, and will reward you, which will make reading this book worthwhile.

George Michael
Merrimack, NH

ABOUT THE PICTURES AND PRICES

Most of the pictures in this book are of museum quality, but many are not. Prices are suggested on many items, but are not included for museum or private collection items. Those quoted reflect the market in the Northeast section of the country from Pennsylvania through New England. Provincial tastes limit the interest in antiques and collectibles across the country. Therefore, one shot pricing for the entire country is not practical. Make sure to research trends in the area where you are going to make a purchase and where you might chose to sell an item later.

Gilbert, rosewood veneer, 8-day mantel clock, c. 1860.

Shoenhut ringmaster, part of a circus, c. 1920s.

Shaker chest, c. 1850-1860, Enfield, Connecticut.

Introduction

HOW TO ENJOY COLLECTING

If you purchased this book with the intention of learning something about antiques and how to collect and enjoy them, you have just embarked on one of the most interesting adventures in your life. There is no mystery to antiquing. Newcomers to the field are fascinated by the actions and know-how of the old timers in the game. They do not realize that once they too were taking the plunge which would involve them in a business which combines a form of gambling, suspense, intrigue, and adventure, which is really quite harmless in its nature. Yet, it is very rewarding to those who have the fortitude to stick it out and learn the rules.

Before getting involved, you must judge how deeply you want to get into the nitty gritty of antiquing, and then try to hold the line in conformance with your plans. Some have likened the antiques business to a disease which gradually possesses you, drawing you in deeper until there is no retreat or escape, but do not let this deter you. Along the way you will have lots of fun, meet many interesting people, win a little, lose a little, and above all, come away with at least one very important advantage—you will be more aware of the beauty in art and antique objects. If this awareness is the only profit you receive, you will be well rewarded.

This quality of "awareness" is the most important asset you can have in the antiques field. Some people are born with it—they have an affinity for the arts and can translate and relate their feelings to them quite easily. Others have to acquire this affinity through study and hard work. Still others acquire it by buying and selling. My motto has always been, "The more rapidly you lose money on antiques, the more rapidly you learn about them. You never forget your lessons."

Everyone experiences a certain amount of this type of learning. No matter how long people remain in the antiques business, they find they make occasional mistakes. In many cases buying and selling is based on personal judgment alone, since one-of-a-kind items keep turning up, and you must gamble on your feelings toward the piece. Frank Rowe once told me after such a losing experience, "When you find you have made a mistake, sell out, and get out." My father once told me, "You make your money when you buy, not when you sell; goods well bought are half sold." I keep this in mind at all times, but there are many occasions when factors such as a possible eventual buyer, personal emotion for the piece, or just the gambling spirit make me plunge into items which later prove to be duds. A dealer once remarked about one of his mistakes, "I showed it to the world, and nobody wants it." This is why it is so important that you judge the type of collector-dealer you want to be, before you get involved in serious buying and selling.

There is no separation between collecting and dealing. Even though you may not have a shop with a shingle hanging out front stating that you are in the antiques business, you will find that before long you will be buying and selling to upgrade your collection. Items bought when money was tight will eventually give way to better items acquired through good buys or during a period of more affluence. This swapping off can make you money as well as providing an outlet for any gambling instincts you have, and will give you the satisfaction of creating a collection of which you can be proud.

Everyone has an instinct to collect something, and this urge can be directed in several ways. First, there are those who collect to impress their friends with something of interest or beauty, which can also be used as decoration. There are those who collect only functional items, such as chairs, tables, chests of drawers, and beds, and those who collect decorative pieces like oils, glass, and fine porcelain. Others combine their desire to enjoy the items they buy with the idea of treating them as an investment, with liquidation for a profit in the future. Then there is the final category of people who are outright dealers, those who buy and sell for profit alone, along with the pleasure of having quality items pass through their hands. The person who stuffs cupboards full of creamers or salt and pepper shakers is a delight to auctioneers and deal-

ers who otherwise would not know what to do with many of the items available for sale. Collections of this type are mostly dust collectors, and unless they are of really high quality can represent only the satisfaction of a squirrel-like need to stuff something away.

People who collect to impress their friends are usually affluent people who have little thought of buying, selling, or upgrading their pieces. They collect art for art's sake and enjoy it on that level, which is a very good one if you can afford it.

Those who collect functional items probably make up the greatest proportion of buyers today. People have learned that if you are going to buy a table, chairs, chest, etc., it is much more sensible to buy old than new. New furniture is worth about half its price when it is delivered to your home, and it continues to depreciate rapidly. Good antique furniture will almost always rise in value, and you can usual sell it at a good profit if necessary. In the meantime, you can enjoy the pieces, whether they

Everyone has an instinct to collect something.

are furniture or decorative, since all of them have a much warmer and more comfortable look because of the patina which comes with age.

Those who treat antiques as an investment are wise in their choice. We are continually made aware of fantastic increases in value as auction sale prices are reported. Quality antiques, have always risen in value faster than stocks, and provide a much greater return than bank interest. If you buy quality, you need have little fear of a decline in value. It is much more pleasurable to enjoy a fine oil painting on the wall than it is to read figures in a bank book, especially with the realization that the painting is increasing in value much more rapidly than your bank account. Quality items can always be liquidated rapidly for cash, so they represent a very fluid form of capital investment.

People who buy and sell as dealers are the ones who do most of the work acquiring good antiques for those who want them. They are the ones who

Auctions are a way of life in America. Most important is the period before it begins—inspection time—when one should inspect everything and have questions answered about the items going up for sale.

scrounge about in attics, barns, and cellars and spend long hours at auctions, shows, and flea markets, searching out the means to their living. It is a rather thankless job in many respects, but the rewards are more than financial, and you must be willing to spend long hours. Many dealers have to empty attics, which are roasting hot from the summer sun and no ventilation. Others have to paw through mountains of rusty junk in garages and barns, often risking their lives by lowering pieces down from haylofts. The best buys at flea markets are made when the dealers are setting up, sometimes as early as 6:00 A.M. and this means rising very early to be there for the first crack at the new merchandise when it is being unwrapped. Dealers will often spend long hours staffing booths at shows and flea markets as well as running a shop at home. You have to be quite dedicated to the field to be a dealer—you will earn everything you work for, but the work will be fun.

Perhaps the greatest introduction to antiques is professional instruction in the field in which you are interested. This is very important in developing the most important attribute in the business—being "aware" of what you see. If you want to specialize in collecting ceramics, it would be advisable to take an eight-week pottery course at whichever local school, university, arts and science center, or historical society sponsors one. Although you may never become a fancy or recognized potter, at least you will learn the makeup of ceramics, recognize the problems faced in making and decorating such pieces, and acquire a feeling for quality. And when you begin collecting, it will not be difficult for you to separate the good from the bad. This advice also applies to those who are interested in furniture, oil painting, pewter, brass, silver, copper, iron, jewelry, sewing, and rug making, or any other craft. Your courses of instruction will give you a better appreciation of the problems faced by an artist, and this will result in your being better able to judge quality work.

Above all, read the many good books available and become a frequent visitor to museums and restorations in order to see, firsthand, the items in which you are interested. An excellent place to begin your education is at an auction—you can sit and listen to the auctioneer describe the pieces sold, you can note the interest and activity in bidding, and you can learn the price at which representative pieces sell. Go to good shows and shops

Go to good shows and shops and talk with the dealers.

and talk with the dealers. You will find them friendly, interesting, and full of information. They are business people who want to cultivate you as a buyer and friend. The old clichés, which deal with the reliability of dealers and auctioneers, are as dead as dodo birds. There are scoundrels in every business—the antiques business should not be singled out as a particular area in which many of them are active. I find that dealers and auctioneers arc much more reliable to do business with than people in private homes who often could care less if they never saw you again. The dealers and auctioneers want you to come back and they will treat you as a valued customer if you are responsible in your business dealings with them.

One of the most confusing aspects of the antiques business is determining just what constitutes an antique. There are many descriptions, but perhaps the following will clear up some misconceptions. In my view, an antique is an art object that is wholly or partially handmade. We buy the work of an artisan's hands and appreciate the feeling, depth, and dimension put into the work. This applies to all fields of art—furniture, glass, paint-ings, ceramics, silver, pewter, and the rest. One can draw a comparison with an oil painting which has depth, dimension, and feeling and says something to us when we look at it. One can purchase a printed colored picture and hang it as a wall decoration as well, but one can see instantly that the print stamped out by a machine cannot compare with the painting done by hand. This applies to all fields of the decorative arts as well. Quality is achieved only by handwork. Those items made by machine must fall into the collectibles category.

We must also talk about quality, as handwork alone is not enough. Quality is made up of three things—good taste, good design, and good construction. Taste includes form, proportion, color, and decoration. The form of any piece must be pleasing to the eye—such as the shape of a teapot, its handle, legs, cover, and finial. Proportions must be harmonious. Color is important, not only in glass and ceramics, but in the patina acquired by wood, brass, silver, pewter, etc. Early painted furniture must exhibit color that has aged naturally. In American furniture, decoration should enhance, not overpower, a piece.

Rare tin toy, surrey with a fringe on top. Sold in New Hampshire in 1969 for $250. A really fine example complete with horse and driver. I have not seen one since.

Cranberry glass Jack-in-pulpit vase.

Anything worn by a famous movie star in an equally famous movie will command big dollars. Here is Ingrid Bergman's armor from Joan of Arc.

18th century mahogany tea table, with label of Thomas Burling, New York, c. 1870. One will note the birdcage construction below the dish top. Value: $20,000-$25,000

When one looks at the French Louis furniture, the rococo carving meets the eye before the body on which it is done. This is all right for French and other continental furniture, but is not accepted as well on our native work.

Purity of design is most important. Furniture was the largest item in the home, so the decorative arts of any period were designed to conform to the furniture. Hence our design periods, which are indicated in the furniture chapter, outline the span of years in which particular designs were most popular. As the artisans moved from one style to the next, many pieces were created with features from two or more periods, creating what we call transitional furniture. The purist will not want it, as it is not pure in design.

The last requirement is good workmanship. Whoever creates the work must do it well. This sets the fine artisan apart from the untrained. All these features must be in harmony to create quality antiques. Your awareness of these rules will grow as you go from auction to auction, shop to shop, and show to show. Suddenly objects will speak to you rapidly—you will recognize quality items at a glance, where once you needed to study them.

I have not mentioned age. Most think that an item a hundred years or older is an antique. This rule was established back in 1930, only to determine if duty had to be paid on purchases made overseas. The year 1830 was selected because at that time, machines began taking over many of the chores for artisans. The year 1830 was used as the determining date until 1966, when President Johnson signed a law, which uses the 100-year rule not to designate an antique, but rather to indicate when duty should be paid. In other words, if you leave the country for more than 48 hours and return with something more than a hundred years old, you will not be required to pay duty. This does not necessarily mean that the item is an antique.

Some prized items such as pressed glass (see Chapter Two) have value in the context of rarity and design. Much handwork was involved in making pressed glass. Some items, such as mechanical banks, have risen greatly in value, but only because they are rare and perform an interesting function. On the whole, you will find the handmade item is much more desired than its machine-made counterpart.

At the beginning of the industrial age, in the 1820s, manufacturers found that machines could turn out products more rapidly and were willing to sacrifice quality for speed and quantity to satisfy growing demand. In rural regions, however, away from the seaports and large cities, we know that many relied on handcraftsmanship as late as the period of the American War Between the States, as most could not afford the new machinery and perhaps they did not want to use it either. Handcraftsmanship has never died—it is still with us today.

A paperweight made by Domenick Labino at his home in Ohio in the 1970s will command far more money than most made in the last century. When the Dedham (Mass.) Pottery closed in 1948, you could have bought fine handmade and hand-decorated plates there, for but a few dollars; today most are worth hundreds. The Dorchester Pottery, near Boston, closed its doors in 1978. Its work is commanding many dollars more than much older work. The famed Mount Washington-Pairpoint Factory of New Bedford, Mass., closed in 1958, left behind a heritage of glass, porcelain, and silver, which is eagerly sought by collectors. These are but a few examples showing that age alone has little effect on the desirability and price of antiques.

Something that was a monstrosity 200 years ago may be just an older monstrosity today. Age is a factor that affects the law of supply and demand. The work of a fine eighteenth-century cabinet-maker is valuable not just because it is 200 years old, but because of the quality which creates desirability. This is what sets the price—desirability, not how old it is.

If the piece meets the requirements of being handmade and of good quality, one cannot always be sure it is worth more than contemporary work. I applaud collecting the work of today as we enjoy the creations of artisans whose skills are equal to, or even better than, those of artisans who worked years ago. The handmade items of today can very well be the desired antiques of tomorrow. Many museums are adding contemporary work to their collections now, rather than waiting years when the price most surely will be higher. If your grandfather had purchased a Winslow Homer back when they were selling for $50, you would be a very happy heir, today. A lot of what is collected today was saved by chance. Many pieces were thrown in the dump or disposed of in other ways. Today, educated as we are in the field of collecting, we can call the shots much better on what will survive into the future as desirable items.

Folk Art Oil on canvas by John Neill, Ogunquit, ME. Neill was a fixture at Perkins Cove, selling paintings from a beat up old Plymouth vehicle, after World War II until the early 1990s, when he passed away. There is growing interest in Neill's paintings. This, of lobster traps at Perkins Cove is perhaps one of his best. Value: $700-$1,000

Educated collecting is a little like betting on a horse race by studying the past performance of the participants. You should check on the awards and recognition won by the artist, and check each particular work in the light of good taste, good design, and good construction. You can then visualize if it meets what you feel will be the desires of collectors in the future, since they will be little changed from what they are today as far as art appreciation is concerned. You can then begin buying the works of those you feel meet the test with the hope the artist will someday "arrive" and be recognized, thus, making his works more desirable. In the meantime, most such investments are small when compared to investing in antiques, and the items can be enjoyed just as much in your home. Whether the artist "arrives" really isn't of great importance as long as you enjoy his work. You can only hope for the other.

When collecting either antiques or contemporary work, insist on all the documentation of the piece which is available. The past history of ownership of an old item can help in tracing its maker

someday. Insist that present-day artists sign their work in some manner, and preserve this documentation. We must begin creating birth certificates for our antiques and collectibles so research on them in the future will be made easier. It also helps to raise the value when works can be traced to important craftsmen as well as important owners. Borrowing an etching pencil from your local police department to inscribe your social security number on your valued possessions is becoming popular today. This should not hurt the value of it if the number is put in an inconspicuous place, and it will aid in identification and help curb the increasing wave of fine arts thefts. The name of the maker can be put on with the same etching pencil if need be.

Collecting antiques should be fun and owning them should be even more pleasurable. Yet there are very few people who really know how to enjoy antiques. Many people worry about them because of their value and the thought of possible fire and theft is always on their minds. If you cannot enjoy an antique, you should sell it to

Learn, look, and examine.

someone who can. If you find that any items are a source of concern when you are away from your home, or when there are children about, it is high time you sold them. Some people are so concerned that they hire "antiques sitters" as a protection when they leave their homes. This defeats the idea of enjoyment and if you are going to get this involved with material possessions, think twice before embarking on a collection. You should have your items appraised. Use the appraisal to insure them under a less expensive fine arts policy, and then let your insurance agent worry about them when you are away. This is why you are paying for insurance.

At the back of this book is a bibliography of the latest available books, which will be of great help to you in pursing further information and instruction in your chosen phase of antiquing. This book is intended as an introduction to the identification, collection, and enjoyment of antiques and collectibles. I hope it lays a good groundwork for you to use in the future. Above all, if I have been able to make you more aware of what you are doing and have shown how to judge a piece in the light of its contemporaries, I feel I have accomplished this goal. Personal tastes in antiques and appreciation of them differ sharply. Just as you would not attempt to buy such a personal thing as clothing for another, neither can you presume you know his artistic tastes, since these may vary greatly from yours. Learn, look, and examine. Do not be casual in your appraisal, as many good pieces are passed over because of this.

The possible fields for antiques and memorabilia collecting are limitless. Let your eye be your guide to quality, and let your experience at shows, auctions, and flea markets be your guide to values. You must be immersed in the business to buy and sell wisely—a part-time, on-again/off-again collector will not keep himself advised sufficiently to do well at it. Talk to dealers and collectors in the field in which you are interested. Go to museums to see the objects on display and study their characteristics. Above all, read good books on the subject. You will find that there is a wealth of material that will help you, if you will only seek it out.

Pedal-operated metal automobile, whose design dates it to the early 20th century.

Chapter One

FURNITURE

Introduction

Historical Overview

To attempt to explain the various details that must be studied in furniture of all areas would require space far beyond the bounds of this book. Its purpose is to make you "aware" of what you see. You must study history, to gain the knowledge of when the first example of a style or period was produced.

In seventeenth-century America we managed to keep abreast of the motherland in design, since commerce brought with it manufactured items, which could be copied. Design books became plentiful in the middle of the eighteenth century,

Carved blanket or dower chests of this type were made in the 17th century. The carving and decoration heighten the value. A concentration of these seems to have been made in the Hadley, Massachusetts to Connecticut area. However, it is known they were made in Boston and elsewhere.

and we were faithful in following these, so that the settlers here could live in the manner of their forbearers. The original thirteen colonies were the center of production until about 1820. The colonization beyond into Ohio, Indiana, Illinois, and the Louisiana Purchase (which became U.S. property in 1803) meant that craftsman of all kinds helped in creating new settlements. It is unlikely that highly styled furniture would have been made until affluence was there to support it. You must content yourself with the study of the country pieces made during this time, gauging when the first real prosperity hit a community and created wealthy patrons who would demand the latest and best. The machine age began at about this time, and with the exception of those who still worked apart from modern civilization with hand tools, you may run into the mass production pieces which saturated the country—especially after the railroads came in and made mass distribution possible.

An unusual situation occasionally comes about because of an event in history. At the time of the Revolution, Connecticut owned a strip of land that extended from its western border all the way to what is now Ohio. Congress later granted parts of this land to New York and Pennsylvania as it intersected their borders and then granted new land at no charge to the Connecticut residents who wanted to pack up and move West. This land in the northern Ohio area is now known as the Western Reserve. Much fine Connecticut and other New England furniture can be found in this part of Ohio, since it was taken there early in the nineteenth century. Some claim the first Hitchcock-style chair was made in Ohio, but research shows it more likely was made up of parts furnished by Lambert Hitchcock from his factory in

Connecticut. He is known to have made chair parts and shipped them unassembled from about 1815 to 1825, when he decided to make complete chairs at his factory in Riverton. Much early Ohio furniture has the look of New England, as it was made by the Connecticut craftsmen who moved there.

Pennsylvania was dominated by a fine school of workmen who worked in strict adherence to English design. This work reached its greatest heights during the Chippendale era, and some feel the finest work in this country was done there and then. Baltimore housed many fine craftsmen who gave birth to ideas in style and veneering, which were soon copied all over the colonies. One has but to see the elegant inlay work, the dainty Pembroke tables, and the magnificent banquet tables to realize how important Baltimore was as a center of fine furniture. Charleston and Annapolis had the wealthy clients a community needs to inspire great cabinetry, and the amount of it left in those areas speaks for itself. A trip to the area's museums and historic homes is highly recommended for further study of this work.

The growing ports of Mobile and New Orleans were definitely influenced by the French and Spanish furniture and artifacts that were easily imported over the sea—a far easier method than overland transport in those days. It inspired local cabinetry in the same style, and further study is now in progress to document such work.

We have read that John Alden was our first cabinetmaker—whether this is true or not is academic. What is most apparent is that if the Mayflower had

Design Periods in America	
Pilgrim	1620-1670
Jacobean	1670-1694
William and Mary	1694-1710
Queen Mary	1710-1750
Chippendale	1750-1775
Federal	
Hepplewhite	1775-1800
Sheraton	1795-1830
Empire	1810-1870
Victorian	1840-1870
Renaissance	
Revival Eastlake	1870-1890
Mission	1890-1920
Art Noveau	1895-1920
Art Deco	1920-1940

been loaded with all the furniture and artifacts attributed to it, it could never have left the dock. The Pilgrims came with the barest of necessities and it is unlikely there was any furniture aboard. Actually, not much of our seventeenth-century furniture has survived. Most was made from easily worked pine and some from the plentiful oak, birch, and maple. I refer to the early part of the century as the Pilgrim period, for want of a better designation. Furniture was quite crude, yet functional. More time was needed for tilling the soil and hunting than for decoration of household artifacts. Much early furniture has probably been lost through attrition, and over the years was just thrown out as old and out of style. Most of what has survived has been snatched up by museums and for use in restored homes.

Toward the latter part of the century (at the time of the restoration in the 1660s) we were influenced by the prevailing English Jacobean styles of heavily turned oak furniture, and its counterpart was made here. The rest of the periods came under the influence of cabinetmakers who worked independently. Although some were fortunate enough to have their names attached to the styles in which they worked, and influenced cabinetry on both sides of the ocean.

Bible boxes were in most homes, as owners would lock up this precious book despite the fact most felt thieves would not steal a bible. They were made of pine and hard woods. Value: $300-$500

Identifying Furniture Style Periods

Do Your Legwork

Throughout furniture identification we see the importance of leg design in each period. This is perhaps the most important feature for rapid identification. I have explained these leg stylings with accompanying illustrations and further explanation of design techniques. We must be careful in using the word "style" as there is evidence that cabinetmakers, especially in the countryside, refused to let go of some designs and continued to work in them long after new styles came into popular use. It is best to refer to a piece as being of "Queen Anne-style" since we know that such pieces were made almost until the nineteenth century, though the most popular years for it were during the first half of the eighteenth century. Some changes in methods of workmanship might give an indication as to whether the piece is early or late, but sometimes this type of attribution can be hazardous.

Leg designs graduated from the heavily turned ball-type construction to the more graceful, yet ruggedly designed William and Mary legs, whose turnings were influenced by Dutch design. Early in the eighteenth century, at the time of Queen Anne,

William and Mary turnip foot chest, Massachusetts, c. 1700. Original teardrop pulls and brasses. Value: $5,000-$7,000

the graceful cabriole leg and varied type pad feet were conceived as a break away to light and airy furniture, more in keeping with the delicate monarch herself. There are many leg variations in this period more fully explained in the illustrations.

Noted cabinetmaker Thomas Chippendale was the son of a cabinetmaker, and his son followed in his footsteps as well. He was influenced by his contemporaries and freely copied their ideas. His first work, *Cabinetmaker's Guide,* published in 1754, influenced work on both sides of the Atlantic for many years. In fact, his designs are the most reproduced today. Names such as Matthias Lock, Batty Langley, and Sir William Chambers are lesser known to collectors, yet all pioneered forms adapted by Chippendale for which he was credited.

Chippendale continued to use the cabriole leg, but gave it a new look with a ball and talon or ball and claw foot. The idea for the claws embracing the ball came from the Orient, where it was symbolic of a dragon's claws encompassing the earth. Most refer to this as the "city-style" Chippendale, whereas the simpler country pieces featured nothing more than cutout boards, often called a bracket

Swing-leg game tables are popular. When one sees five legs, it is not from New England. This Chippendale table features the ball and talon feet on the cabriole legs; a changeover from the plain Queen Anne feet. If the feet have bird talons, they are ball and talon. If they have animal claws or paws, they are ball and claw.

It is common knowledge that in cased pieces of the 18th century, all four legs should be alike. Note this strange combination, with the rear legs pointing in the same direction as the front.

Leg Styles at a Glance

William and Mary period leg, c. 1700, with trumpet turning and stretcher.

Ogee leg, which appeared late in the eighteenth century, so named from the ogee curved molding, which was popular at the time.

Cabriole leg with pad, duck or Dutch foot. This type of leg appeared c. 1715 in England. A shorter version, which appears on many cased pieces, is called a bandy leg.

Square tapered leg, a mark of the Hepplewhite period, c. 1775–1800, though used later in America.

Bandy leg with ball and talon foot, c. 1750–1775, Chippendale.

Bracket base, c. 1750–1775, Chippendale, made simply from cut-out boards. Most country cased pieces feature this type of base.

Simple turned leg of the Sheraton period in America, c. 1800–1830.

Fancy turned and reeded leg, Sheraton period, c. 1800–1830. From the last turning there should be at least 3″ extending to the floor.

Outswept legs in Empire style, most often associated with American cabinetmaker Duncan Phyfe, c. 1820–1840.

Chair with sabre leg, so named because of the curve resembling a sabre, c. 1830–1840.

base, for legs. This can be found on cased pieces, such as chests, desks, bookcases, and the like. There are short cabriole legs with talons or claw feet, and these are referred to as bandy legs. These designs lasted until about the time of the American Revolution, though some country cabinetmakers worked with them until the new design books found their way to the rural areas.

The Hepplewhite period is characterized by the simple square tapered leg, which many feel is the purest in design. These are found on chairs, tables, and some of the delicate cased pieces, such as a lady's secretary. The large cased pieces are

Four graduated-drawer chest, New Hampshire, with French legs. Hepplewhite period. Case in mahogany; Birdseye-maple drawer veneer, c. 1800-1815. Value: $6,000-$8,000

Hepplewhite banquet table with bellflower inlay on the legs. The leaves drop to the center and another basic drop-leaf table can be inserted to lengthen it. Late 18th century, mahogany.

equipped with French legs. These are the only two legs identified for this period.

Leg heights are important in all pieces of furniture. Many were damaged in careless handling; others may have been left on dirt floors in cellars, and some were too tall for their new surroundings, so out would come a saw to take them down to size or even them off. This hurts a piece of furniture, as the change is quite visible to the eye, which is interested in good proportion. There are no set

Porringer-top worktable, Connecticut, cherry. The legs and feet mark the period as 18th century. Value: $1,200-$1,800

rules for the height and width of most furniture, so you must judge the piece with your eye—either the proportion is pleasing, or it isn't. You may find evidence of new wood where the saw has been at work. The cutting may be very evident unless the legs are cut properly at the termination of a turning. No one can help you on this, so use your own judgment and before long, your eye will help you detect tampering.

Marquetry and Veneer

Not long ago, the public was indoctrinated with the idea that the only good furniture was that made of solid wood. The horrible veneering of walnut and oak on our twentieth-century furniture gave rise to this idea. With older antiques, however, you will find that veneered pieces will usually command a higher price than solid wood. In the Queen Anne and Chippendale periods, when veneering was at a minimum, there are naturally little comparisons to be made. The Federal period brought with it a revival of this work, and in this era comparative pieces are valued according to the beauty and workmanship in them—not on whether they are veneered. The striking figured maple and birch most often used made furniture works of art, not just functional pieces. In this respect, I feel that Federal period furniture is still highly underrated today, and before long will, in many instances, surpass the value of comparative pieces from the preceding periods. Age alone does not make a desired antique. Artistic beauty, as a result of fine handcraftsmanship, will become more and more of a deciding factor in value. We are at the threshold of this renaissance now; so Federal furniture represents a much better buy for investment than the furniture which preceded it.

In American furniture, it is unlikely that one will find marquetry work in the Queen Anne and Chippendale periods. Some early Queen Anne pieces are veneered, but those I have examined, especially in northeastern Massachusetts and southern New Hampshire, show evidence that they are English. There must be exceptions, but in my long experience, I haven't seen one to convince me it is American. However, George Hepplewhite in his *Cabinetmaker and Upholsterer's Guide* freely used marquetry (veneering and inlay) to beautify his pieces. In America, eighteenth-century furniture is more beautiful with the highly grained woods veneered to dress it up. Nowhere did this style reach greater heights of expression than in the northeastern section of the country, where such woods were plentiful. Fine figured maple furniture was found as far south as Pennsylvania and west to Ohio. The ultimate work seems to have been done during this period in the Boston, Massachusetts to Portsmouth, New Hampshire region, where classic pieces were made to satisfy the retiring captains, ship owners, and wealthy merchants along the seacoast.

Charles Montgomery in his *Federal Furniture of the Federal Period* (Viking) indicates that one should be careful in indicating that a wood used for veneering in American furniture is satinwood. While he was director of Henry Francis DuPont's Winterthur Museum in Delaware, he had samples of veneer chemically analyzed. No satinwood was found. Practically all of the furniture was decorated with figured birch, one of the many maple varieties, holly, or, in some cases aspen. Though satinwood was used in foreign furniture, it was not in favor with American cabinetmakers. This is largely because satinwood comes from the Caribbean and was expensive to import. Also, it does not have the striking graining of North American wood.

Separate shops were set up to make inlay and veneer woods. These were sold to many cabinetmakers in the same area. Such marquetry may help confirm attribution to a maker, but cannot be used as the only guide.

In some pieces, the woods have been shaded to a black color to highlight the design. This was done by toasting the pieces of wood in hot sand to acquire the desired tonal quality. Few cabinetmakers had the time to devote to such specialized work, and were very happy to have someone else do it.

Construction and Design

Bowfront chests were constructed in a manner that made it impossible for them to lose their shape. First, three or four two-by-six-inch pieces of lumber were stacked one atop the other, the length of the drawer. The boards were then glued together with animal glues, after which the craftsman outlined the curve of the drawer front on the top boards, cutting the front in the exact shape desired. Because there is no stress on the wood, it never attempts to straighten itself. The front was then veneered with the desired wood. To determine that a chest is an early piece, look at the backside of the drawer front: the lines of the

Tiger-maple veneer on the drawers of this bow front Hepplewhite chest enhances its looks and value. Case in mahogany-stained birch, Massachusetts, c. 1800. Value: $4,500-$6,000

A very clean-lined Queen Anne chair of the early 18th century. Note that during this, and the following Chippendale period, American side chairs must have slip seats. If a chair is upholstered over the frame, it could be a bad job done on an American chair, or one which comes from overseas. Sold for $1,550.

several planks glued one atop the other are very evident. If they are not, the piece is probably not of the pre-1830 period.

Chairs became quite comfortable in the eighteenth century and the upholstered wingback with overstuffed cushions was the rule. To be proper, American side chairs of the Queen Anne and Chippendale periods should feature removable slip seats. If one is upholstered around the framing, so that the seat cannot be removed, it is either European or a reproduction. Often, one will see an American chair of these periods authentic in every detail except the slip seat, which may have been reupholstered years later and done improperly. (I have seen this in several major museums.) Removing upholstery will leave tack holes around the frame; so most slip seats are left alone.

Backs of side chairs may be shaped in a "spoon" fashion for greater comfort. Others may feature a split spindle or banister back, which is nothing more than a combination of upright

Design Periods in England

Until the middle of the eighteenth century, the names of furniture styles and periods had been taken from those of monarchs. Actually, most dealers in the British Isles still identify eras according to the ruler's name at the time. The following chart will help if you wish to do the same.

Elizabeth I	**1558-1603**
James 1	**1603-1625**
Charles I	**1625-1649**
The Cromwells	**1649-1660**
Charles II	**1660-1685**
James II	**1685-1689**
William III	**1689-1702**
Anne	**1702-1714**
George I	**1714-1727**
George II	**1727-1760**
George III	**1760-1820**
George IV	**1820-1830**
William IV	**1830-1837**
Victoria	**1837-1901**

(George, The Prince of Wales, became Regent in 1820 at the time of his father's great illness.)

Hudson Valley Queen Anne chair, painted black. The pad, duck, or Dutch feet (take your pick), appeared on this early 18th century furniture. Note the bold baluster turnings on the front rail.

supports. Drop-leaf tables were very popular as they conserved space. The cabriole leg was the rule in fancy furniture. Some of these legs appear on late Queen Anne furniture, though most are ascribed to Chippendale. One must identify what surrounds the ball before identifying its type. Those with animal claws or hairy paws may be identified as ball and claw, but when surrounded by birds' talons, the proper designation is ball and talon.

During the Queen Anne time, the English gradually did away with pegging the joints, whereas American craftsmen pegged into the beginning of the nineteenth-century. Dovetail joints in cases and drawers were more widely spaced than those of later years. Pine was most often the secondary wood used in America, whereas deal or other soft wood not native to our

Queen Anne mahogany drop leaf table, New England, 18th century. Sold at Butterfields in San Francisco, March 24, 1993, for $19,800.

shores appears in the English furniture. Little walnut was used in England at the time, as blight had hit the trees in France, where most of them grew. Perhaps the most telling feature is the width of the boards used in drawer bottoms and on the backs of cased pieces and the direction in which they run. England had long before run out of wide boards, as their trees had suffered indiscriminate cutting for centuries. As a result, they used two or three boards to make up a drawer bottom, with the grain running from front to rear in the drawer. The Americans still had huge pine boards available and usually used a single piece with the grain running from end to end. These would be chamfered or chiseled down at the edges and slid into slots in the drawer sides and front. Also, most English case work has the backboards running vertically, while the Americans ran them horizontally. Some vertical work was done in Pennsylvania, and states farther south where the English influence was great. Actually, if you could study pieces side by side, you would note that American furniture is basically lighter and more graceful than English counterparts of any period.

Identifying Regional Styles

Once you have learned your periods, you may accept the new challenge of studying the regional characteristics of furniture. The different cultures abounding in America resulted in the variety of tastes evident in many types of artifacts. New England furniture is characterized by its delicate style, slender legs, and good proportions. When it is veneered, it is done in good taste with highly figured woods. Dimensions are very important to this aesthetic, and this detail was unsurpassed elsewhere. New England sideboards feature more leg and less body, whereas those from Philadelphia are heavier bodied with shorter legs. Much carving was done, but not in the heavier rococo style that was the mark of Philadelphia work. Southern craftsmen relied heavily on dark stains in the manner of English work, but northern craftsmen were more content to use natural finishes and allow the wood grains to show in their own color. Northern five-legged game tables are a rarity, whereas they were the rule in the South. Charleston furniture is styled much like that of Boston, since many cabinetmakers from New England sought the more temperate climate and carried their influence with them. New York cabinetry was influenced for years by its Dutch heritage and culture, and the designs approximated much of what was being made overseas—much heavier in concept than that in New England.

Regional tastes are strong, and dealers travel all over the country buying pieces that are not appreciated in one area and selling them in areas where they are sought after. New England furniture has little appeal in New Orleans, yet the French furniture from overseas finds a ready market there. One

Slant-top maple desk by Dunlap circle of cabinetmakers, New Hampshire. Late 18th century. Note scroll cutouts in skirt, houndstooth molding and fine-carved shells in the interior section.

Cherry slant top desk, made in the Norwich, CT area, c. 1770s. The ogee feet are not found in Northern New England furniture. Value: $4,500-$6,000

will hardly ever find French furniture in an old New England home—it just does not look proper in the colonial setting.

For years, Empire and Victorian furniture was shipped by the truckload from New England to the South, where there was already a market. It is only within the last twenty years that pieces from these periods began to find favor in the North.

Much fine furniture found its way overseas. Benjamin Frothingham worked in Charlestown, Massachusetts, and labeled his pieces as Charlestown N.E. Some years ago, a fine-labeled highboy from his shop turned up in Copenhagen, Denmark. Another great highboy now in an American museum was found in South Africa, and in 1952, a fine slant-top desk bearing his label showed up in England and was brought back to be sold at an auction in New Hampshire.

Woods and Decoration

Woods may help in provenance. You will find upper New England furniture in pine, maple, and birch. Mahogany was favored in the coastal cities of New York, Philadelphia, Baltimore, and Newport (where it appealed to the wealthy). It was easier to obtain by sea from the Caribbean than other woods, which were transported overland by ox cart. Cherry was used extensively in Connecticut

and it was also favored in New York and Pennsylvania. Walnut was in use from New York to the South as it was a common wood in these areas. Beech, poplar, and hard pine were used in the South as well.

Historians tell us that stringing (a striped inlay), flowers, eagles, and other decorative devices were used just about everywhere, but the cabinetmakers in the major cities of Portland, Portsmouth, Salem, Baltimore, Annapolis, Boston, Newport, New York, and Philadelphia brought the style to perfection.

Walnut and mahogany were favored woods in England early in the eighteenth century, but in this

The late Roger Bacon felt that highboys and chests on chests of the early 18th century were all painted; some with decorations, such as this example. It is dated, Boston, c. 1735.

Rare NH slant-top desk in cherry. Large cherry wood was not found in NH when this desk was made. The knots on the drawers indicate the cabinetmaker did not have enough big boards to avoid using these, c. 1770. Value: $4,500-$6,000

country, the artisans skillfully used the lighter-colored and highly figured maples, mahogany, cherry, and birch in their work. American craftsmen used little or no marquetry, preferring to paint or japan (lacquer and gild) the cased pieces for beautification. Carving was relegated to fans or shells on drawers and perhaps some cutout work on the tops of highboys and fancy finials. Late in the period, Philadelphia craftsmen carried this even further with carvings on the knees of the legs.

Early maple gate leg table c. 1700-1720; made in Massachusetts, with vase and ring turnings, found in a Rhode Island home. Value: $1,800-$2,200

Size

Dimensions are important, as good proportion makes for a good-looking piece. Dimensions also affect value. Perhaps the most desired width for a slant-top desk, five- or six-drawer chest, or high-boy top of the eighteenth century would be an even 36". Those that are wider command less money and smaller ones usually command more. You must be careful in any "just like" attributions, as the width of the piece is very important in relation to value. Short, squat legs, which lower the body of a chest to the floor, do not give the graceful proportion of a tall, well-defined leg. Perhaps the great expression of this is in the cased pieces made in New Hampshire, which, for some reason, feature high legs, which enhance the dignity of the pieces to which they are attached. Another New Hampshire characteristic is the wide moldings, which are apparent at the tops of highboys and chests on chests. Traveling a few miles over the border in any direction will reveal narrower moldings made by nearby contemporaries. Maine furniture is styled very much like that of Massachusetts, as Maine was part of the Massachusetts Commonwealth until 1818 and must have been influenced by this.

Knowledge of these kinds of details can help you make reasonable attribution in the light of known facts. In a region that was full of fine

C. 1770, five graduated-drawer chest in maple with bracket base, Acton, Maine. One must examine a chest with these proportions, as it may be the top to a chest on chest, to which feet have been added. Look for the age of the wood, construction, and tool marks. Value: $2,750-$3,500

cabinetmakers, the work on some pieces of furniture is so similar that you would be hard put to specify the area of craftsmanship.

Identifying Pre-1820 Handmade Furniture

Construction Techniques

You should always get beneath any piece of furniture to examine the leg and base structure, since this is the first place that will receive damage in moving or handling. You must examine the age (or patina) of the wood, to make sure it is the same in all sections and that there are no replacements. Wood reinforcing blocks are glued at important joints to strengthen them. If corner blocks are held in with screws, you must determine if this is later construction or merely bracing which was added later to reinforce a weak spot. If screws are used, they must be of the hand-cut variety, usually with the point tips cut off. In the old days, holes were drilled before the screws were put in, removing the necessity of a point. The slits in the screw heads will usually be off center as they were made quickly by hand. Machine screws are cut dead center; this gives them away.

The Thomas Willing Chippendale carved mahogany card table, Philadelphia. The carving attributed to the Garvan Carver, c. 1760-1770. One sold recently for over $1,300,000.

Sotheby's.

The drawer bottoms should preferably be single board and the grain should run from side to side in the chest. If the bottom has several boards running from front to rear, be suspicious, as you are most likely looking at an English piece. The drawer bottoms should be chamfered, or narrowed down at the edges, and should fit into slots at the drawer sides. The drawer sides should be dovetailed to the front and rear boards—generally, the wider and cruder the dovetail, the older it is. By the Federal period, dovetails were highly refined. The front dovetail is often hidden with a molding or cockbeading, which surrounds the drawer front. This is referred to as a "hidden dovetail," and it does not detract from the piece. The drawer bottom boards should show signs of hand planing or rough saw marks. Saw marks which are straight up and down and parallel to each other are evidence that the board was cut on an up and down jigsaw. This was a two-man saw manipulated by a man standing atop the log and a man beneath in a pit, with the saw stroke moving up and down. The circular saw was reinvented by the Shakers in the 1820s, so boards which show the marks of a circular saw must have been cut during that time or later.

Some experts can feel the leg of a piece and determine if the piece is old. New wood will still be quite round, while wood which has aged over

Considered one of the finest pieces of furniture made in America, is this tea table by Robert Harrold, Portsmouth, New Hampshire. 18th century, Chippendale. One is in the State Department reception room in Washington. Only six are known to exist.

the years will be dry, with wood cut against the grain drying more slowly than wood cut with it. As a result, there is a slight oval shape to a turned leg if it is old, but you must sharpen your senses to work with this clue.

In American work, backboards on cased pieces should run horizontally, and usually are of pine, hewn and chamfered. Rough hand-cut nails generally hold them in. However, such nails are now being duplicated, so do not use this as an absolute means of attribution. In Centennial furniture, the backboards are often a dead giveaway to the age of the piece. Many pieces were made with thin machine-cut wood, and they most likely came this way. You may suspect that fakers later replaced these with old hewn pine to mislead unwary buyers.

Examine Pieces Closely—Determining the age of a chair poses particular problems. You cannot merely examine it from the outside. You must examine the frame construction, since this is where the truth lies. This often means ripping out a dust cover. If you are not permitted to examine the interior framework, stay away from the chair, unless you are paying a reproduction price. Reinforcing blocks to strengthen the legs against the frame were glued on early pieces; in later construction, corner blocks were fastened with screws. The age of the wood is important. Look for any tack marks where the upholstery was changed over the years. Look for hewn marks on the inside wood, as most were left a little rough and are not as smoothly cut as a machine-driven saw would have left them. To judge by the leg backs alone is hazardous unless you know your woods and patina, and have a feel for the correctness of the piece. In fact, even collectors this knowledgeable turn the pieces over.

It is difficult to determine the age of wingback chairs when one cannot cut the dust covers beneath to examine the construction. One can be fairly safe if you find the chair quite heavy when you lift it. Most likely this is a repro, perhaps a hundred years of age, but nevertheless not in period. After lifting literally hundreds of these, I have found that the eighteenth-century chairs had much less wood in them, which has dried out considerably, making the chair much lighter than the repros. You can get the feel of the weight by going to auctions where authentic chairs are sold. Once you lift a few, you will feel the difference.

"Married" Pieces

If you are buying a chest-on-chest or highboy you should check to make sure it is not a married piece. Due to family disagreement on who should get the furniture, it would sometimes be divided with separate halves going to different owners. A new frame would then be built to hold the upper half, creating a phony chest and a top would be put on the lower section. In the case of a highboy, this lower unit is often miscalled a lowboy. Over the years, dealers and buyers have been reuniting sections, even though they are not original to each other. You should pull out a drawer from each section and examine the dovetailing to make sure it matches perfectly. Moldings and beading on the upper and lower cases should be checked. Backboards must be identical and must show the same age. The base should show no signs of tampering. Holes for the brasses or pulls should be cut or drilled identically. Above all, the proportions must be right—be sure the molding supporting the top

Rare William and Mary highboy, burl-veneered maple, Theophilis Pickering, Salem MA, c. 1725. The only period when six legs were seen on highboys. Value: $10,000-$12,000

section on the base is not too wide, and that the height and width of the top is proportioned well in relation to the bottom. Of course, the wood must be the same, but diligent refinishing can make them match. Study the wood in both sections and make sure they originated in the same cabinet shop. It has been suggested that more than one man may have worked on such big pieces, so there may be variances. Although this was very likely, the work would have been divided by specialty—with one person cutting, one dovetailing, one carving, etc.—so all similar work on the two pieces should check out as the same.

Often called a lowboy, this Queen Anne piece should be called a "dressing table." Check the top board. Often, when the two parts to a highboy were separated, the bottom section would have a top on it to create this type of table. Value: $5,000-$7,000

Hardware

The type, age, and condition of brasses are important. From the teardrop pulls of the late seventeenth century, the turn-of-the-century style advanced to bale handles with brass plates behind. The pre-1830 brasses or knob pulls featured a threaded post. This was inserted from the front of the drawer to the inside, where it was held on with a hand-cut nut, often round. Later brasses would be held by a bolt, which would be inserted from the inside of the drawer and fastened to the bale handle or knob at the front. After you have seen really old

Highboy in the style of William Savery of Philadelphia, Chippendale period. Mahogany with flame finials and broken arch top. Value: $12,000-$18,000

Details on top of a highboy made by Henry Clifton of Philadelphia in 1756. It sold at a Foster-Hall auction in Maine, during July 1974 for $37,500.

Block-front chest, three drawers with three shells, made by John Townsend of Newport, RI. There has been discussion on whether it should have the bale handles as exhibited, or wing brasses, mahogany, 1762.

brasses, you will have little difficulty in telling them from the new. However, new brasses do not fault a piece too much, as most collectors will accept them as long as they are in the proper period style. Many museums have new brasses and knobs on their furniture—perhaps because they came that way, and perhaps because of the problem of theft.

Wooden and brass knobs were used extensively in the eighteenth century, especially during the last quarter. They were very popular all through the Federal period, and a great deal of Empire furniture appears with them. Glass pulls were introduced in 1825 by Bakewell of Pittsburgh when he developed a pressing machine to make them. The Boston and Sandwich Glass Company of Cape Cod is known for its fiery opalescent drawer pulls.

American Chippendale country chest on chest in tiger and other maples. Original bale brasses and escutcheons. Sold May 17, 1975, at a Richard Borne auction for $2,600. It would bring many times that today.

Chippendale chest on chest, maple, Maine, c. 1770s. Bracket base with handcut wing brasses. Value: $5,500-$7,000

These became quite popular and appear on much late Sheraton and Empire furniture. After this time all sorts of metal, wood, and glass pulls and handles with back plates were used. There is such a variety that I would be lost in attempting to discuss them. Since most were not handmade, they have little importance in the collecting scheme.

You should check the inside of the drawers to determine if the pulls are original. Pull knobs were quite often replaced with bale handles, and an additional hole would have been drilled. Early artisans hollowed out the holes on the drawer interiors so that the bolts and nuts would not tear clothing. If you find a drawer with one hole hollowed and one just drilled to accommodate the bolt, it is obvious that the brass is a replacement. Sometimes two new holes have been drilled to accommodate a bale handle, and the single hole that once held the pull knob will be quite obvious from the interior, though it will be covered by the back plate at the front of the drawer.

American Style Periods

Pilgrim

During the Pilgrim period (1620-1670), cabinet-makers used whatever woods grew locally. Oak was favored in England at this time, so it was only natural that this wood was used here as well. A clue to provenance is that white oak prevailed in England, while in America both red and white were used. Furniture made from red oak is most likely American, since it is doubtful that anyone would have shipped this wood back to England at the time.

Naturally, pine was a favorite as it was plentiful and easy to work with primitive tools. Oak gave way to walnut and mahogany early in the eighteenth century, due to the demand of the wealthy for fine furniture such as that made in England. However, out in the country, maple, hickory, birch, cherry, and other fruitwoods were utilized, as they were readily available at literally no cost.

The Pilgrim period, with iron utensils and simple furniture that would have been found in most "keeping" rooms in an early American, 17th century home.

Jacobean

The Jacobean furniture of the early seventeenth century was rectangular and low in proportion, reflecting the low ceilings popular at the time. Most legs were straight with some turnings, and a melon shape was popular. Legs were braced with stretchers and were most often close to the floor. The later Jacobean period brought with it much carving and even caning of chairs.

Some refer to the Jacobean period as the Carolean period, which was characterized by the introduction of S and C scrolls with mixed Dutch, Portuguese, Flemish, Spanish, and French-Italian influences. Spiral-turned legs appeared, and geometric moldings were favored. The Dutch had perfected the turning lathe, which made the spiral moldings possible, at a time when the English and other artisans were still carving them totally by

Jacobean-style chair.

hand. At this time, padded backs appeared on chairs, and bun or ball feet were the rule. Needlepoint, velvet, leather, and brocades were used for upholstering. The great wood carver Grinling Gibbons left his mark with workmanship which has perhaps never been duplicated. Motifs included acanthus leaves, roses, crowns, and scrolls.

During this time, artisans produced crude stools; benches; trestle tables, which were long dining tables; low box type chests; bible boxes; and simple bed frames with rope supports for a feather or corn husk filled mattress. There was little attempt at beautification, but we do find good examples of carving in specific areas. In the western Connecticut/western Massachusetts sections, a school of carvers is recorded near Hadley which left us a fine heritage of their work. Some pieces are called "sunflower" chests because of their floral decoration, and others are simply called Hadley chests as a means of identifying the school of work they represent.

Oak was a popular wood for this work, and because of this, many pieces have survived. English counterparts of these chests are also collected, and you must determine their provenance by the decorative motifs. Study of the decoration that existed at the time, both here and overseas, is a great help in attribution. To do it solely by workmanship at this early period is hazardous.

Historians tell us that the term "Jacobean" might be applied to several periods in the seventeenth century. The name is loosely adapted from *Jacobus,* the Latin name for King James I, who reigned early in the century. James I was succeeded by Charles I, who was later beheaded by Cromwell and his associates. Some refer to the years 1649-1660 as Cromwellian, as they feel there was a definite change in design to reflect the absence of the monarchy, which until then had supported and inspired craftsmen. Furniture from this period is characterized by stiff lines, with little embellishment, but this should be of little concern to the American collector as there is little available either here or in England.

Until recently, styles of this period were not much in favor here in America, since the cased pieces are bulky and the chairs and settees are quite uncomfortable. Also, one would find it almost impossible to acquire a complete set of chairs, or other multiple items, as time has taken its toll of many of them. Our practice of wanting complete

Another of "Hadley" chests made c. 1690. The decorations are quite fanciful.

Shelburne Museum, Inc., John M. Miller photographer.

sets held down interest in such seventeenth-century furniture. The English reproduced much of it in the nineteenth century, and you must be careful in your purchases if you want the early work. Perhaps the best clue to look for is pegs in the framework. The English were using pegs to join furniture right into the Queen Anne period early in the eighteenth century, but at that time, such work began to disappear. However, almost all seventeenth century work should show pegs. Also, you should check the under frame of any furniture to look for new screws or angle-cut braces. In the early days, craftsmen glued crude blocks of wood at joining points, whereas later work shows machine-cut braces held in by screws. You should look for early marks left by saws, planes, and chisels. Later work done by machine will be perfectly smooth, with very tight joints.

William and Mary

James II, the son of Charles II, seemed to have little better luck in ruling than Charles I, and he fled the country, leaving his daughter, Mary, to rule with her husband, William, who was Dutch. Though they ruled only from 1688 to 1702, William and Mary managed to have an influence on furniture and other art styles. Many Huguenot craftsmen were coming into England at this time to escape religious persecution caused by the revocation of the Edict of Nantes. The Dutch and French influence was immediately felt, and for the first time, furniture took on graceful lines and propor-

tions. It featured a combination of curved and straight lines and chair backs were heightened. The seats were most often square, with backs slanted for comfort. Turned legs with vase and ring, trumpet and inverted cup designs became the rule. Ball and bun feet were still used on low chests for strength, but longer legs with stretchers framing them became the rule for the taller cased pieces. The chests and highboys were soon decorated with inlay, painted decorations, and well-grained veneers.

Some royal furniture was gilded, and some appeared with marble tops. The cockleshell was popular in carving, and some chair legs had feet with toe, and even ball and claw, carvings. China cabinets were popular, as antique collecting became a pastime for the wealthy. Tall clocks appeared, and the game tables introduced at the time of Charles I became the rage as cards and

Catherine of Braganza of Portugal married Charles II at the time of his restoration to the throne in 1660. She brought with her, as part of her dowry, highly carved furniture which influenced British cabinet-making throughout the rest of that century. For those concerned about the caning, remember this was used at the time of the Egyptians. Value: $800-$1,200

other games of change swept the nation. The long, rigid refectory tables of the preceding years gave way to graceful gate leg and other drop-leaf designs. One of the most important designers of the period was a Huguenot, Daniel Marot, and as a result, his work shows the influence of the Louis XIV styles then prevalent in France. This was a period of high style and represented the transition from the rigid and functional to the graceful and beautiful in furniture.

Queen Anne

The advent of Queen Anne to throne in 1702 brought with it a further refinement in style, with the pieces becoming perhaps more delicate and beautiful than those of any other period. The heavy underbracing of the preceding periods gradually disappeared, and graceful cabriole legs, designed from the architectural cyma curve, became the rule. Anne ascended the throne after the death of William of Orange, who had given Parliament the power of absolute rule in England, reducing the monarchy to a titular role as far as governing was

Classic mahogany drop-leaf table in Queen Anne style. The single board top and leaves, illustrate how meticulous the cabinetmakers were in selecting their wood. Value: $1,800-$2,200

Illustration of Queen Anne style.

Living room of the late Roger Bacon, the dean of the 17th and 18th century furniture in the country. Note the Queen Anne table and chairs.

concerned. With the monarchy no longer dictating style, cabinetmakers exercised their own imagination, yet most came up with a refinement of the continental styles which were still most appreciated. The Dutch influence was strongly felt during Anne's reign, and we are fortunate that it was, since it left us with a heritage of furniture. In America, cabinetmakers in Boston, Portsmouth, Newport, New York, and Philadelphia rivaled their counterparts in England. The Americans were able to work with a wider selection of woods, using native as well as mahogany and other exotic woods from the Caribbean. Proportions were more delicate to fit the smaller homes in this country.

Some feel that little or no furniture in this style was made in America before 1730—that it would have been shipped from England. As I have written, veneered Queen Anne highboys are in the older settled sections of the country, so many must have been shipped here.

Queen Anne tap table, Rhode Island, 18th century. Tables of this type made for inns and taverns were made extensively into the 19th century. Maple. Value: $2,200-$2,500

Chippendale

Until the middle of the eighteenth century, the names of furniture styles and periods came from the monarchs. It was about this time that the name of Thomas Chippendale became quite prominent in cabinetry. He borrowed designs from others and carried them to perfection in a blending of functional use, as well as beauty. Chippendale might be called the first true English style which evolved from many others, and which was carried to perfection by other cabinetmakers as well. Here in America, the craftsmen seized on this departure from the reserved Queen Anne style, and turned out classic pieces using our beautiful woods. This was the era of the famous Goddard and Townsend families in Newport, and their creations in the Chippendale style are considered to be the epitome of cabinetmaking in this country.

Chippendale favored mahogany and used curves freely. He continued the use of the cabriole leg and placed the ball and claw and the ball and talon foot firmly in leg design. He favored carving over veneering for beauty. The back rails of chairs were most often of serpentine or curved shape, and many are characterized by pronounced ears at the juncture of the side posts and crest rail. Chair arms were curved and often flared at the ends, and the supports

Tilt top tea table w/piecrust top. Chippendale, c. 1750-1775. Those with plain rims are called, dish top. Mahogany. Philadelphia. Value: $2,750-$3,500

were angled forward at the side rails of the seat. The ladder-back design was carried to its greatest height, and many featured intricate piercing and carving on the rails. Chippendales' carvings featured acanthus leaf (which was brought to its fullest fruition early in the nineteenth century), scrolls, French rococo, fruit and flowers, and even lion heads. The breakfront made a dramatic appearance in Chippendale's time, and he furthered the making of sideboards, which are generally credited to Thomas Shearer, another English designer.

Other designers of note were also in great favor during this time. Perhaps Chippendale was most influenced by Thomas Johnson, a well-known designer and carver in London. Johnson was a master of the French styles that we label as Louis XV. Sir William Chambers went to the Orient, and on his return pioneered the use of oriental influences in furniture, and this caught Chippendale's fancy.

King-size bed frame in Chippendale style. It is English, not too old. It is unusual in that the form was not made during the period. Seen at St. Thomas in the Virgin Islands. Value: $500

Butterfield & Butterfield.

Chippendale-carved, tiger-maple chest on chest, New Hampshire, c. 1750-60. The sharp ankles and knees, plus the spoon handle carvings would suggest it was made by someone who had apprenticed with the Dunlaps. Value: $30,000-$40,000

The wingback chair made its appearance in the early 18th century. The ball and talon feet mark this piece as Chippendale. This is one of the most reproduced chairs in the country. A quick check will help you. Get behind it and push it up from the back. If you cannot lift it from the floor, most likely it is a repro. If it comes up easily; then you must cut the dust cover and check the wood construction and tool marks. The old chairs have less wood, additionally, they have no springs, hence the lighter weight. This chair is identified as American, Charleston SC, mahogany with yellow cypress and pine. c. 1770.

Highly grained or decorated furniture is much in vogue, today. The bolder tiger-maple striping sets this Chippendale desk apart from the others. Massachusetts, late 18th century. Value: $8,000-$12,000

Striking pair of Chippendale side chairs with ball and talon feet. The seats are upholstered down around the seat rails, which signify they are not American, c. 1750-1775.

The "Chinese Chippendale" design was created as a result. Chambers published his *Designs For Chinese Buildings, Furniture, Dresses, Etc.* in 1757, and Chippendale was quick to use it. Robert Manwaring published the *Chairmaker's Guide* in 1766 and this, along with a furniture stylebook done by Matthias Darly, had great influence on Chippendale. Robert and James Adam were primarily architects, but wealthy patrons had them design furniture to match their house designs. The shops of Chippendale and another up-and-coming cabinetmaker, George Hepplewhite, were used for its manufacture. Needless to say, both were influenced by the Adam styles, about which little is known in this country as so little of it was made or sent here. The Adam brothers returned to the use of fluting in legs after excavations in Greece had uncovered such designs, and they are also credited with stressing the use of veneers and inlays to beautify furniture.

Federal

Hepplewhite

George Hepplewhite, another noted London cabinetmaker, was responsible for a radical departure in furniture style, doing away with the curved legs and fancy carvings of Chippendale's time. Though contemporary with Chippendale in his early years, Hepplewhite took his inspiration from the then recent excavations at Pompeii, which prompted a revival in interest in the classic lightness, grace, and elegance of pieces unearthed. He

Chippendale side chair in country style with the squared legs. The rib-band back and slip seat are consistent with an American style, c. 1750-1775. Value: $750-$1,000

did away with bizarre decoration and trusted to purity and simplicity of line to create a whole new idea. Louis XV had died, and across the channel, the French designers noted the change in tastes and paralleled Hepplewhite with their version of the Louis XVI style. Both featured the slender tapered leg, often with a spade foot.

Bow front chests made their appearance and the convex fronts were often terminated at concave corners, another Hepplewhite form. A favorite of the Prince of Wales, Hepplewhite utilized a feather carving on many pieces, inspired by the feathers on the prince's hats. He adapted the Crusader shield as a shape for the backs of chairs and also for mirrors. Short, curved arms were used on chairs, as was a rail above the seat to reinforce the back. Chairs were usually upholstered with the material extending over the frame and covering it entirely. If you should find a Hepplewhite designed chair with slip or removable seat, be cautious, as this is not the norm. Some say Hepplewhite's styles reflected the austerity of the period after the Revolutionary War. Be that as it may, there are students today who consider his styles perhaps the most classic of all. Such beauty was created with simplicity, using the coloring of well-grained woods, either veneered or solid, along with restraint in any carving. New appreciation is growing for work done in this style in America, since from Boston north to Portsmouth, New Hampshire, it was brought to full development in beauty and fine cabinetry.

Chests of this period most likely would feature the "French leg," or outturned tapered leg, often reinforced with a pronounced toe. The cutouts on the skirts of such pieces are important, as this work determines much of the value, based on the ingenuity of the maker. Though we generally record

Hepplewhite banquet table with birdcage Windsor chairs. Bellflower inlay. The huge leaves are dropped to the floor to make it a round table. It will seat 12. Table: $5,000-$7,000; 6 chairs: $3,000

Four of a set of eight Hepplewhite dining chairs with tapered legs and shield backs. Made late in the 18th century. Value: $3,200

Thomas Shearer, an English cabinetmaker, is generally credited with making the first buffet/server, just before our Revolution. Hepplewhite created the design with tapered legs. His design book appeared in 1789, two years after his death. Though veneering of wood was not popular in the periods before, it made a grand entry in Hepplewhite's time.

Four drawer chest in maple, made by member of the Dunlap circle of cabinetmakers in New Hampshire, during the late 18th century.

that the Hepplewhite style was going out of favor in America at about 1800, we have found documented pieces made in this fashion as late as the 1830s, despite the advent of two period changes at the time. This was still an era of hand construction, and one would go to a cabinetmaker and order the pieces made up as he saw fit. It would not be unusual to have pieced made-to-match earlier ones handed down in a family. Because of this, it is much safer to refer to a piece by style, such as "Hepplewhite style," as you cannot be sure whether a piece was made during his lifetime or during the time his designs were most popular. This would apply to all periods. The Dunlap family (a group of cabinetmakers in New Hampshire from 1740 to 1830) is known to have worked in the Queen Anne Style as late as the 1790s, as this is what their customers wanted.

Several features in Hepplewhite furniture should be mentioned. The long, tapered legs on tables and chairs often boast an enlarged square foot. This is called a spade foot and was used on both sides of the Atlantic.

While the preceding periods had produced tall chests and highboys, they went out of favor during Hepplewhite's time, and none has appeared in his style. Some of the four drawer chests made in the north shore of Massachusetts and the Portsmouth, New Hampshire areas are fast approaching (and in some cases have exceeded) the values of chests of

previous periods. These are outrageously beautiful pieces most often made in mahogany, or mahogany stained birch, and veneered with striking figured birch or maple woods. Those featuring a drop panel, which is nothing more than a decorative rectangular or oval veneered decoration beneath the bottom drawer, are highly sought because this distinctive feature is rare.

Research I have done on the drop panel feature has uncovered the names of several makers: Joseph Clark of Greenland, New Hampshire; Judkins and Senter of Portsmouth, New Hampshire;

A family of cabinetmakers, the Dunlaps, are well known for the classic furniture they made between 1740 and 1830. Illustrated is a tall chest on chest, with the fishtails, inverted C scrolls, and spoon-handle carvings for which they were noted. The sharp ankles and deep knees make one wonder how they could provide enough support. Their pieces are in major museums throughout the country.

Nathaniel Appleton of Salem, Massachusetts; and Spooner and Fitts, Athol, Massachusetts. Fewer than 100 cased pieces featuring the drop panel have turned up in the country. There are clock cases which have it. The research has indicated that this drop panel decoration did not appear on any Boston furniture, but cabinetmakers there, such as the Seymours, featured a raised panel decoration at the tops of secretaries. Portsmouth furniture of this type did not feature a raised panel, but Salem work featured both upper and lower panels.

Duncan Phyfe

In his wildest imagination, no one could conceive that a baby born at Loch Fannich in Scotland in 1768 would grow into a craftsman who would revolutionize the style of furniture not only in this country, but also throughout the world. This small town, just thirty miles from Inverness, was hardly known until Duncan Phyfe left it and came to Albany, New York, in 1783. During the long voyage with his family, a brother and sister died, reflecting the hazards of travel during that time.

When Phyfe was sixteen, he entered a cabinet shop as an apprentice. When he was qualified, he opened his own shop. He was lured to New York City early in the 1790s as he was told this was where the money was. Located on Broad Street, among many other cabinetmakers, he was hard put to make ends meet until a member of the John Jacob Astor family saw and liked his work and gave him orders. Soon other wealthy people became his patrons; by the turn of the century, he may have been regarded as the outstanding furniture craftsman there.

New York was a growing community after the Revolutionary War, and our increasing trade with the French brought with it the latest styles from the continent. Phyfe worked from the design books of Hepplewhite and Sheraton, but soon turned to the incoming French Directoire style. Gradually, he developed his own ideas and incorporated them into his furniture. In this later work, one rarely sees a straight line. He is best remembered for his curves and reverse curves in chair and table legs and backs to chairs and sofas. His decoration included carving, marquetry, and reeding. Many of his pieces feature brass paw feet. Most of the furniture was mahogany and featured carved acanthus leaves, which were popular at the time.

The out-swept legs often rode on casters, and the pedestal-based table in this design is felt to have made its first appearance in his shop. His imagination in carved decoration ran from the lion mask to the cornucopia and oak leaf. Many panels are done in drapery, whorled fluting, thunderbolt, wheatear, leaf and dart, and palm leaf. The rotating-top, tilt-top game table appeared during this period; it is possible Phyfe helped pioneer it. Phyfe liked the lyre design and often used it in the base of a table and on the backs of chairs. Often, the strings are of brass or whalebone, and some features are highlighted with ebony.

His sofas featured short legs that most often terminate in a bulge. Most seats were upholstered, but some were caned. Carved eagle and lion heads were featured, but not limited to his furniture alone.

The Phyfe style has never died. Many furniture firms feature reproductions in their catalogs and showrooms. Naturally, because this style has been popular since the beginning of the nineteenth century, one must learn how to identify the period pieces. In Phyfe chairs, the seats were always curved or rounded; apparently he designed them this way to allow for the elasticity of the cane. The supports underneath the cane were mortised into a dovetailed groove in the seat rail that gave it the

Federal period mahogany inlaid Pembroke table, dated by the owner at 1790. Value: $2,500-$3,500

strength he wanted. If the cornucopia motif is used, it is generally accompanied by the laurel, which complemented it.

If a chair features the receded Sheraton leg, most often the back carving includes the thunderbolts, wheatears, drapery, and fluting. The joining of the chair legs to the frame is most often reinforced with glue blocks, whereas the more modern brace is nearly triangular and screwed with relatively new-looking screws.

Phyfe made many Pembroke-style tables and many worktables, but most featured the receded Sheraton leg and not the pedestal base for which he is best known. He made an early extension dining table that was the forerunner to those we enjoy today. They did not appear until about 1820.

The furniture purist does not pay much attention to the Phyfe style unless the master himself labels it. Most of his pieces were well labeled, generally along the inside of a framing member. Chairs and sofas may reveal this labeling if the dust cover is pulled back, but since most people do not want to disturb the cover, it is possible there are many authentic Phyfe pieces whose owners do not know their importance or value. Most competent appraisers can tell from the outward appearance if the piece is old or new and if it should be checked further.

One feature that seems native to Phyfe and New York State is the winged claw feet that appear front and rear on sofas of the period. If you see one with feet like this, it's time to lift the dust cover to look for a label.

Sheraton

The name Thomas Sheraton looms large as one of the foremost eighteenth century cabinetmakers who worked in London. He issued *The Drawing Book* in 1794, which set a pattern of style in furniture that was to remain quite popular until 1830. At first, he used the tapered leg, which had been popularized by George Hepplewhite, another London maker, but soon brought forth his own design—the turned and receded leg. This was patterned after furniture designs uncovered in excavations taking place at that time in Italy and Greece. It was a return to a more classic style.

During this period, the trade between this country and the Orient began to grow, and soon the Oriental influence was felt in our decorative arts.

Bamboo furniture became popular, and soon furniture makers were turning our local woods out to resemble the bamboo in legs, arms, and spindles of chairs and other pieces. Rush seats were most popular on the chairs, and soon the name "fancy chair" was applied to those with this Oriental look. Because they were popularized during the Sheraton period, it was only natural that the term "Sheraton fancy chair" came into being.

Actually, there is not much fancy about them—they were low in cost, and had greater appeal to those of limited incomes. They found their way to the common homes, to the farms, and in the servant's quarters of the wealthy homes. Today they are more highly regarded, as they are handmade, rugged, and of quite good quality to use. Age is in their favor, for those who wish to equip their homes with period pieces. It would be safe to say that all were painted originally, and some will be found with decoration and stenciling. The front legs must have button feet and must be in good shape, and the bolder the turnings, the better.

Ladies, or box desk with reeded and turned legs marking the Sheraton period, c. 1800-1830, mahogany. Research by Joseph Hammond has convinced historians that most were made in the Portsmouth area. A few were made in Empire style with rope legs.

Sheraton couch with reeded and turned legs. The back rail is veneered with figured birch. One will note the eight legs—one sees few couches outside this period with this many legs. Again, since the rear legs do not match the front, it is American.

This is a period worth collecting right now. Prices have not yet ascended beyond the cost of much of today's fine new furniture. The carving as well as the marquetry, using many beautifully grained woods, can be considered works of art. There are many Sheraton tables selling for relatively little money. Bow front chests have become more expensive, but there are many flat-fronted

At left is a dressing table with turned legs, Sheraton, c. 1820-1830. The Empire influence creeps into this style as they overlapped for some years. The raised drawers and scroll back are Empire; birch and maple, New England. At right is a corner washstand, very English in its look, George IV, early 19th century. I have never seen an American example in this form. Table: $500-$750; stand: $450-$600

Sheraton table with reeded and turned legs; cherry and tiger maple. The feet below the last turnings in this period should be at least three inches, which would suggest these legs are at the minimum, c. 1820-1830. Sheraton pieces which are pegged can be assigned to the 1800-1820 period. Value: $600-$800

Sheraton game table, with plume inlay. Reeded turned legs, c. 1800-1830. Note the long feet, which continue after the last turnings, Salem or Boston. Value: $2,750-$3,000

legs; out-swept legs with brass paw feet; and other variations. This is the last period with distinctive feet. Leaf and fruit carving became popular. The scimitar or sabre leg, patterned after the Roman sword, is a design used to this day. Though some very graceful pieces were made in the Empire period, the earlier gave way to some rather horrible ideas such as the scroll leg or elephant trunk style. This plagued the upper sections as well as the bases, on pieces that otherwise are good in design. It was during the Empire period that the machine age set in, so that less handwork was required. Good taste and design seem to have gone out the window. During this and the later Victorian period there was much carving, but most of it was done by machine.

examples of the period which are quite beautiful and will have excellent value 20 or 30 years from now. Some of the prettiest worktables are Sheraton; many were made to hold candleholders as well as whale oil lamps, which appeared in the period.

The Sheraton designs overlapped with the incoming Empire designs, and many transitional pieces incorporate features of both. Rope legs, acanthus leaf carving, and scroll backs are most often ascribed to Empire design, but these appear on otherwise identifiable Sheraton chests. Actually, the designs were used as late as 1840-1850, when in New York State, Pennsylvania and Ohio, cabinetmakers refused to work with the fancier legs and decorations that appeared as early as 1810 in the Empire style.

Empire

By about 1810, a European influence of design was felt in America. Cabinetmakers had been content to work with English styles to the end of the century and beyond, but gradually they entered into the early nineteenth century period, which is called "Empire." A variety of leg styles appeared—the curved curule of the Roman magistrate chairs; animal, dolphin and fish legs, inspired by the Egyptians; rope, twist and carved

Empire-styled secretary with turned legs, c. 1830-1840. The front corner posts and overhanging top drawer, mark the period. The piece is mahogany veneer on pine, New England.

Empire-styled couch in style of Duncan Phyfe. The winged claw feet are an indication of NY State Design. Vintage, c. 1820-1830.

Transitional bow front chest with Sheraton and Empire features. Reeded column posts and scroll back are the latter. This is a country NH piece, which features then expensive mahogany with crotch mahogany veneer on the drawers, c. 1820-1830.

Prior to our Revolution, our furniture was inspired by the tastes and styles of our mother country, England, and it was not until after our separation that we began to develop our own tastes. After 1800, American tastes leaned strongly toward the French. France and America entered into trade, to the discomfort of the English and soon our seaports were deluged with the latest fashions from France. New York became a leader in the furniture revolution, and soon the best of the French Empire or Directoire styles were being copied here. Decorations in carving featured the acanthus leaf, pineapples, animal and bird feet, flowers, lyres, cornucopias, and scrolls. Heavy cornices and moldings were prominent. This is a rather enigmatic period, since some good design was created, as well as some that was outright monstrous. In the early part of the period, which extended from about 1810 to 1830, furniture with tasteful proportions and decoration was made by such artisans as Duncan Phyfe and Henri Lannuier in New York and Anthony Quervelle and Henry Connelly in

Philadelphia. When machines came into general use, about 1830, the art of hand craftsmanship began to die out, and with it, the true lines of beauty in furniture. The Empire styles that came after began to show the effects of poor design and construction, and by the time the Victorian designs achieved a foothold, the look of fine furniture had all but disappeared.

During the Empire period, mahogany was most favored as a wood. When it was not available, country workmen would often veneer simple pine with mahogany to create a more expensive look. Four-poster beds were quite popular. Some were made with a simple tester frame on which a skirt would be hung, while some were made with the full canopy. The poorer people settled for high legged beds made with posts as much as four or five feet from the floor, and those which featured pineapple or cannonball carvings at the tops were popular. The tall posts were often reeded in Sheraton style, and acanthus leaf carving was used to beautify them. You may see canopy-topped beds with reeded posts at the foot and tapered posts at the head—this is perfectly all right, as reeded posts were difficult to make, and the artisans possibly felt the head posts were pretty much out of sight anyway.

Sleigh beds made their appearance, and set the stage for the look of future beds. Until the appearance of the Hollywood-style bed in this century, most beds were very conventional, with a headboard, footboard, and spring and mattress of some kind. Rope springing beneath the mattresses gave way to coil springs and flat springs at about the time of the Civil War. A man by the name of

Handmade maple and cherry trope-legged table, early Empire, Maine, c. 1825. Note interesting leg carving and ball feet.

Samuel Pratt is credited with inventing coil springs for furniture in the 1820s, but they did not seem to make their appearance as bed springs until the aforementioned time. At least we know that furniture upholstered with springs did not come before the 1820s. Attribution as to the age of chairs and sofas can be often be based on this, unless there is evidence that springs were added later.

Horsehair as an upholstery material came into full use, though it is known that Thomas Shearer featured it in the third quarter of the eighteenth century. The fetish for putting animal paws and bird feet on chairs, sofas, and cased pieces has never been explained. Some approximated the grotesque, and in later years—in fact, right up until the 1950s—many pieces were thrown into dumps and otherwise disposed of. Renowned cabinetmakers like John and Thomas Seymour, who worked in Boston during the Federal Period (1770-1830), left some elegant works of construction for us to marvel at today, but some of these have animal feet that detract from the aesthetics of the whole piece.

Victorian

Queen Victoria was a buxom woman and some feel that her ascent to the throne prompted the massive furniture that appeared at about the same time, 1840. Some designers reverted to the styles of Chippendale and the cabriole leg with ball and talon foot made a dramatic return. Others were plainer in concept, but carving, mostly done by machine, became the favored decoration. Decorative veneering and inlay all but disappeared. The machines made mass production possible and reduced the output for fine handcrafted furniture to a few scattered shops throughout the country. However, away from the cities, good furniture of this period was still made by the country cabinetmakers who could not afford machinery, or would not bother to use it. Such pieces may show evidence of good handwork and may be prized accordingly.

There was delicate Victorian furniture, and some that was heavy and cumbersome. You must judge it on the merit of quality as outlined in the Introduction. However, a problem exists so far as age is concerned. As this styling extended for such a long period and has been reproduced so much in this century, you cannot always be sure in judging age. This merely underscores the problem of collecting machine-made items which may be reproduced at will. Several large furniture companies in the 1920s and 1930s did nothing but make fine reproductions of Empire and Victorian styles, and many of these pieces are now touted as 125-year-old originals based solely on the fact that someone's grandmother owned them.

This was a period popular for its marble-topped pieces and you should insist on the often used colored marbles from overseas. Mahogany and walnut were the most popular woods, but some rosewood has appeared on American pieces. Secondary woods were pine, ash, poplar, chestnut, and elm. Much more elm wood was used than is generally realized, as it was an inferior wood for burning, and could not be relied on for surface construction of any furniture. However, once dried properly, it was strong and fairly stable. If elm is used on a surface, and exposed to the elements of heat and cold, it is prone to split. Leg styles

Victorian corner chair. Pieces of this style may be difficult to age.

reverted back to the late seventeenth and mid-eighteenth centuries, reviving the heavy ball and cabriole leg with various styles of feet. The graceful sweep of the Louis XV leg of the mid-eighteenth century is very evident. Rounded forms were used on chair backs and carvings of grapes, flowers, swags, and even rococo motifs were used for adornment.

The increased affluence of the populace in the growing industrial complex brought the need for more closet space in which to hang clothing. Since such space was at a premium in older houses, the wardrobe experienced a great revival. The Dutch and Germans had been making their *kas* and *schrank,* the French, their armoires, since coming to this country and settling outside the New England area. The Northeast had few counterparts of these until the Victorian period. The well chest became popular, with raised small drawers offsetting the larger ones. Mirrors became a part of almost every bureau. Dark stains which hid the beautiful wood graining, were the rule, as some felt it would make the massive pieces look smaller.

While fine furniture was being made for the well-to-do, there was a lower quality being turned out for the masses. Little has been written about the pieces then being made for the industrial worker, whose funds were limited. To lump this furniture together with Victorian-style antiques is not wholly appropriate. At least one historian, years ago, suggested classifying the entire Empire and Victorian periods into an American theme, calling it American Home. However, the others had grouped the Hepplewhite, Sheraton and Empire periods together as the Federal period, and this is generally accepted today. This encompasses the work between about 1770 and 1830, when the machines began to take over.

The reasons were many. It is not easy to classify this pine furniture—bedroom sets, drop-leaf tables, kitchen chairs, and benches—as Victorian. Can we honestly identify sleigh beds and rockers, Morris chairs, and platform rockers with the basic Victorian furniture? There were many oddities created, such as beds which dropped out of phony chests of drawers and even a set of shelves on an iron frame

Renaissance Revival carved rosewood center table, attributed to Alexander Roux, New York, c. 1850-1860. The incoming Gothic designs were a revolt against the rounded forms of the Victorian period which preceded. Architectural carving was a mark of the period. Value: $2,500-$3,500

which could be swung parallel to each other to form a tabletop. There were shapes in chairs and settees not found in Europe; such as arrowbacks and Hitchcocks and the Shaker styles, created by the well-known religious sect. Painting and stenciling furniture were quite popular, and often one will see a bedroom set decorated with the scenes at a farm, where an itinerant painter might take lodging in return for his work. Is this a technique which can be ascribed to those who did honor to Queen Victoria? The last of the monarchs to lend a royal name to a period style cannot be credited with (or blamed for) all that was done then.

In short, I feel that the era from 1830-1890 could be designated the American Home Period, leaving the more classic designations to those who enjoy them overseas.

Renaissance Revival

As early as the middle of the nineteenth century, there had been a revolt against the massive Victorian designs. Cabinetmakers such as John Belter, Joseph Meeks, and the Herter brothers in New York City stimulated a revival in earlier forms, notably those of the renaissance period. Meeks and Belter changed more slowly, being content to work at first with the rounded forms, but highlighting them with graceful design and carving. Belter pioneered the use of laminated wood—what we call plywood today. Backs of chairs and settees were steamed and bent under pressure. While in the proper curve, they were carved, which in turn, released the pressure of the wood fibers to attempt to straighten themselves. None has gone out of shape since then. One may examine such fancy chairs to see if the laminations are visible at the edges of the backs.

The Herter brothers and others worked toward the end of the century in the Renaissance Revival forms. It was not until 1972 that the public became much aware of the furniture made during the period 1870-1890. Charles Eastlake had refined the Gothic Renaissance Revival forms into furniture which would fit into the average home. Jonathan Fairbanks, curator of the American Decorative Arts at the Museum of Fine Arts in Boston, staged an exhibition of pieces designed by two noted architects, Henry Hobson Richardson and Frank Furness. He suggested the use of the term "Eastlake" to denote the furniture of the period,

setting it aside from the term "late Victorian" which had been used until then.

Eastlake

The period between about 1870 and 1890 must be assigned to the influence of Charles Eastlake of England. His *Hints on Household Taste,* published in 1868, refined the Gothic Renaissance Revival forms into usable household furniture for the average person. The Eastlake style was characterized by decorative panels and carving, both by hand and by machine. Rounded forms were out and the architectural Gothic styling was in. Some of the designs approached the grotesque, which held back appreciation of them for years.

Popular during the Eastlake period were these tall chests with corners on piano hinges, which could be used to lock all the drawers at once. Walnut, with burl walnut panels. In the Northeast they were nicknamed, "Texas Highboys" as most ended up there. Value: $800-$1,000

Actually, the Gothic Renaissance Revival style was a revival of Gothic, Italianate, and ancient Greek and Roman forms. Some suggest it was a wedding of Gothic and Jacobean styles of the sixteenth and seventeenth centuries. Walnut became the favored wood. Mahogany, cherry, oak, and pine were used as well during the period. Furniture is characterized by its architectural look. Factories in Michigan, New York, and the South began making poor man's Eastlake and, until recently, this has been regarded as the bottom in design, compared to all the periods.

Other identifying features are the teardrop pull, which reappeared after an absence of about 200 years (it had been last seen during the William and Mary period), and carved "acorn" pulls. Also, bureau drawers grooved horizontally, most often in oak, are a mark of the period. However, one cannot identify Eastlake from leg design, as all types were used.

One of the most interesting pieces made in the Eastlake period is the "Texas highboy," so called, because it was made of walnut, one wood the termites in the Lone Star State did not like.

Eastlake Victorian side chair.

Butterfield & Butterfield.

Working in the Eastlake Period were the Herter Brothers in New York. This walnut center table sold at auction in 1992, at Butterfields, for $30,800.

The revival of Gothic Renaissance forms began in the middle of the 19th century. However, in England, Charles Eastlake wrote his Hints on Household Tastes *in 1868, refining the architectural designs into furniture for the average home. Hence the Eastlake Period, c. 1870-1890. The top of this mirrored chest reflects this design and is dated by it.*

I have seen these highboys with six and seven drawers, with a corner post attached to a piano hinge. There is one keyhole in this post. When it is closed against the drawers, all can be locked from this single point. In the 1950s, most sold for five to ten dollars apiece. They are well into three figures now. They are much in demand everywhere, as they offer a lot of drawer room in such little floor space. The bracket-based five- and six-drawer chests of the late eighteenth century have risen so much in price, buyers are settling for the walnut version. Most are decorated with burl walnut panels in lighter woods, almost the color of bird's-eye maple, though some maple was used to decorate desk interiors.

Many of the pine sets from this period were decorated at the factory. This decoration will heighten value if well done and in good condition. Out in the country, some pieces can be found

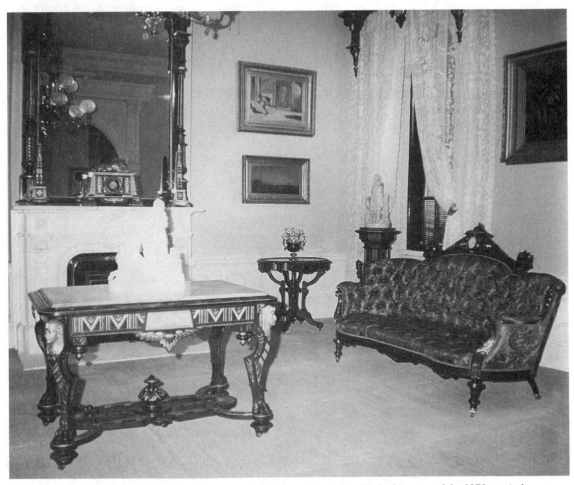

At the 100th birthday celebration of the Metropolitan Museum of Art in New York, this room of the 1870s period, was exhibited. All furniture has the Gothic style of Eastlake.

which were decorated by itinerant artists or even by an artistic member of the family. I have seen some with scenes of buildings on the farm along with trees, flowers, and animals. These must be treated with the same care as oil paintings. They can be restored by a good artist if there is not too much deterioration.

Wooten Desks

The Wooten is called the "King of Desks" by none other than Eileen Dubrow, who is known as the country's foremost collector of them. Having a close association with Wells Fargo, as one was in each office, they have been spread all over the country since they were made in the 1880s. The form is Gothic Revival, which translated to simpler terms is Eastlake, as his design features appear on them. Most were made of walnut, and often inside drawers were veneered with maple as well as burl walnut. An interesting note is that Wells Fargo is known to have marked all its possessions in all its offices, yet no Wooten desk has yet turned up so identified.

Wooten desks were made in Indianapolis. The first patent was issued October 6, 1874, and by 1875, the company was in full production. Business people, as well as presidents, were among the first customers. The desks were made in three grades—standard, extra grade, and superior. The latter featured exquisite carving. Hardware was of Berlin bronze.

Some of the Wootens were built with cylinder tops; these came in twelve styles. In 1877, Joseph Moore, former Wooten manager, obtained rights to make the desk, and also in the same year, Henry Wiggers of Philadelphia patented a desk closely allied to the Wooten. One of these is in the Heinz House at the Henry Ford Museum. The desks were last advertised in 1885, with the company going out of business. Some say the walnut trees needed to make them were disappearing, but history tells us there was a great recession in the mid-1880s—perhaps this is more the reason. Wooten desks have turned up in England, as well as in barns on old country farms, all covered up.

The famed Wooten desk was made in Indiana, mostly in the 1880s period, at the time of Eastlake design. Most were made as storage desks and safes for Wells Fargo, but many found their way into the hands of royalty overseas. Wood is walnut, with various light woods for veneers on the drawers. Value: $5,000-$7,000

Mission

About 1890, the oak period began, lasting until about 1930. It was inspired by the simple, straight lined furniture found in the Spanish missions on the West Coast and in Mexico. Made on square lines, the pieces are rugged indeed. Many town halls and other public buildings are still outfitted with Mission chairs, desks, and tables, since they are functional and nearly indestructible. Most of the pieces would not win any beauty awards, but the clean lines are reminiscent of the comfortable Hepplewhite, which is enduring in quality.

The most conventional furniture for the home was made in this period. The round oak table, pressed back chairs, side-by-side cupboard/desk combinations; Hoosier cabinets; entire bedroom

Oak became a favored wood, about 1890, with the mission styles coming into vogue. Mass production of such items like this side-by-side, brought quality furniture within reach of just about everybody. It has been said that over 50% of "oak" furniture is not really oak, but rather chestnut, elm, poplar, and even plain birch with a stamped oak grain. Value: $450-$850

sets, ice boxes, and sliding door bookcases were in disfavor until the early 1970s. Then, the values of furniture from the previous periods had risen dramatically. Those who wanted to outfit their homes with nostalgic pieces from the past began to take an interest in oak.

Later, attention was directed to the arts and crafts production, which had been limited to but a few makers. The names Gustav and L & JG Stickley of Fayetteville, New York, Limbert in Michigan, and the Roycrofters in East Aurora, New York, began to assume importance as collectors recognized the superior design and craftsmanship. Since then, many books have been written, analyzing the good, better, and best of oak furniture, and these serve as good guides to buyers.

One must pay attention to labels and marks to determine maker. Gustav Stickley not only made furniture, but also published *The Craftsman* magazine in which he detailed the measurements of lumber and offered to sell fittings, pulls, textiles, and other parts and pieces so his furniture could be copied exactly, at home. He indicated in his own writing that each piece of his furniture bears a shop mark, which is a pair of joiners' compasses enclosing the motto "ALS IK Kan," along with the written signature, Stickley, within quotation marks. The original name of the community in which he did his work was Eastwood, New York. Further, he stated that he had no connection with any other factory, to dispel any thoughts that his brothers Leopold and J. George were part of his concern.

Early in the twentieth century, Elbert Hubbard assembled craftspeople who worked in furniture, pottery, lamps, ceramics, and metals, making some of the most desired pieces of that period. The factory went out of business in 1940, but has been revived as the Roycrofters at Large Association in East Aurora, New York. The early Roycrofters furniture is well marked, either by carving on the wood or by a diamond-shaped bronze plate—an R within a circle, topped by a double cross. Mission-style oak was the mainstay of the business, but under Mr. Hubbard's direction, new ground was broken in designs which contributed to the direction of the Art Nouveau and Art Deco periods. Hubbard was a philosopher and his wife, Alice, fought zealously for women's rights. In their memory, the Elbert Hubbard Foundation was formed and the original "campus" which the Roycrofters inhabited is alive again. The location has been placed on the National Registry of Historic Places. One should note the new Roycroft mark features R's back to back. Hubbard is known to have developed the Larkin Club, where he worked before going out on his own. On May 7, 1915, the press announced that the Lusitania had been sunk by a German submarine. Hubbard was on it.

One cannot talk about oak without mentioning the Larkin Soap Manufacturing Company. It began operations in 1875, marketing soap, then eventually branching out into other products. One could exchange soap wrappers for premiums, which included furniture, lamps, rugs, curtains, silverware, linens, and china. The Buffalo Pottery Company was organized in 1901, and began firing in 1903, making pottery items to be used as premiums for the soap wrappers. The furniture work extended into the 1920s, and much of it what is collected today came from the Larkin factory in Buffalo.

The pieces were marked with a paper label, many of which, unfortunately, have come off because of improper care. After World War II, the furniture made its way to cottages, cellars, and chicken coops, as well as the dump. Oak was not in favor. However, with the renewed interest since 1970, the Larkin pieces are considered very desirable today. Copies of the catalog reveal that a round oak table could be had for sixteen soap

Limbert game table in oak. It was made by Limbert Arts and Crafts Furniture, which was located in Grand Rapids and Holland, Michigan. Sold in 1995 for $450.

wrappers. The other premiums are astounding when considered against today's prices.

There is English oak in this country as well. One designer, who is quite well known, was William Morris. An artist and writer from a wealthy family, he was born in 1834 and died in 1896. Morris was interested in design, and in 1857, opened a studio with several partners. Here they designed stained glass, tiles, tableware, textiles, and furniture. This work was the forerunner of the arts and crafts movement. Morris was a contemporary of Charles Eastlake and was influenced by the revival forms popular at the time. The Morris chair is named for him, as he designed it. The favored wood was oak, though mahogany and other hardwoods were used on both sides of the Atlantic. Morris perceived furniture that was suitable as well as functional—well designed, in a way that could be mass-produced. The name "Morris" is generic now. None will be found with his name, as his studio only designed them; others did the manufacturing.

Art Nouveau

Late in the nineteenth century there was a growing interest in designs from the Orient. Trade with Japan brought new ideas in forms and decorations, and the Europeans were the first to incorporate them in their decorative arts. Even the entrances to buildings captured the spirit of what was soon to be called the Art Nouveau style. Flowing lines, floral decoration, and a sculptured look became the rage with architects, as well as with decorators and artisans.

Louis Comfort Tiffany studied in Paris and returned to create some of the best pieces in this period. One could list the names of many lesser-known designers, but their work is not as well recorded, making identification of the artist almost impossible. During this period, the arts and crafts movement flourished, creating much that is high on the collecting list, today. These designs persisted until the 1920s, when new ideas originated after World War I.

Art Deco

In 1926, an exhibition was staged in Paris, titled, *Arts Decoratif,* which introduced new forms into the art world. Nudes appeared in bronze, glass, ceramics, and wood. Photography came into its own during this period, and those who typified the

19th century, Enfield, Connecticut, Shaker teacher's desk with side drawer. Value: $800-$1,200

Early 20th century Art Noveau mahogany gilt mounted vitrine cabinet. Value: $600-$800

"flapper" era have left a profound record of clothing, artifacts, furniture, and decorative objects which exhibited free flowing forms and great nuances in color. Walnut waterfall furniture was in vogue and blonde oak was soon to follow. The years 1920-1950 are designated as the deco period, which was phased out after World War II in favor of much experimentation in design that has yet to be labeled.

Other Styles and Influences

Shaker

To broaden our knowledge of the Shakers, whose industry helped create many artifacts that

Unusual Shaker cupboard, Enfield, Connecticut colony, 19th century. Functional designs were a mark of their work.

are high on the collectible list today, we must recall the movement that started here late in the eighteenth century when Ann Lee left England with a band of followers and founded the first colony at Mt. Lebanon, New York. A celibate sect, it grew nevertheless, and locations for colonies extended all through New England and as far away as Kentucky. The Shakers supported themselves as food and herb growers, and also by the manufacture of furniture and other household items. Their furniture is light and delicate, yet very strong. The lines are simple with no ornament, and in this simplicity projects great beauty. They worked with the woods at hand, and created pieces like chairs, cupboards, desks for the Eldresses, tables of all kinds, and just

19th century pine Shaker cupboard, Mt. Lebanon, New York. This was the first colony established in this country by Mother Ann Lee. Value: $16,000-$18,000

about everything which was made of wood. Their buildings, which still stand today in some places, were designed with strength and durability in mind. They can be found in their original state at Canterbury and Enfield, New Hampshire; Sabbathday Lake, Maine; Hancock, Massachusetts; Chatham, New York; and Pleasant Hill, Kentucky. Most of the groups sold off their material possessions as their numbers dwindled during the Depression. Shaker furniture is high on the desired list today, not only with private collectors, but also with those who are busy restoring Shaker buildings to their original look. The largest colony is in Canterbury, where twenty-seven buildings have been preserved by a foundation set up for this purpose.

At a seminar in Canterbury, New Hampshire in 1991, June Sprigg, curator of Hancock Shaker Village, gave much insight on Shaker artifacts. According to Ms. Sprigg, there were never more than 6,000 Shakers in the movement in this country, in villages stretching from Maine to Kentucky. Thus, if they made everything attributed to them, none would have ever slept. Some oval boxes made as recently as 1987 have been doctored with red paint and aged. Reproduction Shaker seed packets are being made, wrinkled and aged to fool most anyone. Baskets are altered with Shaker-style handles.

A popular item is the Shaker oval box. The walls are a single piece of thin wood, bent and joined with overlapping "fingers" which are nailed (most often with copper nails) to fasten them. Some feel the fingers should point only to the right, but it was affirmed they could point in either direction. Iron nails were used early in the nineteenth century; the copper nails came later. It is possible there are some cribs and cradles, despite the Shaker vow of chastity, as they often took in young children to raise them.

There are no Shaker decoys, card tables, or game boards. They did not decorate buckets. Samplers with birds or crowns are not theirs. Double beds were made until the 1830s, but not after that. The Brother Gregory rockers with ten spindles are being reproduced. Practically all Shaker ladderback chairs have inclined backs.

Moravian

Anyone who has visited Bethlehem, Pennsylvania, marvels at the early stone architecture; some of it dating back to 1741. Buildings here and in

The Moravians settled first in Bethlehem, Pennsylvania as early as 1741. One should visit there to see the historic buildings they left as part of their heritage. Christmas music is a big part of present day celebrations in this city. Noted are the trombone choirs which still play. Pictured is a trombonist's chair with added footrest on each leg, which helped rest the players during long sessions.

Kemerer Museum.

nearby Nazareth marked the founding of the Moravian colonies in the new world. Later, this religious group expanded its missionary work to Winston-Salem, North Carolina and into Ohio.

The history of the Moravians goes back to the fifteenth century when an independent religious community was set up under the guidance of Johan Hus in Germany. August 13, 1727 is celebrated as the foundation of the renewed community at Herrnhut, not far from Dresden. The oppression of religious groups prompted many to migrate to the American colonies.

In Bethlehem, the Kemerer Museum has many items attributed to the Moravians. As with most furniture items made by religious groups, the designs are quite austere. There are not many clues to determine provenance as many other religious groups who settled in Pennsylvania made similar pieces.

Bethlehem is the home of the Moravian Archives, a place where one can research and study the history of this movement. The cemetery is revealing; the stone markers lie on the ground and reveal that anyone, including blacks, were welcome as members. Some are identified as such on the stone, evidencing the all-encompassing work of the Moravian brotherhood. Moravian antiques are not plentiful, but one can study their form and proportions at the Kemerer. It is well worth a visit.

One may visit a settlement overseas at Christianfield, Denmark. The architecture is much like that in Bethlehem and many artifacts made by the Moravians are displayed. It is preserved as a national historic landmark.

Biedermeier

When a piece of nineteenth century furniture sells for $154,000, a lot of interest is aroused as to what it is and why it brought so much money. In this case, at the November 21, 1984, Butterfield & Butterfield auction, a rather heavy "Biedermeier-style" secretary realized the highest price ever received for something not commonly found in America. Most know little about this Continental style, which was popular during the first half of the nineteenth century in Germany and Austria. The term "Biedermeier" actually originated from a popular cartoon character who came to symbolize the German bourgeoisie of that period. Eventually, the term was applied both to the period in general and to the period's social, political, and decorative style.

The Biedermeier design was adapted from French Empire style, but is characterized by a less formal simplicity. The pieces are smaller in scale, made of light-colored indigenous woods; surface ornaments such as ormolu mounts were used sparingly. One of the reasons this secretary brought such an extraordinary price, is that it broke all of these rules. Its architectural style and walnut wood are unique. Although the piece was identified as

Austrian, some Austrian museum curators suggested it is not Viennese, but provincial. Inlaid with the coat of arms of a baron, it was probably commissioned by a newly ennobled baron, explaining its opulence of scale, ornament, and design.

One will find Biedermeier furniture in this country, but it is not plentiful. The best places to look are where the Germans settled: New York State, Pennsylvania, Ohio, and the Carolinas. I have seen some in Denver and on the West Coast.

Zoar

In 1817, a group of separatists from the Lutheran Church in Germany came to America and eventually created Zoar Village in Ohio. The group was active until 1898. Since this was a river town, those who stopped there on ferries and freight launches became customers for the furniture, pottery, and other artifacts made in the community. Zoar furniture is quite rigid and stiff in appearance and is rugged. Unlike the Shakers who developed their own designs, the Zoars, along with other religious sects, generally made furniture in the style of the day, not bothering to beautify it with marquetry or carvings.

The community is being restored today, and more is being learned about what was made there. There is a limited amount of furniture than can now be documented, so you may never know if you possess a Zoar piece unless you do your homework. There are pieces at the Cleveland Museum of Art, where a booklet is available on the history of this sect.

An Austro/German design of the period was Biedermeir. This is an incredible design for a desk made, ostensibly, overseas. There was much Biedermeir-styled furniture made for the common pocketbook. The style was used throughout the 19th century. Value: $3,500-$5,000

Another example of Biedermeir furniture is this fruitwood architectonic secretary abattant, made in the 19th century from fruitwoods and Circassian walnut. Value: $10,000-$12,000

19th century, pine side chair attributed to the Zoar Colony in Ohio. Most chairs made by religious sects were stiff and uncomfortable. Value: $450-$600

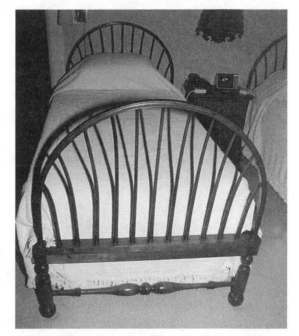

Wallace Nutting is known for his reproduction furniture. This is one of a pair of twin beds he made to duplicate the backs of Windsor chairs, which were used in the bedroom. Value: $800-$1,000

Wallace Nutting

Few people involved in antiques and collecting do not know the name of Wallace Nutting. A Congregationalist minister, he began collecting American furniture and decorative arts as early as 1905. His first book, *Furniture Treasury,* published in 1928, is well illustrated and shows a wide range of what to collect. It is still available in bookstores, which testifies to its value as a guide to collectors.

In later years, Nutting acquired the Wentworth-Gardner House in Portsmouth, New Hampshire, and used it as a showroom in which to sell antiques to museums and other serious buyers. This led to further acquisitions, such as the Saugus Ironworks in Saugus, Massachusetts, and the Webb House in Wethersfield, Connecticut, both of which have since been fully restored and opened to the public.

In 1917, Nutting began making reproduction furniture, and it is said that he lost a fortune in the venture. However, many of his pieces are turning up today, and are highly sought, though none is much more than 80 years of age—dispelling the notion that something must be old to be good. I have seen what I feel is a rarity in Nutting furniture, a marked pair of beds made to resemble the backs of Windsor chairs. These were done on special order for someone who wanted to have them match the other Windsor-style furniture in a room. The beds are in a home in Holyoke, Massachusetts.

Nutting is best known to some collectors for the color photographic prints that bear his name. They give us a look at life as it was, and are still as decorative today as the day they were issued. The Wadsworth Athenaeum in Hartford has a permanent installation of Nutting's collection of early American furniture.

Centennial

During the third quarter of the nineteenth century, there was a revival of interest in the styles prevalent during the Revolutionary period almost a hundred years before. Fine reproductions were made of period styles popular then, using the same woods and same types of veneers and inlays. Another revival took place during the 1920s and 1930s, and the work was so good that anyone but an expert can be easily fooled. Old handmade drawers were often taken from undesirable Empire-style chests and incorporated into good period frames made from old wood. Appraisers long ago labeled such work "Centennial," and the name is in general use today. Many a poor chest or desk was altered with a new base, frame, legs, or feet, and was completely restyled to make it more desirable. Unscrupulous dealers have passed these on without saying too much about them—in one estate appraisal in Boston, eleven of the twelve cased pieces of furniture were Centennial, yet they were bought as antique.

There must be some dealers who genuinely do not know that they are handling a reproduction, so they cannot be accused of misdealing. Actually, in many cases the furniture is just as finely made as its predecessors and should be regarded as fine work. It should not command the same value, but you should not ignore it, as it represents that which was classic in form and work. There are Centennial collectors who want nothing else, and they must confine their buying to the Boston and Philadelphia areas since this is where most of this work was done. What our Bicentennial has produced to match is anybody's conjecture. The rule in buying is to look for as much handwork as possible, and to buy only quality in taste, design, and construction.

Twentieth Century Furniture

Not much can be said for the styling of furniture during the late twentieth century. America's burgeoning population gave growth to mass production which inundated us with very mediocre pieces, and supply seemed much more important than quality. The walnut waterfall, blonde oak, and gray oak became the hallmark for those who wished to be modern. The era spawned a host of factories which brought back "colonial" designs in maple and birch, but the reproductions left a lot to be desired as the workmanship was not good and the wood colorings ranged from red to very light blonde. Quality furniture has always been made, but buyers have always been limited because of cost. Concerns such as Paine in Boston and Mayfair in Albany continued to turn out impeccable pieces, and their work is gathering a lot of attention today from those who regard it as classic in the same manner as you would assess a classic car, boat, or airplane. Private cabinetmakers have

Lacquered black wood furniture is still popular today. The three-part cabinet, pictured, is handmade and hand painted. Purchased in Kowloon, in 1986 for $300. It was shipped to New England for $125.

Walnut and ash conoid bench made by George Nakashima, c. 1958. The study of custom cabinetmakers of the 20th century is ongoing. Much of the work made by them commands higher prices than similar antique items.

always been at work, and from time to time these individual pieces turn up to please their new owners. Those which are labeled are a prize, and if you should locate some of these, attempt to document their history if at all possible, while information might still be available. These pieces may be classics in museums someday, and such documentation will be very important.

It is not likely that there will be a return to the golden age of anything, as quick sale and profit seem to be the motivating force in our economy. Handcrafted furniture will always be with us and there is greater interest in it today, but we can never hope to enjoy it on the scale it reached before 1830. You must live with your nostalgia if nothing more.

Areas of Collecting Interest

Chairs

Branch

There is no question that many years ago, crude chairs were made with available materials. One of the most interesting is a type of chair that was popular in the nineteenth and early twentieth centuries. Made of branches from which the bark has been peeled, it offered utility with very little comfort. Most had a simple handmade cushion to soften the bumps. Many of this type were made all across the country, though in the East they appeared most often in New York State. Some say branch chairs

---

Collecting Tips

There are some very good buys in furniture that has been repaired or restored. This is usually acceptable to the buyer as long as much work is not evident or objectionably visible. A drawer front that is obviously new will hurt a piece. A new frame or legs beneath a chest, well cut, done in good proportion, and refinished so they cannot be told from the upper section will be quite acceptable, though a top price should not be paid. Interior bracing work (new drawer slides and the like) will not harm value too much as long as it is out of sight. However, your leniency over the liberties taken with a piece may not be shared by the next buyer when you wish to dispose of it.

You are lucky if you find a labeled piece of early furniture. Witness this label from Michael Allison, New York, early in the 19th century.

The indented mark of Jonathan Bird, 1792, Charlestown, SC, found on a tilt-top candle stand.

If you are prone to refinishing or decorating pieces of furniture, remember that as much effort must be expended on a poor piece as on a good one. If extra work is needed, it is best to seek quality, as it will be more rewarding as far as ownership and eventual resale are concerned. Always buy a piece with the thought that you may have to sell it someday, and you will be more cautious and better satisfied with your venture into this area of antiques.

gave rise to what is known as the Adirondack chair. The mountainous areas of New York State were full of vacation hotels and homes for which local craftsmen created low-cost furniture.

The tradition for this design seems to have originated in central and eastern Europe, as far back as the sixteenth century. They appear in paintings and sketches of the period. Hardwoods, such as walnut, hickory, and, in this country, maple, seem to have been the favored woods. Oak does not bend well, so the makers did not use it.

When the West was settled in the last century, branch chairs, or twig chairs as some call them, made their appearance in abundance. There were no furniture factories out there, and what came in by railroad was too expensive for the average settler. Each is a unique piece as the design conforms to the wood used in the same way that the shape of a stone wall depends on the shapes of the stones available. A chair like this is not overly valuable, but it is a good conversation piece. All should be saved as early examples of our culture.

Windsor

All through the eighteenth and nineteenth centuries, various types of country chairs appeared. The earliest of the type we can collect easily is the Windsor. According to one story, George III in England saw a spindle back of this type in a farmhouse near his castle and became so enamored of its beauty that he commissioned many to be made for Windsor Castle. This is unlikely, as he did not ascend the throne until 1760 at the age of twenty-two. Historians tell us the Windsor chair form has been with us since about 1740 and well executed in both England and America. The Windsor is one of the most popular to collect today. Identified by its multi-spindled back, it comes in many forms and shapes, and it seems to have been adapted to just about every functional type of side chair or armchair known. The spindle-back chair is not original; counterparts have been identified in early Greek and Roman civilizations. That it was successfully revived in England is not disputed, but most feel it was brought to its fullest form in America. The rarities are the fancy writing armchairs which were made originally for use in classrooms and public buildings where political and public meetings were held.

Some call the bowback armchair a "sackback," but I have never found out why. Some of the best

Branch rocker, typical of furniture that was made in the Adirondacks for summer homes. Eventually, furniture of this type was made in factories, but most pieces I have seen are labeled. Value: $450-$600

Early 20th century stick or branch chairs are popular. Most are inspired by examples such as this from the Adirondacks in New York. Value: $350-$450

examples were made in Connecticut with knuckle arms and boldly turned legs.

The earliest American Windsors were of loopback, bowback, or what some call horseshoe back style, just a simple bowed structure. The straight-line backs seem to be of later origin. They range from three spindles to as many as thirteen, which I saw on an English chair, and are valued accordingly. There is a basic rule that the greater amount of handwork expended in making a piece, the greater the value, so those with more spindles are more expensive.

Armchair, typical of the early 18th century with split spindle back. This is quite a good example as the baluster turnings on the front rail are very bold, New England.

Some historians contend that Thomas Chippendale popularized the first straight crest rail-top chair in the middle of the eighteenth century and since this is not disputed, we can assume that those with straight backs came after this time. The straight rail was popular in the seventeenth century in the Jacobean and William and Mary styles, but during the Queen Anne period (early eighteenth century) and into the Chippendale period, the rounded back was the accepted form.

A theory has been advanced that the Windsor chair actually originated in Windsor, Connecticut, in the seventeenth century and that the style was adopted in Britain. Some feel it was not fancy enough for the English home, but more suited to the colonies. Some feel they were the outgrowth of the Carver and Brewster chairs; the former feature spindles above the seat and the latter, spindles above and below.

The most popular type collected today is the birdcage Windsor, which features a series of squared spaces at the top. Spindles are doweled into the seat back and through the crest rail where they are sheared off. On the birdcage, another rail is installed beneath the top rail, several inches below. The spindles run through this rail as well, but are cut alternatively to form the squared spaces. Some call these chairs pigeonhole or pigeon coop Windsors, but birdcage is the more accepted term. Windsor chairs with legs coming visibly through the seat plank are generally attributed to pre-1800; those with ends of the legs hidden in the plank should be dated after 1800.

The most popular Windsor chair is the seven-spindle, but it appears with five to eleven spindles. The eighteenth century forms feature widely splayed legs and H stretchers, whereas those after 1800 most often have leg-to-leg stretchers. None has been found with button feet. Those with heavy bulbous turnings on the front round, with the large carved disc between—called the baluster turning—are not from New England, but rather show the Dutch influence in New York State and Pennsylvania. Any Windsor with a cabriole leg most likely comes from overseas. Early examples were constructed of durable oak, which gave way to pine plank seats and hardwood spindles and legs. These would be hickory, oak, ash, maple, or birch. Usually they were painted, but bringing them back to natural wood, if properly done, does not depreciate their value—that is, if they are nineteenth-century.

If eighteenth-century, they should be examined to make sure finishing does not destroy a good patina. Quite often, a chairmaker would use many different woods to use up stock in his shop, knowing all would be covered by paint anyway. Be prepared for surprises if several woods show up in the chair you refinish.

Another popular form is the step down Windsor, whose crest rail is cut into a series of steps at the ends. These are not as valuable as the birdcage, but are found in many interesting varieties.

The desirable raised comb back is most often found in rockers.

The fan back is quite good—simple straight spindles fanned out to meet the crest rail. One with nine or eleven spindles is quite valuable.

Clocks

If you want to collect clocks of the late eighteenth and nineteenth centuries, you will do well to concentrate on those of American make. Piece for piece, they will command more money than their foreign counterparts. The tall or grandfather clock is one of the most desired, made everywhere in the colonies. Try to determine whether the works were made by the clockmaker, since many grandfather clocks were assembled from parts bought somewhere else. Works and dials were imported from England, and many American makers merely made the weights and pendulums, then had a cabinetmaker prepare the cases and assemble the clocks for sale. Osborn's Manufactory in Birmingham, England, was a prolific concern, and many so-called American clocks house their works. However, as long as a clock is incorporated in an American case with native weights and pendulum, it is regarded as American. The desirability of these clocks is determined by whether the works came from England or were handmade in America, and the latter will command the most interest and value.

Until about 1850, clocks were powered by weights whose gravitational fall drove the hands and striking mechanisms. When the mass production of spring-wound timepieces became practical, it was impossible to make a shelf clock that would run more than 30 hours with one winding due to the short distance a weight could fall. The tall clocks could run for eight days on one winding because of the long distance the weights could drop to the floor. Spring-wound mechanisms made the eight-day shelf clock a reality. Throughout the nineteenth century, various types of wall, shelf, mantel, and tall clocks were made, along with the clocks designed for commercial or industrial uses. Church and tower clocks were in demand, and many made way back in the 19th century are still keeping time.

Construction and Design

There are similarities between tall clocks made in Europe and those made in America. The Sheraton-style cases made in England are much the same as those made here, so it is advisable to check the works first to see if they are stamped with a maker's name. In upper New England, you will find that the makers used can-type weights made from tin, which were soldered after being filled with metal, stone, or even beach sand. Most of the many Pennsylvania clockmakers used solid cast-iron weights in the manner of the English clocks.

Tall clock by Samuel Milliken, Bradford, Massachusetts, c. 1740. Most American tall clocks in the 18th century displayed brass faces. Value: $12,000-$14,000

However, most of the Pennsylvania clocks are quite tall, some standing as high as nine feet, and the English clocks are more the height of those made in New England. So if you find a tall clock of New England height (in the seven-and-a-half-foot range) with iron weights, you could be looking at one made in England. Can weights are generally a good sign of American make, but you must realize that clock weights are interchangeable, so you must do some research to verify the place where the clock is reputed to have been made.

Mantel clocks took on different sizes and shapes. Most were made of wood, but marble, china, and iron cases are common. Some were made with scenes painted on the inside of the glass fronts, and this can heighten the value, especially if the work pictures some important place or person. Some had special movements or different means of powering the clock. One such device resembles a wagon spring—very few were made, and those appearing now command high prices. Some clocks

Elegant tall clock by Jacob Godshalk, Philadelphia, c. 1755. The Philadelphia cases were perhaps the fanciest ever made in America. Value: $32,500-$35,000

were made with alarms, and these are of interest. The cases gradually evolved in style, keeping pace with furniture changes. Those made in the later nineteenth century in what is called "gingerbread" reflect the last true period change, that of Eastlake. They were made in these fancy styles as late as the 1920s, with the designs often pressed into the wood by machine.

School and regulator clocks have experienced a revival, and those with calendar devices are interesting, but are in short supply. China cased clocks are often a product of foreign manufacture, notably German. Many have American works, however, which suggest that the cases might have been shipped here for final assembly. There are some French marble and iron-cased mantel clocks with American works, and you have only to read the dial to confirm this.

Clockmakers

Even if a clock is signed with the name of a noted maker, you must do a little more research to document it. Witness the case of the famous Simon Willard, who worked in the Boston area during the Federal period. A master clockmaker, he was responsible for training many apprentices. Those who came from his shop are regarded as next to him in importance as craftsmen. Clocks by one such apprentice, Lemuel Curtis, often sell for more than the master's, but Willard is revered for his clocks and many fine ones grace homes and museums, not only in New England, but throughout the country.

Willard was known for creating masterpieces in unusual cases, such as his famous lighthouse clock, one of which is in the White House. Shaped like a lighthouse, this clock features a face at the top, surrounded by a glass dome, with the pendulum and weight hidden by the tall body. Some scholars wonder if he was actually responsible for such oddities as this, or if they were the creation of apprentices, with the works somehow appearing with Willard's name. In the absence of written proof, much of this was only conjecture until new evidence came to light.

An issue of the *Boston Evening Transcript* of Saturday, March 28, 1928, carries a revealing story about Simon Willard which should give rise to much conjecture and cause some uneasiness among owners of Willard clocks. It was written by a Charles Messer Stow, a highly regarded antiquarian of his time. He tells of visiting the showroom of Israel Sack, who was then in Boston, and he reprinted a bill of sale which was attached to the door of a tall clock. It read:

Clock Manufactory, Simon Willard, at his clock dial in Roxbury Street, manufactures every kind of clockwork, such as large clocks for steeples, made in the best manner and warranted; price with one dial, 500 dollars; with two dials, 600 dollars; with three dials, 700 dollars; with four dials, 900. Common eight-day clocks, with very elegant faces and mahogany cases, price from 50 to 60 dollars. Elegant eight-day timepieces, price 30 dollars.

Timepieces which run 30 hours and warranted, price 10 dollars. Spring clocks of all kinds, price from 50 to 60 dollars. Clocks that will run one year, with once winding up, with very elegant cases, price 100 dollars. Timepieces for astronomical purposes, price 70 dollars. Timepieces for meeting houses, to place before the gallery, with neat enameled dials, price 55 dollars. Chime clocks that will play 6 tunes, price 120 dollars. Perambulators are also made at said place which can be affixed to any kind of carriage and will tell the miles and rods exact, price 15 dollars. Printed by I. Thomas, Jun. Worcester.

The advertisement tells us of many items made by Willard that have not yet turned up. Where is a clock that runs one year on one winding, where is the clock that plays six tunes, where is the perambulator device that tells the miles traveled with the baby, who ever knew that Willard made such devices? What will give comfort to Willard clock owners if the following statement, printed by Willard and inserted inside the same case, is true? It reads:

I believe the public are not generally aware that my former patent right expired six years ago, which induces me to caution them against the frequent impositions practiced in vending spurious timepieces. It is true these have Patent printed on them and some with my name and their outward appearance resembles those formerly made by me. Thus they are palm'd on the public. Several of them have been brought to me for repairs, that would certainly put the greatest bungler to blush. Such is the country inundated with, and such I consider prejudicial to my reputation; I therefore

disclaim being the manufacturer of such vile performances. S. Willard.

When Willard retired from business in 1839, he sold his tools and goodwill to an apprentice, Elnathan Taber. Taber was allowed to print Simon Willard on the face of the clocks he made, and these were sold by Simon Willard, Jr., at his store in Boston. All of this should be cause for reflection by owners of "Willard" clocks, as well as dealers and appraisers. In light of the direct writing by Willard himself, you cannot be too careful in attribution to the master. You must apply some of this thinking to other makers as well.

Simon Willard is known to have put his works in many different cases, such as the one pictured. All of his clocks are well marked.

Early in the nineteenth century, three noted clockmakers joined forces in one concern, though later they went out on their own. Each was a true craftsman and each left us a legacy in fine timepieces. Seth Thomas, Eli Terry, and Silas Hoadley made up this partnership and, along with other makers such as Chauncey Jerome and Joseph Ives, brought to the industry the mechanization that made volume production possible. The Connecticut peddlers clock came into being—a shelf clock that sold for about $10 at a time when a tall one cost $100. These clocks were sold door-to-door, bringing a timepiece within the reach of almost everyone.

Tall clock made by James C. Cole, Rochester, New Hampshire, c. 1815 in pine case. Charles Dennett of Rochester made fancy cases for Cole and some of these are in major museums in the country. Value: $5,000-$7,000

Performing

Performing clocks are experiencing a revival. Years ago, just after World War II, cuckoo clocks were important collectibles. There was plenty of competition for those carved of walnut in fancy styles. Returning servicemen brought home many of them, which flooded the market, lowering the value of both old and new.

The cuckoo clock is said to have been invented about 1730 in Germany by a craftsman named Anton Ketterer. Most were made in the Black Forest region, a picturesque area along the Rhine. Perhaps they reached their peak in interest at the time of our centennial in the 1870s, when many were exhibited. Soon, almost every parlor had one,

Simon Willard's famous lighthouse clock. Reputedly, the glass dome shades were made at the Boston and Sandwich Glass Company. Value: $100,000-$130,000

which is the reason so many turn up today. The huge output of new cuckoo clocks has reduced the value of old and new. Most hang on a wall, little used, as they have to be wound every day.

At auction recently, some of the earlier clocks in carved walnut, which match the Eastlake period furniture, achieved prices not seen but a few years ago. None made after that time seem to complement the furniture of this century, so it may be awhile before their turn comes.

American shelf clock by Elnathan Taber who was an apprentice to Simon Willard and later took over his business in 1839. Value: $3,500-$4,000

Regulator

The word "regulator" was used to describe an accurate wall clock. According to Brooks Palmer, author of the *Book of American Clocks,* the term was applied to many Connecticut-made clocks, many thousands of which were made. The octagonal frame around the face seems to have originated in the middle of the nineteenth century, though the greatest production came late in the nineteenth and early into the twentieth centuries. Hardly a schoolroom or office was not equipped at some time with a regulator clock. Some ran eight days on a winding, others were geared to thirty days.

Seth Thomas, with Eli Terry and Silas Hoadley in partnership, began making clocks in Greystone, Connecticut, about 1808. They made wood as well as brass movements. In 1813, Thomas sold out his interest to Hoadley and moved to Plymouth Hollow, where some of his most desirable clocks were made. In 1866, to honor one of its most popular residents, the name of Plymouth Hollow was changed to Thomaston, so it is reasonably easy to date his clocks, depending on the town name that appears on the label.

All regulators are quite desirable today, but those with names of the better makers, such as Thomas, are the ones sought by collectors. Oak cases are the best, and condition must be good. Copies of these clocks made in Japan have recently flooded the American market. Once in awhile a cache of them turns up which had been stored away by some institution that replaced them with electric clocks years before. Quite interesting are those with an S and T forming part of the hands. These clocks were made in a variety of sizes; thirty inches was the standard size for schoolroom

Edward Howard of Boston is noted for the wall clocks he made in five sizes ranging from 30 inches to five feet. Most are in wood, but at North Station in Boston, they had a marble case Howard, five feet long. It disappeared when the station was remodeled.

Orrery

An orrery is a clockwork mechanism that reproduces the daily motion of the earth and periods of the moon. The idea was to show the sun and planets on the same plane with relative motions, rather than showing their size and distance from each other. One can wind the clock mechanism and watch the revolving of the planets. Through scientific calculation it is also possible to establish their relationship to each other in future.

The first orreries were made by the noted English clockmaker Thomas Tompion and his nephew by marriage, George Graham. The first was made for Queen Anne. It was called a tellurium and was made of silver and ebony. Later models feature extended arms with planets and their satellites attached showing their position at all times.

Orreries were expensive and were found at first only in wealthy homes. In time, less expensive models were designed for school use. By the middle of the eighteenth century they were quite common in the British Empire. The larger models are fixed; other models were designed to collapse and could be carried from place to place.

Most are wound with a hand crank, not a key. The better orreries are made of metal, but in the nineteenth century they were also made in wood, paper, and papier-mâché. Variations of type are endless. Those made in England are the most collectible, so England is a good place to look for one.

clocks. They keep good time, and the brass works in most will outlive any present-day owner.

Lacquered Furniture

When trade with the Orient began centuries ago, the Europeans brought back many decorated pieces of furniture, as well as other decorative art objects. They found great favor on the Continent and in England, so it was only natural that this style was duplicated. Artisans were taught to beautify furniture in England in oriental design, but the wealthy wanted none of that. When furniture was ordered from an English cabinetmaker, quite often it would be sent by clipper ship to the Orient to be lacquered and gilded in this fashion. One might wait two years to end up with the piece in his home.

Here in this country, this was too much of a luxury, and the Orient was too far away. So in our seaport cities, japanners, as they were called, were trained to do such work locally. Today, this

Queen Anne scarlet lacquer bureau bookcase with rare blocked base c. 1720. Most likely, England. Value: $16,000-$18,000

Lacquered furniture pieces began to arrive from the Orient as part of our clipper trade, which expanded during the 19th century. Popular were the sewing stands which contained, under the lift top, all the necessities for the lady of the house.

Two clear glass whale oil lamps c. 1840s, which would be described identically, but dimensions prove they are not. These are pressed, have a dome top, heart-shaped design, hexagonal bulbous knop and hexagonal base. Be careful in pairing up items of any kind. Value: $175 ea.

furniture is as highly prized as the oriental. Black japan lacquer was made from linseed oil, umber, asphaltum, and turpentine to thin it. The gilding was done with gold leaf or powder, and then protected with a mordant varnish. Some refer to this type of decoration as chinoiserie. It became a favorite not only on furniture but also on woodwork, silver, porcelain, pottery, wallpaper, cotton, linen, and other textiles as well.

Some historians believe that all Queen Anne furniture came painted, japanned, or decorated originally. Pieces that do not have this or another painted finish, in their opinion, have been refinished to the detriment of the piece.

Lamps and Lighting

Fuel-Burning

A great deal of the world is still lighted by oil, which means that many of the lighting devices we consider antique are still in use in various lands.

Fats and oils of all kinds were common fuel for early American lamps, and many homes were lighted with them well into the nineteenth century. Lard was a popular fuel at the end of the eighteenth century, but this gave way to whale oil early in the nineteenth century. Whale oil was made by rendering the blubber from a sperm whale. In the mid-1830s a new fuel, camphene, was introduced and widely accepted because it was cleaner burning and gave off less odor and smoke than the whale oil. Camphene was made of about one part turpentine to seven parts alcohol. Lemon, balsam, and juniper were among the other ingredients introduced to camphene fluid to give it a better scent and burning quality. Unfortunately, camphene was quite volatile and many fires were started by careless people who put it into lamps other than those designed for it. Camphene lamps look almost identical to whale oil lamps, but you can tell them apart by the length of their wick spouts. Camphene lamp spouts are longer in order to keep the flame farther away from the fuel supply.

The Argand lamp was invented in Switzerland during 1783 and was the first radical change in lighting since the beginning of time. Until then, fats and oils were burned in the open, either in cruzie or Betty lamps or hardened into candle form. The new principle allowed fats to be burned through a wick, using a draft of air introduced beneath the wick and a glass chimney to draw the air upward. All oil lamps operate on this principle to this day. However, it was not until the first oil well was drilled at Titusville, Pennsylvania, by Colonel Edwin Drake, beginning the petroleum industry, that petroleum oil lamps began to dominate lighting. Coal oil (a residue from diggings at mines) had been used before that time, but it did not have much impact, as production was limited.

The birth of kerosene as a fuel during the growing industrial age brought with it a tremendous surge toward making lighting devices, notably the glass oil lamp. These lamps could be pressed out cheaply and soon practically every home had one or more. The multitude of such lamps, made in glass as well as in metal, provides enough informa-tion to make another book. However, here are some tips that can be useful. Any colored glass is important, as well as the type of decoration, especially that of hand-painted shades. Some people collect lamps by pattern. The popular "Gone with the Wind Lamp" which made its appearance in that movie, was actually not around at the time of the Civil War. This is the double-globed type, usually with painted decoration on the upper and lower sections. The upper globe has quite often been broken and replaced with a reproduction. If this is well done it is acceptable, but if the replacement is obvious, it harms the value. Many lamps were made with bases of metals of all kinds and even of marble and alabaster, either in simple turned style or else fancied up with figurines. These must be judged on their quality and appeal.

The astral lamp was designed to carry fuel from a font to the burner via a tube, which made an overhanging light possible. A special fuel, called astral oil, was created for this lamp. Many of the old astral lamps are high on the desirable list since they

American, c. 1840s, clear pressed glass camphene lamp. Wick is extended, as camphene is very volatile and heat must be kept away from it. Value: $250

One of the many decorative lamps made by Louis Comfort Tiffany in New York, early 20th century. Lily lamps, such as this, are priced according to the number of shades. Value: $12,500-$15,000

were made with cut glass shades and prisms for elegant homes.

The advent of gas and electricity for lighting at the end of the nineteenth century caused the slow demise of oil lamps as lighting devices in America, but it was not until after the implementation of the rural electrification program in the 1920s and 1930s that they made a rapid disappearance. Most country people keep a supply of oil lamps in case of power failures, and oil lamps keep turning up at auctions when old estates are liquidated.

The hand lantern was a necessary device, whether it burned oil or used a candle. The early pierced tin lanterns date back to before the Revolution. At the turn of the century these gave way to lanterns faced with glass as the glass industry grew to meet the demand. The Dietz Company is still very much in the lantern business, and advertises that it has a plant in Hong Kong, which turns out over a million units a year—mostly for the underdeveloped nations. More lanterns are being made today than at any other time in history, so you must never regard the oil lantern as a disappearing item. However, some of the old ones make good collectibles, especially those made for the railroads. Some utilize brass, and these are the best. You can see a great collection of lanterns of all generations at the Canal Museum in Syracuse, New York.

Old coach lanterns and automobile lights are rising in value. The early ones burned carbide gas, which is given off when calcium carbide is moistened with water. Kerosene was used in some as late as World War I, and many have turned up from government warehouses still dressed in their khaki color. These must be judged on interest and condition. As is the case with many types of collectibles, pairs of lanterns are more desired than singles.

Electric

The most desirable of the electric lights are those which are popularly called "Tiffany type" lamps (see Chapter Two for more information on Tiffany). These feature shades of iridescent or colored glass set in either leaded or bronze framing. Those made by Tiffany are commanding huge prices. The workmanship in the coloring, design, and iridescence of his lamps is unmatched. Some of the lesser types are referred to as oyster shell shaded lamps and are quite Gothic in their look. The coloring and design in the glass is most important in judging their values.

Aladdin Lamps

Aladdin is one of the great names in lamps of the early part of this century. Practically every farm home had one or more. Now they are being sold at auctions and by dealers as collectible antiques. A club called the Aladdin Knights of the Mystic Lamp has been organized.

Victor Samuel Johnson formed the Mantle Lamp Company of America in Chicago in 1908. He was born in Minden, Nebraska, in 1882 and died in 1943. In 1949, it became the Aladdin Industries and today is headquartered in Nashville, Tennessee.

The company gained fame at the Panama-Pacific International Exposition in San Francisco in 1915 by being awarded a gold model for its Number 6 lamp. The company advertised it made the best kerosene lamp in the world and offered

There are collectors of electric lamps. This Aladdin lamp of the 1920s is typical of a wide range available. There are clubs which promote the Aladdins. Value: $450-$600

$1,000 for any lamp that could equal it. The offer was never collected.

Sixteen models of Aladdin Lamps were made from 1909 to 1968. They can be found in combinations of bright nickel, satin brass, Old English brass, and glass. Most are identified easily by the special 12-1/2" tall chimney designed for this company alone. The extra height created better combustion. In an Aladdin kerosene mantle lamp, the kerosene is burned primarily not to produce light, but rather to produce heat. The heat of the nonluminous blue flame causes the nonburning mantle to incandesce and emit its pure white light.

Aladdin table electric lamps are a new area of collecting interest. Some of these have soared in price. In the bibliography you'll find a book by W. Courter in which you can see pictures and obtain information on what you should seek.

Radios

Old radios fall into the collectible category since most date from after World War I. Early sets were completely battery-operated, but also very popular were the crystal receivers that were put together by children as well as amateurs. High-power stations were set up in the 1920s, among them WGY in Schenectady, XERA in Del Rio, Texas, and WLW in Cincinnati, all with 500,000 watts of output. If you compare this with

R.C.A. Regenerator reciever.

the maximum of 50,000 watts allowed clear-channel stations today, you can understand why it was easy to build almost anything to receive such a strong signal. The TRF (tuned radio frequency) receivers were the rule until the mid-1920s when the superheterodyne came along to replace them. Tinny magnetic speakers gave way to the more resonant dynamic speakers, and electricity became the universal power for them.

If you are looking for exotic early radios, concentrate on early Atwater Kent, Majestic, RCA, and Polle Royal. There are many others that are good to collect whose names disappeared years ago. Perhaps most desired are the Scott all-wave receivers of the 1930s. They were built on two chrome chassis: the upper tuning section, and the lower amplifying section. As many as thirty tubes were in these sets, guaranteeing worldwide reception of the highest order. A sleeper is the Philco 690 XX made in 1937. With six speakers, it heralded the oncoming hi-fi boom and could tune the world. The less expensive 490 XX had four speakers, woofers and tweeters, making it quite a set as well.

There is growing interest today in short-wave reception. The old sets were designed to pull in the farthest stations. I would look for the early Scotts. Those built today probably cannot exceed their quality and reception.

Sliding-Door Bookcases

Very popular with the collecting set today is the sliding door bookcase. Most were made in separate sections so that one could add them to create any

Atwater Kent radio with refinished dome, table-type model.

height desired. The door lifts and slides to the rear over the books, making it self-storing and handy. One will find a drawer in the bottom section quite often, though many bookcases were made without them. Oak is the favored wood; most such cases were made between 1890 and 1930, when oak was very popular.

Oak fits in with the décor of many homes where this is the wood collected. Also, it is easy to move these cases, as each section lifts off. I have never seen one with locks, so one assumes that most books were not considered valuable enough to steal at the time. Most popular widths range between 36 and 42 inches. They were made by several companies, so it would be difficult to assign provenance if they are not labeled.

I have seen these bookcases in walnut and mahogany, but these do not have the value of oak. One will find them when law offices are sold out at auction, and they turn up in house auctions as well. Remember though, that these are being reproduced today, in oak as well as other woods. Prices of new ones are about the same as the old, which means the value of the olds should stabilize. Best advice is not to buy old or new for investment, but rather for use, as reproductions generally diminish the value of the old. Many buyers prefer the new ones, which do not need to be refinished.

Spool Cabinets

Collectors seem to like any furniture which has a lot of drawers. They are put to use to hold collections or as storage chests that take up a minimum of space with maximum capacity. One of the favorites at auctions just about anyplace, is the spool cabinet. The earliest seem to have made their appearance in the Eastlake period, c. 1870-1890, and were made extensively into the 1930s. Years ago, most communities had at least one dry goods store, which sold towels, sheets, and pillowcases along with yard goods, patterns, thread, and needles. The spool cabinet was a necessity as a storage and display piece of furniture. The earliest were made in walnut and oak and seemingly these would continue to be the favorites. One will see them mahogany stained, but most likely less expensive woods were used underneath this coloring.

These cabinets range from the tabletop type to those that rest on the floor. The more drawers the better. Some spool cabinets from the Eastlake

A spool cabinet which details what is in the drawers. This is a fine example dating from the late 19th century. Value: $450

period feature acorn-carved handles and teardrop pulls, while most feature knob pulls. I have seen them in wood, brass, and glass. Those with the original lithographed labels on the drawers and especially those in good condition will command more dollars.

If you purchase such a cabinet, it is best to leave it in original condition. Restoration might hurt its look and the interest in it if you ever wish to sell it.

Tea Wagons

The small table on wheels is called a tea wagon. Its history is not clear. We do know that tea drinking did not come into vogue until the seventeenth century, and most vessels, utensils, and furniture relating to it did not appear until then. The early tea table is small, often with a tilt top, and in many shapes and forms. None from our colonial period had wheels. The caster did not appear until the middle of the eighteenth century, but was not used on most small utility tables. Casters were generally reserved for larger pieces, making them easier to move. The tea wagon seems to have appeared late in the nineteenth century, perhaps as late as the 1890s. No manuals on the preceding Eastlake and Victorian furniture picture them. Hence the term "antique" can be only loosely applied. Tea wagons are machine produced and have been made extensively right up until today. Most are in mahogany or walnut finish, though they can be made of almost any wood stained to resemble mahogany or walnut. Early in this century, they could be found in almost any furniture store. Their popularity experienced a revival as the

TV snack table during the early days of TV. This was nothing but a modern version of an older form. The dark-colored woods disappeared, and the sleeker Scandinavian modern design took over.

Older tea wagons are judged by their style, wood, and condition. The fancier the better, and true mahogany or walnut makes them more valuable. Wheels have narrow solid rubber tires and these must be in good shape. Some were painted and stenciled by owners over the years. Good decoration may enhance value.

Wicker

Wicker is a generic term, not a raw material, that includes wood, rattan, and manmade fibers. Very little is known about wicker furniture, though it is collected readily today. The earliest pieces, made as far back as the time of the early Egyptians, were made of rattan, and this material was used extensively into this century. New developments in the industrial age changed the way wicker and rattan furniture were made, so be aware of the different types and weaves when buying.

Late in the last century, it was felt that tightly woven wicker furniture (known as Cape Cod style) was the best because it was stronger. A machine was invented to twist paper on wire into a cord which could be woven on yet another machine, developed by Marshall B. Lloyd in Michigan. Much of what is called wicker today is really this kind of tightly woven papier-mâché. That is why knowledgeable buyers look for the open weave, sometimes called a Bar Harbor weave. Paper is not strong enough to be woven into an open design, so if you want rattan, look for the open weave. Naturally, the arms of a chair and other areas where reinforcement is needed will be tightly woven, whether the chair is made of rattan or paper. But if the non-stress areas, such as the back of a chair, are made in an open weave, you can feel safe that the chair is not made of paper. The Bar Harbor weave was used at first to cut down the cost of manufacturing wicker, but today it assures the material used, which is most important.

One danger in buying a paper wicker is that it cannot be dipped to remove paint. The paper will soften in the mixture, causing it to lose its strength. If you have tightly woven pieces, you can check to see if they are wood or paper by getting underneath and piercing with a knife blade. This is advisable before any restoration is undertaken.

Assortment of wicker furniture.

FURNITURE GALLERY

Transitional side chair with Queen Anne base and Chippendal back, c. 1750. Though upholstered around the side rails, this is American. The owners know the reupholstering was done incorrectly.

Lyre-based Federal-period table, mahogany, and gilt bronze mounts. In the style of Charles Honore Lannuier, New York, c. 1830. The out-swept legs on a pedestal base were used extensively in the period, by many cabinetmakers, among them, Duncan Phyfe. Value: $4,000-$6,000

The Gothic-styled base of this table marks the Eastlake period. Walnut with white marble top. Practically all American furniture has white marble tops. If you see a colored marble, your first instinct is to regard it as European, until it is checked. There is colored marble dug in this country, but not enough to satisfy a big demand. Value: $450-$600

Bow front Sheraton chest, c. 1820-1830, mahogany with figured birch veneers. Cookie corners, reeded posts. Some in this period featured scroll backs. Its value in 1970 would have been between four and six hundred dollars. Value today, in the $2,500 to $3,500 range.

Rare is the couch with square-tapered legs in Hepplewhite style. Casters appeared mid 18th century in England and were used, as well, in this country. Value: $3,000-$4,000

Taylor & Dull photography.

Bombe, four graduated-drawer chest; mahogany, Boston area; 18th century. Sold by Sotheby Parke-Bernet galleries on Oct. 26, 1957 for $4,500.

As nice a 19th century Shaker chest as one can find, Enfield, Connecticut. The cabinetmakers worked with pine, maple, butternut, birch, ash, beech, and other local woods. Value: $18,000-$22,000

Bombe-shaped secretary with bandy legs and ball and talon feet. This design is credited by historians to only have been made in the Boston area, in this country, c. 1750-1775.

Shaker eldress's desk made for them for private storage and use. The Shaker rocker exhibits a feature that must be present to be Shaker—the chair legs must be slotted to fit over the rockers. Stools of the type pictured could have been used for climbing into high beds, or as prayer stools.

Originally, a drum-top occasional table, this was cut down to make a coffee table. Claw feet, mahogany, with an eagle inlaid on the top, Empire period. Value: $300-$500

Mahogany Empire period bed by Prudent Mallard, New Orleans, c. 1840s. He worked with Duncan Phyfe before opening his own cabinet shop. Much of his furniture was as high as 14 feet. It is of interest that all four posts are carved alike. Value: $8,000-$12,000

The sabre leg is a mark of the Empire period in this country. The vase splat was popular. These were made all over our country in the 1803-1850 period. Value: $125

Worktable, with rope-carved legs, three drawers and drop leaves. Though it looks like many sewing tables with a lift top and false drawer, this example is really a three-drawer table, Empire period. Value: $600-$800

One of a pair of Empire game tables which sold for $2,750 at Morton's in New Orleans. The striking claw-footed pedestal base, is all hand carved. Period about 1830-1840. American, possibly Anthony Quervelle, Philadelphia.

Mahogany Empire period bed by Prudent Mallard, New Orleans, c. 1840s. He worked with Duncan Phyfe before opening his own cabinet shop. Much of his furniture was as high as 14 feet. It is of interest that all four posts are carved alike. Value: $8,000-$12,000

Empire ormolu-mounted mahogany tric-trac table, early 19th century. It could have come from either England or France. Few of our cabinetmakers indulged in such classic decoration. Value: $15,000-$20,000

Couch featuring dolphin feet and arms; American, Empire period.

18th century, paneled-corner cupboard, made of pine. Its French design suggests it may have been made in Canada. Value: $1,800-$2,200

Hunt table, Maryland, late 18th century; made of cypress and pine. These tall serving tables were used outdoors at the time of a foxhunt, so riders could reach their food and drink without dismounting. This form is very English. None has appeared in New England, as the foxhunt tradition was not alive in the North. Value: $1,500-$1,800

Snake foot mahogany, tilt-top, dish-top tea table, c. 1770. Made in Portsmouth or Dover, NH. Value: $1,200-$1,800

Tambour desk, so called because of the tambour doors, which recede onto the body when closed. Late 19th century, American. Value: $4,500-$6,000

The most spectacular slant-top desk of them all. In carved ivory, made in China for Catherine the Great; now in Pushkin Palace. There are carved heads of former Czars and Czarinas, in colored relief.

During the period of Louis XVI, late 18th century, French designs were copied all over the world. Furniture, like these chairs, came from overseas. Here are two of a set of six Italian neoclassical, parcel gilt and painted armchairs. In 1994, Butterfields estimated them between $12,000 and $18,000.

Four-post bed with tester, New England. The reeded posts and acanthus leaf carving mark it Sheraton, early in the 19th century. Most often the rear posts did not match the front, as we see here. This form is perhaps the most reproduced for beds of this type, mahogany. Value: $1,800-$2,500

Three work tables. At left, the fancy spool-carved legs are very Empire, but the top features cookie corners, which appeared in Sheraton furniture. Center piece has the tapered legs of Hepplewhite and is most likely a sewing table with lift top and false drawers at the top. Table at far right exhibits rope-carved legs in Empire style. All are early 19th century pieces. Values from left: $800; $600; $800

Mahogany tambour secretary, New England, c. 1800. Its upper section is nicely scrolled and finished with flame finials and diamond-paneled doors. The three drawers are carved. The piece terminates with legs, which are Sheraton. Value: $7,000-$9,000

Tilt-top candle stand in mahogany. The spider legs mark it as early 19th century, New England. Value: $600-$800

Impressive drop-leaf table, rope-carved legs, c. 1830s. Single-board drop leaves are 19", wood is cherry, Southern New England.

Birch drop-leaf table with turned legs, c. 1820-1830. Double ball turning dresses it. This large width in birch boards is rare and unusual. Bought in NH the year after the Civil War ended, for $1 at auction.

Massachusetts tap table, estimated c. 1800. Single pine board top measures 36" x 27". This form was made extensively through the 18th and 19th centuries. Value: $1,200-$1,600

After the Revolution, we were friendly with the French, who had assisted us. The furniture they sent here influenced our Sheraton and Empire period styles. This is a gilded armchair, which was made in the French Style in Philadelphia, c. 1800. Value: $3,000-$4,000

Classic New England worktable with two drawers and drop leaves. Mahogany and mahogany veneers. The long legs, past the final turning, give this a classy look. Legs are rope carved, c. 1830-1840.

Unusually tall four-post bed with no tester. It features ball and talon feet. Most likely it is 18th century, from England.

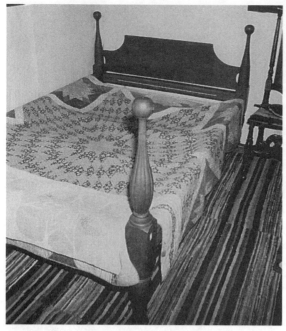

In the 1840s, the tall posts all but disappeared from beds, giving way to the shorter versions with all types of carving at the tops—cannon balls, lemons, eagles, pineapples, bells, and the like. Most had rope springs. At a show in 1975, it sold for $800.

Rarely is there any discussion of furniture made in New Jersey. Pictured is the chest I use—made in New Jersey, c. 1830-1840, in walnut. The large drawer at the top indicates it did not come from upper New England. Provenance is known, as the family in New Jersey owned it ever since it was made. There were lots of fine cabinetmakers in NJ. However, most often, one must go there to see their work. Value: $2,200-$2,800

Game table in the style of Charles Honore Lannuier, New York. The carved legs and claw feet, add to its desirability, c. 1830-1840.

Fire screens were a necessity when one sat or read by the fire light. The curule leg is standard in Empire design, influenced by the excavations which were done early in the century in Egypt. Panels can be painted, or feature needlework of one type or another. Value: $1,700-$2,250

A simple country bed in spool design, which originated in the growing industrial period, of the 19th century. Spools of all types were created for the spinning mills, and the form spilled over into furniture and continued throughout the century. Value: $250-$300

Double bed in cherry, New York State. It sold at auction in 1985 in Fayetteville, New York for $450. The posts feature the pineapple carvings.

Papier-mâché armchair, c. 1850-1860 with mother-of-pearl inlay. It is black lacquered and came from the Orient. Value: $600-$800

Side chair, attributed to John Henry Belter, New York mid 19th century. Belter pioneered the use of laminated wood, which was steamed and bent under pressure, then carved. The wood fibers were cut and the backs would never lose their shape. One should look for the laminations on the back frame. Value: $5,000-$7,000

Harp of David, mid 19th century, made by Harp-O-Cord Company, Columbus Ohio. 20" in height. Value: $400-$600

Rococco Revival carved rosewood etagere, attributed to Alexander Roux. New York, c. 1850-1860. A near identical example, with label, is at the Metropolitan Museum of Art in New York City.

Small oval lamp stand, tilt top, with spider legs, which became popular after 1800. Wood is mahogany, Connecticut. Value: $600-$800

Drum-top table in classic style, made in New York. The carved legs and claw feet add to its desirability, c. 1830-1840. Value: $4,000-$6,000

An English drop-leaf table with drawer with legs in George IV style, c. 1820-1840, mahogany. Not much furniture from this period is available in this country. Value: $1,800-$2,200

The sack back Windsor armchair is most desirable. A lot of spindles and knuckles on the arms improve the value, 18th and 19th centuries. Value: $1,800-$2,200

Washstands were made extensively in pine for the farm and factory homes. These examples were photographed at a shop in Truro, Nova Scotia, so most likely are Canadian. Values from left: $75; $175

Step-down Windsor chair, in pine and maple. Early 19th century. So called, because of the steps in the back rail. Value: $175-$250

Fan-back Windsor chair, late 18th century. So dated, because the legs are doweled into the seat and are visible. If they terminated in the seat, dating would be after 1800. Value: $300-$450

Ladies' writing desk labeled by Meier and Hagen. Sold at Sotheby's for $750.

Rare Windsor bench with spindle back. Early 19th century, New England. Value: $1,800-$2,500

At many auctions, upholstery is stripped, so buyers can see the frame and tool marks. Most would be reupholstered anyway.

Walnut loveseat made between 1840-1870. Thin wood is desired on pieces of this period, along with an oval or cameo back; triple arch, graceful arms and legs; serpentine front with carving and a minimum of upholstery. This example does not meet the requirements to be a good one. Value: $200-$300

Falling into the deacon's bench category is this New England example, which dates to the latter half of the 19th century. Value: $200-$350

Sack back Windsor armchair with plain arms, early 19th century, New England. At right, is a mid 19th century, New England arrow-back/comb-back rocker. The rockers can be suspect in a chair of this type. Values from left: $1,800-$2,200; $150

Unusual 19th century. New England side chair in Windsor style, with spindles. I do not know of any name assigned to this form. Sold for $300 at auction.

Writing arm Windsor chair with comb back. The chair legs protrude through the seat, which would date it late 18th century, New England. Value: $2,500-$3,500

*Last half of
the 19th century pine
lift commode, which was made as part of
a bedroom set. Many were decorated at the
factory, and others by itinerant painters in homes. Value:
$225-$275*

*Pine washstand with English mulberry bowl and
pitcher. The scroll back would suggest the second
quarter of the 19th century. Value: $175-$250*

*19th century pine-grain-painted blanket chest with
turned legs. Most often, this type of grain painting was
done in the home. The best are of six single board
construction. Value: $450-$600*

*Strange pieces keep turning up like this chair, whose seat
is the top of a washstand with back and legs robbed from
other chairs. Value: $75*

Pine commode made as part of a bedroom set. The marbleized decoration is what sets it apart from the others. The features of the back suggest the Eastlake period, c. 1870-1890. Value: $350-$500

Pine table with drawer, late 18th or early 19th century, New Mexico. Not much furniture of that period from that area has survived. Value: $800-$1,000

Pennsylvania, 19th century pie safe. Value is determined by the designs on the punched tin sides and doors. Pies and other baked products are kept in them as a protection from animals and insects. Many are still very much in use and they are being reproduced. Value: $350-$600

Underside of lid of desk in Nova Scotia. Teachers have signed it with years they taught, back to the early 20th century.

Pine rocking cradle. Many of these date back to the 18th century. Tradition of these was in the British Isles, hence an attribution here to New England. Hanging cradles will be seen where the Germans and Dutch settled; New York, Pennsylvania, etc. Value: $350-$500

19th century school teacher's desk seen at an antiques shop in Nova Scotia. Value: $350

19th century wooden butter churn with hand crank. There are many styles of churns, but this type is a rarity as they were difficult to clean. Value: $250-$350

The thumb-back chair is one of the most collected and reproduced in this country. The name comes from the shape atop the chair posts. Value: $100-$150 ea.

19th century low cobbler's bench, complete with tools. Almost every home had one of these for the repair of leather items like shoes and harnesses. Value: $250-$450

Settle bed, pine, 19th century. The seat and front lift, then recline forward revealing a mattress of straw or feathers, which can then be reclined as a bed which is self storing. Most of these came out of Canada. Value: $1,800-$2,200

19th century New England pine cobbler's bench, complete with tools. This example is minus the clamp, which held work in place. Value: $450-$600

Side table, walnut and tulip, made c. 1880. The lower shelf with gallery sets it apart from most.

Charles Montgomery Collection.

Folding chair by George Hunzinger, 1835-1898. Hunzinger perfected many folding chairs and other pieces of furniture that could be collapsed.

Stylish chair by George Hunzinger, New York, patented March 30, 1869. His chairs were a revolt against the architectural lines in vogue at the time.

19th century, pine chair, or hutch table, which tilts for storage out of the way. Old paint and width of boards help set the price. Next to it is a small wheel, often called a flax wheel. Value of table: $1,000-$1,200; wheel $250

19th century, pine Shaker tilt-top game or sewing table, Enfield, Connecticut.

Carved leg of an oak console made by the Herter Brothers in New York, c. 1881-1882, for the Vanderbilt family. It was sold at Butterfields, June 7, 1995, for $288,500.

Walnut drop-leaf tables were popular late in the 19th century, until oak took over. Very few pieces are marked. A rarity is this table, the only marked piece ever found from the Thomas Parker Table Company, Merrimack, New Hampshire. It is stenciled under the top. Value: $800-$1,000

Auction goers in NH were shocked in 1969 to see this walnut ladies' desk sell at auction for $250. A few years before, it would have left the block for about $10.

Shawl-back rocker, with cloth tape back and seat. A shawl could be draped over the crest rail, when using the chair. Late 19th century, when bentwood was in favor, Canterbury, New Hampshire, Shaker Colony.

Custom oak dining table and chairs. Originally, these were in the Denman Thompson House in Swanzey, NH. Sold in 1969 for $1,200.

Brass and marquetry inlaid rosewood center table, made by Pottier and Stymus of New York, 1878. Value: $8,000-$12,000

Cylinder desks were as popular in the oak period, 1890-1930, as the roll tops. Some may be found in walnut. Value: $800-$1,400

The press design in oak is popular. Highly sought are sets of chairs like these, with deep impressions and interesting design.

Ebony inlaid mahogany side chair, made by Greene and Greene, Los Angeles. Value: $450-$600

Frank Lloyd Wright oak dining chairs, executed for the residence of Darwin Martin in Buffalo, c. 1904. Wright did not make furniture, he designed it and local cabinetmakers created the finished product.

Server made for Alfred Vanderbilt's Thunder Lodge by Ernest Stowe of Upper Saranac Lake, NY, c. 1900.

Very fine hatbox or bonnet-top dresser in birch. Value: $350-$450

Made in Binghamton, New York, this set of shelves is hinged so that by pulling the top shelf, they will all align into a tabletop. Value: $400-$600

Custom server in oak, all hand carved. Formerly in the Denman Thompson House, Swanky, NH. Thomson was a playwright and his troupe performed before Queen Victoria. Sold in 1969 for $650.

Aaron Willard was a brother to Simon. Pictured is a shelf clock he made, c. 1820. The case is maple.

Brooklyn Museum.

Shelburne Museum.

Very rare Simon Willard pendulum clock. The clock works and bell are in the pendulum.

Miniature clock made by Henry Bauer, Philadelphia, c. 1790-1805, height is 48".

The rope corner columns suggest the Empire period, as this shelf clock was made c. 1840s. Its value is enhanced by gilt decoration. Value: $350-$500

Typical shelf clock made in Connecticut, mid 19th century. Adding to the value is a reverse painting on the glass at bottom. Value: $450-$600

This shelf clock is named a double steeple, because there are two sets on the case. They were made by several Connecticut makers in the 19th century. Value: $250-$400

Iron peddler's clock, bought in Amsterdam. They sold there in 1970 for $35.

Peddler's clock made c. 1840s. These had spring mechanisms which permitted winding only once a week. They were small and many could fit on a wagon. They were sold by peddlers traveling the countryside. Price was $10. Value today: $150-$250

In his books, Brooks Palmer refers to these as "black clocks" as the cases are of black wood, iron, or marble. They were made c. 1880s in Connecticut. Value: $250-$400

The cases on many oak clocks are quite fancy; they are often referred to as "gingerbread cases." Pictured is a most unusual example of a corner clock made in Connecticut, late in the 19th century, with the stylized case.

Most historians agree that mirror clocks originated in New Hampshire. I have seen none from any other area. They dated in the second quarter of the 19th century. Value: $600-$1,000

Seth Thomas Ship's clock in brass, 19th century.

Wag on wall clock, 17th century. The mechanisms were just rested on a shelf prior to encasing them in the wall clock bodies, Germany. Value: $1,750-$2,250

The girandole design is credited to Lemuel Curtis who had been a Willard apprentice. Only about 30 originals were made. They are being reproduced and we picture a fine example made by Joe Kopcych, who lived in Bridgewater, MA, in 1969, when this was made. Value: $2,500

The 1920s brought with it many art deco clocks which appealed to sportsmen, patriots, sailors, and the like. This golfer's clock was priced at $185 at a shop in Wisconsin, early in 2001.

Two wall clocks by Elmer Stennis who worked just South of Boston. Reproductions he made in the 1960s and 1970s have risen in value. He was committed to the state prison at Walpole and continued to make clocks while incarcerated, as well as after he was released. Value: $700-$1,000

Even the Viennese show great appreciation for the work of Boston, 19th century clockmaker, Edward Howard. This timepiece is on display at the Museum Technesches in Vienna.

There are many foreign made clocks in this country. Pictured is a Sevres porcelain and bronze dore three-piece clock garniture which was sold at auction in New York by William Doyle for $6,000 in the 1970s.

At left is a crystal and silver inkwell with clock; center, is a 19th century French bracket clock and at right, a 19th century porcelain and bronze elephant clock. They are typical of many clocks brought to these shores by tourists and dealers.

The pillar and scroll clocks were among the prettiest in shelf design. They were first made in Connecticut by Seth Thomas, Eli Terry, and Silas Hoadley, early in the 19th century. They are being reproduced today. Value: $1,100-$2,500

GLOSSARY

Acanthus: A plant native to southern Europe used as a motif in carving throughout civilized history. Very popular in French Empire-style furniture.

Acorn: A turning based on the shape of an acorn.

Apron: A board, which joins the understructure of cased furniture, tables, and chairs—often cut out for beautification.

Armoire: A cupboard for the storage of clothing.

Ball foot: A simple ball turning that was joined to the bottom of chests by a turned dowel.

Baluster: A turning, often done with bulbous swellings. Very popular in the late seventeenth and early eighteenth centuries.

Banding: A contrasting narrow stripping of veneer used for beautification. Popular during the Federal period, especially on drawer fronts.

Baroque: The Italian equivalent of French rococo, defining quite busy carvings and decoration.

Bombe: A chest or secretary base with a rounded bulging front and sides. Believed to have originated on American furniture in Boston.

Bun foot: A flattened ball with slender ankle above.

Cabriole: A shaped leg based on the cyma curve, with wide knees and narrow ankles terminating in various feet. Used extensively in the Queen Anne, Chippendale, and Victorian periods.

Caryatid: A carved human figure used as support for an upper pediment or shelf in furniture.

Court cupboard: Late seventeenth or early eighteenth century cased piece used for linens and dining areas.

Cyma curve: An S-shaped double curve.

Dentil molding: A series of carved rectangular blocks with spaces between. Often called hound's tooth molding if shaped to points.

Dutch foot: Often called a duck foot. A simple pad used on cabriole legs during the Queen Anne period.

Escritoire: A simple writing desk, with drawers, pigeonholes, secret drawers, and the like.

Escutcheon: A brass plate used for decoration or to surround openings such as a keyhole.

Fiddleback: A violin-shaped splat found as early as the time of Queen Anne, but revived during the Empire period.

Figured: Highly grained wood used in Marquetry.

Finial: A turned decorative device usually found atop cornices of high chests, or even as drops at the front lower section of highboys and lowboys.

Fluting: A channeled carving that is done in straight lines parallel to each other.

Fretwork: Ornamental work created by cutting and perforation.

Highboy: A tall chest of drawers, originally called a tallboy in England; usually standing on high legs and made in two sections.

Kas: A Dutch cabinet or sideboard painted with primitive figures.

Ladder-back: A chair back with the cross splats arranged in ladder fashion.

Lunette: An ornamental design in half moon shapes. Often used in veneering in the Federal period.

Lyre: Design patterned after the instrument of that name. Popularized during the Empire period.

Marquetry: Decorations formed by inlaying various woods, shell, bone, or metals into a wood surface. This is often done in a thin wood veneer, which is then glued to the surface of the piece to be decorated. The rarer "intarsia" is veneering directly to the main surface.

Ogee: A shape made from two cyma curves with their convex sides meeting.

Patina: An aged surface.

Reeding: Convex grooves, carved parallel to each other.

Ribband: A reference to a carved or cutout "ribbon" chair back.

Rococo: From the French *rocaille,* literally meaning "a pile of rocks." Carved ornamentation full of curves and other fancy carving motifs.

Schrank: A German cabinet or sideboard painted with primitive figures.

Serpentine: A serpentine curve used on the fronts of furniture.

Spindle: A turned round such as that used on chair backs and frames.

Splat: The central figure in a chair back.

Stretcher: An underbracing beneath case pieces, chairs, and tables, with reinforcement joined leg to leg.

Swag: A carving of leaves, draperies, or flowers.

Tester: The frame of a high four post bed, to which a decorative skirt is attached at the top.

Veneer: A thin ornamental wood with desirable graining that is glued to a surface of lesser wood.

Chapter Two

GLASS

Introduction

Historical Overview

Glass reputedly originated on the shores of the Mediterranean when a group of Phoenician sailors built a fire to cook their evening meal. In the morning, they found that the hot coals and flames had melted the sand beneath and hardened it into a crude form of glass. There must have been a quantity of soda mixed with the sand, since soda is necessary as a flux to form the melted silica. Since that time, various minerals and elements have been mixed with silica to produce different types of glass, each with its own peculiar qualities. Lime, ashes, lead, and even gold have been used to produce glass ranging from the inexpensive to the exotic. Little is recorded about early glassmaking until the time of the Romans.

Roman civilization developed every known method of making glass objects until refinements in the making of plate glass were discovered in France during the seventeenth century, and then pressed glass was developed in America early in the nineteenth century. At first, vessels were made by molding forms of sand or clay, and hot threads of glass were spun around these in spiral fashion. These were then smoothed out as much as possible, joining the threads in the process. When the blowpipe was invented, artisans soon learned to form pieces and even add decorations, handles, spouts, etc., using crude tools, most of which changed little until the early nineteenth century.

From a collecting standpoint, you should concentrate on those items made after the Revolutionary War since there is not much pre-Revolutionary American glass, as England supplied most of our

finished glass, and very little of this has survived. New Englanders like to take pride in the fact that theirs was the earliest settled part of the country and that the region preceded the others in the manufacture of all types of goods. However, it was quite late in producing one glassmaking concern that remained in business for an appreciable length of

The Portland Vase, the most famous glass artifact in the world. It was made by the Romans, during the first century AD. It is cameo cut, British Museum, London.

time. This was the England Glass Company, located in Cambridge, Massachusetts, operating between 1817 and 1888. The concern then moved to Toledo, Ohio and today is known as Libbey, Owens, Ford.

The earliest production of glass, which might be collected today, was made in the Pittsburgh region. Glass factories had operated in many places during the eighteenth century, but little can be attributed to them. After the Revolution, glass works began to appear in the western Pennsylvania region, notably in what is now the Pittsburgh area. As early as the 1790s, factories were shipping glass via riverboat all the way to New Orleans. It was not until 1817, when the New England Glass Company was organized in Cambridge, Massachusetts that any long-term production of glass originated in New England. The Marlboro Street Works was organized in Keene, New Hampshire in 1817, but was quite small. Still, flasks from that company are high on the collecting list today. Inkwells and decanters are about the only other items made there that can be found and attributed to that works.

Keeping Informed

Some of the greatest forums and seminars held over the past years have featured glass as their subjects. This is where one learns the tidbits that make collecting fun and, at times, confusing. Back in 1978, at the Midwest Forum held at the Henry Ford Museum, Kenneth Wilson, then director of collections, showed a Syrian-made bowl from the 1st century A.D., which closely resembles that work done in New Jersey in the 18th century.

He also demolished the conception that the name "flip glass" should be applied to the large hand-blown tumblers made on both sides of the Atlantic. Flip is a drink made with rum as its base and it is unlikely such a glass, quite large in size, would be used in drinking flip, as a small tumblerfull would suffice to put one under. Mr. Wilson stated that he feels the term is a twentieth century connotation, merely invented to identify the form.

The center of glassmaking in the nineteenth century, as well as today, is in the region, which comprises western Pennsylvania, Ohio and West Virginia. There were many fine companies in this area, making glass in similar metal content, designs, and decoration. Years ago, historians referred to this region as the Midwest or Pittsburgh area when discussing the output of the factories there—just as we make reference to Staffordshire County in England when identifying provenance of pottery which was not marked by the factories in that region. To identify all of these glass companies would require many books. Several are listed in the Bibliography. One book in particular that I would recommend is *Pittsburgh Glass* by Lowell Innes, who is credited with bringing attention to the glass made in the Midwest and Pittsburgh areas and assisting in many museum exhibitions which helped identify it.

Glassmaking Techniques

Glass is a combination of sand, flint, and spar or some other siliceous substance with an alkali or some other material added as a flux (a substance used to promote fusion). Of the alkalis, soda and potash were the first used successfully. Lead, borax, arsenic, nitre, and lime were used later. Sometimes pearl ashes, sea salt, and wood ashes were used. When red lead was used it gave the glass a yellow cast, which could be corrected with nitre. If arsenic was used in excess the glass would turn milky. Pearl ashes were first used to make perfectly transparent glass. Borax was just as good, but it was more expensive and its use was mostly confined to making looking glasses.

The materials used for making glass were first reduced to a powder, either by pounding or by grinding in a horse mill. Then the powder was mixed with flux and calcined under intense heat for five or six hours. The resulting product was called "frit" and could be easily melted in the glass pots, with workmen skimming the scum from its surface. A typical mixture for a fine grade flint glass would be 120 pounds of white sand, 50 pounds of red lead, 40 pounds of pearl ashes, 20 pounds of nitre, and 5 ounces of magnesia. With the addition of a pound or two of arsenic, the material would fuse much more quickly and at a lower temperature. A cheaper mixture could be made by substituting sea salt for the arsenic. Crown glass (a popular product in the eighteenth century) was made from the following ingredients: 60 pounds of white sand, 30 pounds of pearl ashes, 15 pounds of nitre, one pound of borax, and a half pound of arsenic.

Color and Etching

There were many "green glass" factories set up as early as the eighteenth century. A common mixture was as follows: 120 pounds of white sand, 30 pounds of unpurified pearl ashes, wood ashes well burned and sifted, 60 pounds of common salt, and 5 pounds of arsenic. In the rural glassmaking plants, a good green glass might be made by mixing 200 pounds of wood ashes with 100 pounds of sand.

Colored glass has been with us for centuries, and the formulas have undoubtedly changed over the years. The following formulas come from recipes in use at the turn of the eighteenth into the nineteenth centuries, and in general for many years after that.

To a glass mixture (such as the one outlined for flint glass above) add 9 pounds of copper precipitated from aqua fortis and 2 drachmas of precipitated iron for green. To 10 pounds of glass add 6 drachmas of zaffre (oxide of cobalt) and 1 drachma of gold precipitated by tin for bright purple. Varying these formulas, you will find that for amethyst, magnesia was used; for black, magnesia and calcined iron; for white opaque, calcined horn, ivory, or bone; for ruby, gold precipitated by tin; for blue, calcined bones, horn or ivory, magnesia, and zaffre; for yellow, calcined iron or crude tartar and antimony.

After glass is formed, either by blowing or pressing, it must be annealed (heated) in an oven in which it then cools gradually in order to retain its temper and strength. Etch-

Blown deep amber glass flasks, from the Marlboro Street Works, Keene, New Hampshire, c. 1820s. At left is the Masonic and right, sunburst. Value: $250-$600

ing was originally done by dipping the glass body into ordinary melted wax. After the glass was hardened, an artisan would etch the outline of a decoration or picture into the wax on the glass body. It would then be dipped into a lead lined box which contained a fluoric acid which would etch the glass wherever it was not protected by the wax. Initials and monograms could be put on glassware in this manner. After a rinse in neutralizing water to flush away the acid, the remaining protective wax would be removed by dipping the piece in hot water and melting it away. A varnish coating was sometimes applied.

Engraving on glass is generally done by a spinning cutting-wheel, with the artisan holding the glass body against the wheel to produce the desired decoration. The term "copper wheel cut" refers to such a method, with the wheel most likely sprinkled with diamond dust to speed the work. However, back in the early part of the nineteenth century, you could have purchased glass engraved in a more radical, simpler method. While the glass piece was hot, it would be dipped into a mixture of red lead, sand, and borax, heated and fused with what was called a menstrum—a mixture of pure cane sugar, water, and common writing ink, which would hold some oxide of manganese. The mixture might have also been painted on with a camel's hair brush or squirrel's foot. A simple etching or engraving tool would be used to cut away the desired decoration. The etching would appear in reverse, with the cut areas smooth and clear and the untouched areas appearing to have been roughened with a tool. Some artisans felt that clearer cuts could be made in this manner, with less possibility of unwanted glass powder being ground into the body at the edges of the cuts by the wheel.

Identifying the makers of early glass is quite difficult, as most melted the same metals according to the same or very similar formulas. Colors and pattern designs were copied freely, and neighboring concerns would often help each other when large orders came in, with each making up part of the order in similar molds. Workers in this industry were quite transient and always in demand, so they might take their own trade secrets with them from plant to plant, which would account for the similarities of workmanship.

18th Century Glass

Glassmaking Pioneers

Caspar Wistar

Glassmaking in this country was introduced in Jamestown, Virginia, as early as 1608. There were window glass and bottle-making houses in New England and other settled parts of the country after that time, but it was not until Caspar Wistar, a Dutch inhabitant of Pennsylvania, went to Salem County in New Jersey and opened a glassworks there in 1739 that America had a company whose product became well known by name and survived for some years. Wistar made glass in what is now termed the "South Jersey tradition," and under his direction and that of his son's, it survived until 1780, when the fires of the Revolution put them out of business. Not one whole documented piece has survived intact from this output. Designs like the lily pad, cross ribbing, and swirled ribbons originated here and spread throughout the colonies.

Henry William Stiegel

Next to Wistar in influence was a very colorful character named Henry William Stiegel. He came to this country from Germany and managed to marry the daughter of the ironmaster of the Elizabeth Furnace in Lancaster County, Pennsylvania. He opened his glass house in 1763 and began turning out pieces in the German tradition of glassmaking, which makes it difficult today to tell his work from the imported glass made at that time. Stiegel became wealthy, and the title of "Baron" was bestowed on him as a measure of respect by his fellow townspeople. His high

Decorated glass often attributed to Henry William Stiegel, Pennsylvania, third quarter of the 18th century. Much glass of this style was imported, so it is difficult to make a positive attribution to Stiegel. Value: $75-$125

spending habits resulted in his being thrown into debtor's prison, which brought a halt to a very colorful career and the very interesting quality glass for which he was responsible. After the demise of his plant, about 1773, Pennsylvania remained prominent as a location for glassmaking due to the availability of coal and silica. The Philadelphia Glass Works was organized at that time with many of Stiegel's former workmen and this company prospered under varying ownerships well into the nineteenth century.

Robert Hewes

Collectors must take note of an early glass works which, though not successful, established the industrial concept of building not only a factory, but the homes and store for supplies to accommodate the workers. In 1780, a Bostonian, Robert Hewes, selected a site in Temple, New Hampshire, which is in the Southwestern area of the state. The site was chosen because of an abundance of firewood to heat the pots and good silica which melted well for the production of bottles and window glass. It had been rumored that many of the workers were Hessian soldiers who had deserted earlier in the Revolution. The factory was started in May of 1780 and burned shortly after construction. It was rebuilt during the fall of 1780-1781. Ten days after firing, the main furnaces collapsed due to the moisture and frost in the stones. In March of 1781, the Temple selectmen gave Hewes a loan to rebuild and organized a lottery to help, which failed. In the summer of

1781, the furnaces were rebuilt and by the fall of 1781, were in production of crown glass, philosophical glass (glass made for laboratories, i.e., beakers, test tubes, piping, etc.), bottles, and window glass. This was the first crown glass made in America. In 1782, Hewes gave up the experiment and returned to Boston to open the Boston Crown Glass Company.

In 1976, the site was excavated under the direction of Frederick Gorman and Dr. David

Starbuck—an undertaking sponsored both by the Boston University Department of Classical Studies and the Corning Museum of Glass. Hessian belt buckles were found to confirm the existing rumors. There is no authenticated piece of Temple glass in existence, though many feel some window panes in the old houses in the area could well have come from there.

John Frederick Amelung

Another early glassmaker was John Frederick Amelung, who set up his New Bremen Works at Fredericktown, Maryland, in 1787. Lured here by promises of opportunities in the new world, he encouraged other works to follow him into the venture, which survived only until 1795. America had not instituted tariffs against imports which would have given local manufacturers protection from overseas competition. However, Amelung's glass won great favor and there are good etched and signed pieces which have survived.

After the Revolution, many glassworks were built, but there are few records of what they made. Some did not survive long enough for documentation of their activities. It was not until the beginning of the nineteenth century that any really large, successful firms were established—with examples of their work documented. At the end of this chapter, I have listed the names of some whose work might be identified and collected.

19th Century Glass

We might categorize American glassmaking into different periods as an aid to identification. Nineteenth century glass must almost be lumped together so far as content and quality are concerned. Different blowing techniques and types of decorations might aid in determining the origin of some pieces as far as regions are concerned, but due to continuous importation, it is quite difficult to tell American work from that which came from overseas. When mechanical pressing of glass was developed about 1825, glassmakers were able to run wild with mold designs, and pressing techniques could be identified, and glass from the Pittsburgh area took on a completely different look from that made in New England. New England benefited from the likelihood that immigrants would settle at their

Crown Glass

In the days when fashioning glass at the end of a blowpipe was the method of manufacture, everything, including flat pieces such as windowpanes, was made in this manner. It is believed the blowpipe was known to the Romans as early as 50 B.C. and remained the best way to fashion the metal (glass in its molten state) into desired forms until the French and English learned to form glass in sheets by pouring it into molds in the late 17th century. This was done to make the looking glasses from then into the early part of the 19th century and was a very expensive process.

The glass blowers who prevailed throughout the countryside both here and overseas still fashioned their flat glass by first blowing the metal, then spinning the rod in their hands to flatten the bubble at the end of the pipe. When this was extended as far as possible, the flattened glass was further smoothed with simple tools to widen it as much as possible. Once annealed, the cutters would slice it into the small panes, treasured by owners of period homes. However, the centerpiece, where the pipe had been attached, was always raised and often showed the spiral marks as evidence of the spinning. This center cut, often called the bull's-eye pane, is what gave the name "crown" to the glass made in this manner.

first port of call, where work might be available, rather than head into the less developed areas in the Midwest. However, many workers got their start in New England and then went on to factories in the Pennsylvania, West Virginia, and Ohio areas, taking inland techniques and ideas learned on the coast. It is amazing how much we do know about the origin of American glass, when so little of it was marked or otherwise documented.

In collecting glass, you will find it is best to concentrate your efforts in the regions where it was made. If you collect Hobbs and Brockunier, you should look for it in the Wheeling, West Virginia area. If you desire Sandwich glass, there is more of this on Cape Cod and in eastern Massachusetts than anywhere else. You will find the prices are generally lower in such areas since the law of supply and demand keeps them stable. You should look for Keene and Stoddard historical flasks in New Hampshire—looking for one made in Mantua, Ohio, might be rather futile. However, shipments of glass were made to different parts of the country, so you might examine the old records of companies preserved by historical societies and researchers, and you may locate what you are looking for elsewhere. The Boston and Sandwich Glass Company shipped glass to the west coast, so a lot of it can be found there. Some was even sent to Russia and other European nations. However, I have looked for specimens all over Europe (even in Russia) to no avail.

Pressed Glass

In 1825, a patent for pressing glass by machine was issued to Benjamin Bakewell at his plant in Pittsburgh. This was first used for pressing solid objects such as drawer pulls. In 1827, a further patent on pressing was issued to Deming Jarves at Sandwich for an improvement whereby hollowwares might be made. The new technology was adopted around the world, and the resulting mass production created so much glass, in so similar a manner and look, that most historians qualify their opinions on origin unless absolutely sure.

There are some who feel that glass should be judged by its quality and not by the name of the maker. Unfortunately, most dealers and collectors do not agree with this premise. Documentation of glass is highly important, as much is collected by the maker's name. Early colored pressed glass is desirable, but patterns were copied on both sides of the ocean, which makes positive identification

Lowell Innes Collection.

Left, blown cobalt decanter, Bristol area. Its shape places it at end of 18th century or early 19th century. Right, cut decanter of Anglo-Irish influence, first quarter of the 19th century. Note mirror-like characteristic quality of stopper.

Currier Gallery of Art.

Canary-yellow pressed glass, Horn of Plenty butter dish with Washington head finial.

difficult. It was not until Ruth Webb Lee published her *Handbook of Early American Pressed Glass Patterns* in 1931 that collectors had a common glossary to use so items could be advertised in a manner that all could understand. Other patterns have been discovered since the book was published, but it remains an excellent guide. To this day, pattern glass is still made by basically the same mechanical means as that devised early in this century. This has caused a faithful reproduction of many of the old designs possible, much to the consternation of collectors. Collecting an item which can be reproduced has its own built-in set of hazards, so you must arm yourself with great knowledge before venturing far into this field. Read the available literature and talk to dealers to help you discern the differences between original and reproduced glass pieces.

The Horn of Plenty design was popular in the early days of pressed glass. Here are examples made at the Boston and Sandwich Glass Company.

After the Civil War, industrial plants had to turn from making military items to consumer production and glass companies struggled for their survival. Victorian England had been making fancy colored glassware which found favor here. It was not long before this was challenged with local production. America entered what often is called the "Art Glass period," when artistic design and color were the subject of much experimentation. In the 1860s, William Leighton left the employ of the New England Glass Company for a new job at Hobbs and Brockunier in Wheeling, West Virginia. He pioneered in the use of inexpensive lime as a flux for melting the silica. Until that time, glassmakers utilized lead and crushed flint to make what is a superior product. Lowell Innes, in his book, *Pittsburgh Glass* (Houghton Mifflin, 1976), indicates that Adams and Leighton may have worked together on this, with Leighton getting the credit for it.

The New England Companies

New England gave birth to the Boston Crown Glass Company, New England Glass Company, the Boston and Sandwich Glass Company, Portland (ME) Glass Company, and the Mount Washington-Pairpoint Company which was a marriage of the Mount Washington Glass Company and Pairpoint Silver Company in New Bedford, Massachusetts. Another lesser-known company was the Union Glass Works which operated between 1851 and 1924 in Somerville, Massachusetts. Much that was made there is mistaken for New England Glass Company products or Sandwich glass. (There were about thirty-five businesses devoted to the making and cutting of glass which operated in Sandwich over the years, so one must read the books done by Barlow/Kaiser which are listed in the bibliography to learn of the wide range of work done in that community.)

The Boston and Sandwich Glass Company operated between 1825 and 1888 when it closed due to labor problems brought on by its inability to compete with the cheaper glass shipped to New England from the Pittsburgh region. The New England Glass Company closed the same year and its owner, William Drummond Libbey moved it to Toledo, Ohio, where it still operates as Libbey, Owens, Ford. Portland operated between 1863 and 1873. This left Pairpoint and Union as the two

Blown and Pressed Glass

In the early days of pressing glass, it was found to be easier to make a larger piece in two sections. For example, the base of a whale oil lamp, such as those made in the 1830s, would be pressed in a mold. These could be done in many colors, but all would be in the same form. A top section could then be made either in a mold or by hand blowing. After cooking this could be attached to the base by means of a small hot glass wafer— the two pieces were just pressed together and on hardening, would be joined. In this manner, the same base might be used for candleholders, compotes, cake plates and the like—the wafer made it possible to join any two sections together.

What is interesting is that the base can be pressed, while the front is hand blown; hence the term pressed and blown glass, as both techniques are combined in the same piece. This can be puzzling to the novice glass collector, who can recognize the two ways of forming it, yet know that they can't be done together. A good glassblower could make the top section more quickly than it could be molded in a press, and at that time, there was till a lot of pride in doing handwork. Check any glass to see how it was made and decorated, you might be surprised at the several different techniques performed on the same piece.

Famous candleholders with petal top and loop bases, joined by a wafer of glass. This made two colors possible. Boston and Sandwich Glass Co., c. 1840-1850.

Window of elegant glass made by Boston and Sandwich Glass Company, Sandwich, MA. Exhibited at the Sandwich Glass Museum.

decorations, most often figures and background in classic form. Various rules were created to authenticate her work. The four generally accepted rules are that the figure had to be a child with only one arm showing; one leg should appear longer than the other; the child should be standing on a patch of fog or clouds; and there should be foliage, fernlike in appearance, in front of and at the rear of the child. These figures were supposed to be a takeoff on the Kate Greenaway figures which were popularized in her books. The final rule stipulated that all the enameling should be white—any color indicated the piece was not done by Mary Gregory.

In their extensive research, Barlow and Kaiser acquired the diaries of Mary Gregory and her sister, Emma, from the descendants of the latter's family. Indeed, Mary Gregory did exist and she did paint at Sandwich, though she did other painting work at home for other companies in various mediums. She painted between 1880 and 1883. Emma painted for a brief period in 1880. Mary never married—she spent most of her life caring for her mother, though she was not in good health most of the time. What is revealed in the diaries, much of which is reproduced in the book and which I have read from the written pages themselves, reveals that neither painted figures on glass. Some examples handed down in Emma's family reveal winter

remaining works. Pairpoint was closed in 1958, with another works by that name opening in 1969 at Sagamore, Massachusetts, under that name and the guidance of Robert Bryden, who was the last manager at the original plant. The present factory is still working and one may purchase fine glass there.

The Mary Gregory Story

Unless you have a copy of *The Glass Industry in Sandwich, Volume IV,* by Ray Barlow and Joan Kaiser, perhaps the true information about "Mary Gregory" glass has passed you by. Until its publication, rumor, stories, and tales debunking the existence of Mary Gregory were rampant. Proponents said she painted white enamel figures on glass at the Boston and Sandwich Glass Company on Cape Cod in the 1880s. Others felt she never existed at all except in the minds of collectors and dealers who used her name to create a demand for late nineteenth century pieces which had enameled

If Not Mary Gregory, Then Who?

When asked the provenance of all the enameled glass with figures, if they were not Sandwich, Dorothy Lee Jones, director of the museum and former president of the National Early American Glass Club, said, "All of you who have been my friends for the past twenty years know that I have always stated such glass was not made in America—it came from Europe."

More professionalism can be shown by identifying the figured pieces as enameled glass, with no reference to Mary Gregory. It has no resemblance to the work she did. The quicker we relieve this fine painter from any responsibility for much of the shoddy work on such glass, the better.

scenes in dark browns, blacks, and some gray on white opalescent glass.

Enameled figures on glass most likely were made in Europe. This is not Mary Gregory glass; her diary reveals she did not paint figures at the Boston and Sandwich Glass Works.

Mr. Barlow lectured on these finds at the Jones Museum of Glass and Ceramics in Douglas Hill, Maine, several years ago. He brought examples and the diaries to convince the heavy hitters that their classification of enameled glass in the then "Mary Gregory" style should be reevaluated in light of this written evidence. Some pieces have appeared with a bird or flowers, but these were exceptions to their work, the bulk of which was winter scenes.

Waterford

During the nineteenth century, much glass was shipped here from Europe. One could write chapters on this glass alone. However, with our space limitations, we can call attention to a few facts that may be of help. In 1794, George III, still suffering from the costs of the American Revolution, instituted a tax of fine glass. This was to be taxed by weight, but his collectors based the tax on the weight of the product before cutting. The makers were upset at paying tax on powdered glass that lay

Style and design often attributed to Waterford in Ireland. Remember, the original Waterford plant opened in 1794 and closed in 1851. A new Waterford opened in 1951. Hence, most of the old glass attributed to the c. 1900 period must be identified as Anglo-Irish cut, such as this example. The new Waterford is marked. Value: $75-$95

on the floor after cutting and appealed this, but to no avail. Several opened plants in Ireland to escape this tax. They were built in Cork, Dublin, Waterford, and several other places. Managers, workmen, formulas and molds were sent across the channel.

It is next to impossible to differentiate between English and Irish Glass made during the nineteenth century. This is why better-informed collectors identify it merely as Anglo/Irish glass. The pros will rarely mention the name of a particular factory. One which is used very indiscriminately is Waterford. Few realize that this plant closed in 1851. Another was opened with this name in 1951. However, for one hundred years, no Waterford glass was made. So, if your grandmother received some as wedding gifts, it is not Waterford. None of the pre-1851 glass is known to have been marked. Glass made since 1951 does bear the Waterford name. Also, the claim that there are rare, treasured Waterford chandeliers in historic homes in this country is a myth. At a lecture on Irish antiques held at Pennsbury Manor in Morrisville, Pennsylvania in 1970, the speaker revealed that in his two years of research in Ireland and England to prepare for his talk, he found no evidence that lighting devices of any kind were made at the early Waterford plant—this includes chandeliers.

Lacy Glass

The term "lacy" is applied to clear glass which is highly decorated. It appeared about 1828 at the Boston and Sandwich Glass Factory shortly after the method of pressing glass was perfected. At the time, most clear glass showed many imperfections such as bubbles and "straw marks," which are ridges resulting from this primitive manufacture. The extensive figuring on the pieces helped make these marks less evident.

During this period, practically all the companies used lead as a flux—the compound which helped turn silica into the transparent state. Early "lacy" is quite heavy and most edges, where the pieces had to be trimmed and smoothed after they were annealed, are rough. The lacy period in which this heavy metal was used extended until c. 1858. After that time, experiments with soda and lime as a flux resulted in a glass of much lesser quality. Lacy was made overseas as well, and heavily figured glass of this type is still being made today.

Early pressed lacy glass comes in many designs. Lowell Innes tell us that most was made between 1838 and 1858 in lead glass at factories both in New England and the Midwest, as well as overseas. These examples could have come from various glass works.

Art Glass

The art glass period in this country dates from between 1880 and 1900. In Victorian England, glass manufacturers began producing colored glass and our companies followed suit. During this period, some of the finest designed, colored, and decorated glass appeared. Some were given such exotic names as Peachblow, Burmese, Amberina, Crown Milano, Pomona, Diamond Quilted Satin and the like. Some are identified by color, such as ruby, black amethyst, cranberry and others by their finish or decoration, such as enameled or satin finished. Generally, most are referred to as art glass when there is no specific name given.

In 1917, the Libbey Company issued a catalog of art glass which was made the same way it was before the company left Massachusetts during the strike of 1888. It is difficult to separate the early from the later work. Also, from 1920 to 1940, many reproductions of the early art glass forms were made. Most of these were made by machine, so it is not difficult to separate them from the earlier hand blown examples. They can fool the newcomer, however. Libbey is still available in gift shops, today.

Cut Glass

Cut glass of the brilliant period (1890-1915) is the most desirable to collect. This was a period when the quality of the glass metal was at its best. About 25 to 28 percent of its content was lead, which gives the glass brilliance and weight and

Lowell Innes Collection.

Small, clear cut Pittsburgh compote on knopped stem with rayed base. Rim cut on the outside with five scallops. Bowl cut in a single row of large strawberry diamonds and fans alternating with roundels surrounded by a rayed pyramid. Fourteen short panels below this row.

allows deep cutting to enhance its design. The advent of World War I brought with it the need for lead to be used in munitions, hence its scarcity for making glass during this period. The quality never quite recovered after the war, as the new, light cut glass became the fashion, with but a few holdouts in the industry continuing to stress the quality of its metal.

Over the years, the term "cut crystal" took over, signifying that this was a better metal than conventional glass, but not of the quality of the brilliant period. Today's fine glass may include no more than 10 to 12 percent lead, which accounts for its look, which cannot match that of the old. Much European crystal has found its way into this country, some of it good, and some not so good. In France, a conveyor system has been developed which makes it possible to mix the ingredients of the glass metal at the start, melting, and casting it into goblets and the like and then annealing them, with the finished product cut by machine and delivered as an item ready to be packaged and sold, with no hands touching it all along the way.

Cut glass went out of favor for many years as new furniture could be scratched easily by it. It was not until the 1960s that there was resurgence in interest in it. Remember, the signed pieces most often command much more money than those unsigned.

20th Century Glass

Carnival Glass

Poor Man's Tiffany

Frank Fenton of Newark, Ohio, is credited with first turning out an inexpensive iridescent glass in fancy shapes and coloring in 1907. He mixed iron oxide and iron chloride with glass metal to give it its sheen. Other glass works picked up this development immediately, and soon such famous works as Imperial in Bellaire, Ohio; Millersburg and Westmoreland, both in Pennsylvania; and Fenton's former employer, Harry Northwood of Indiana, Pennsylvania, were turning out the poor man's Tiffany. No glass company in New England is credited with making the product. By this time, most New England glass works had closed or had moved to the mid-western area. The first new color in appearance was yellow, or marigold, but chemists soon explored the full range of colorings. Artists came up with designs ranging from the most popular grape through the tiger lily, fine cut heart, sunflower, sunken daisy, shell and jewel, fish scale and beads, open rose, scroll embossed, thistle, star, and singing birds, to name a few. Fruit bowls were popular, along with hatpin holders, powder jars, and pin trays. On the rarer side are ashtrays, banks, jelly jars, paperweights, and electric lamps. Baskets and vases were popular, but most were for decorative rather than functional use. The pitcher

The Carnival Glass Club commissions a limited edition of carnival glass to be made each year as a fund raiser. At the time of the 1968 election, the Nixon/Agnew ticket was featured on this tumbler made by the Imperial Glass Company. Only 1,200 were made. Value: $250-$350

and tumbler sets were favorite premium items and, in some cases, complete dinner sets were made.

In later years this was called "carnival glass," as it was often given away as a prize at carnivals and fairs and was also used as a premium by cereal and tea companies. During the depression years, companies found their warehouses full, with no ready market for distribution. Loads of this glass was dumped into the market and carnival operators seized on it as an inexpensive prize for their games of chance. Long regarded as an inferior product, carnival glass was an item, which had to be sold by the boxful at auctions until a few years ago. Then collectors became interested in it, as there were pieces that showed definite quality, reflected by the handwork incorporated in the making. Most people think the glass was all machine made, but research has proven that up to seven or eight men spent four or five minutes making each well-molded piece. The inexpensive pieces look inexpensive, and those of value look it, so you do not have to be an expert to evaluate most of this glass. Depth of molding, design, color, iridescence, and proportions must be judged in determining quality.

Harry Northwood

One of the prolific makers of carnival glass was Harry Northwood who located his Northwood Glass Company in Wheeling, West Virginia. Some claim that over 1,300 patterns were created between 1909 and about 1920 when the manufacture of this type of ware began to diminish in popularity.

However, Northwood had been experimenting with other glass before this time. He worked for Hobbs and Brockunier in Wheeling, as well as the La Belle Glass Company and Buckeye Glass Company in Ohio. His first factory was in Sinclaire, Pennsylvania, opening in 1896 and moved to Wheeling in 1902. He worked until 1923.

In his early years, he experimented with what is known as custard glass, an opaque variety that came in several colors—custard, blue, and green. Some light blue pieces were decorated with gilded chrysanthemums. Some say this color was produced with uranium at a time when few may have known of its radioactive qualities.

Much of this output was dedicated as giftware, some finding its way into bags of flour to be given as a premium. The smaller pieces were put into twenty-five pound bags and the larger pieces in one hundred pound bags. One tale has it that inspectors found weevils in flour stored near the Ohio River and ordered it destroyed. It was all dumped into the Ohio River, complete with the glass. A treasure lies down there for someone to discover.

Chrysanthemum glass made by Harry Northwood, Newark, Ohio, c. 1922-1923. Deeply molded and gilded, this was made as a premium to be put in bags of flour. It was made in several colors. Very desired, in good condition, today. Value: $600-$750

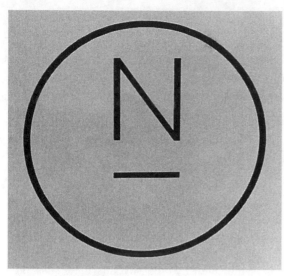

Some credit Harry Northwood with being the first to make the iridized carnival glass, as early as 1907. His glass is among the best to collect and it is marked with the underlined "N" in a circle.

The top favorite seems to be the Northwood pieces, which are well marked with a capital N within a circle, usually at the bottom of the piece. Fenton signed his pieces in script, and these are being reproduced today. Early Imperial glass was marked with a cross, the eight letters of its name appearing two to a section. Newer Imperial pieces are signed with a G superimposed on an I. The most popular colors in order of preference are purple, blue, green, orange, yellow, and marigold. White carnival glass is quite rare. You will find that most of this glass is rather inexpensive. Search for deep cut, well-colored quality pieces if you want to collect carnival glass.

Heisey

Augustus H. Heisey served in the Civil War on the Union side. After the war, he had worked as a salesman for the King Glass Company of Pittsburgh. He married a daughter of one of the owners of the Duncan Glass Company, and became a partner in Duncan and Heisey. In 1893 he resigned, and in 1895 he established his own glass company in Newark, Ohio.

He had three sons, George, Wilson, and Clarence all of whom worked in the business. In 1900, the diamond mark with an H inside was adopted as the trademark and appears molded in most of the Heisey pieces. Many patterns were identified with a number, rather than a name. Between about 1923 and 1930, the company specialized in colored pieces. At that time, some glass was identified by name, such as Flamingo (a pink), Alexandrite (orchid), Moon gleam (green), Tangerine (orange), Zircon (pale yellow), Sahara (canary yellow), and Ivorina Verde (a dark yellow opaque colored with uranium slats). The opaque and frosted glass came later.

In the 1920s, Heisey acquired some of the original Sandwich glass molds and turned out pieces, which can fool the novice. In 1958, Heisey closed its doors, selling its molds to the Imperial Glass Company in Bellaire, Ohio, where they continued to make it with the H inside the diamond for several years.

The most desired Heisey glass is Verlys, which is camphor or frosted in various patterns. None is opalescent or colored. Verlys is an art glass originally made in France after 1930. Heisey obtain the rights and formula from the French factory and produced the glass for a short time. The French-produced glass can be distinguished from the American made by the signature: The French is mold marked, while the American is etched script signed.

Among the rarest of pieces are the Heisey cocktail shakers of clear glass, about a foot tall, with a removable glass strainer at the top. These are unmarked.

Tiffany and Art Nouveau

The turn of the century brought with it a change in style as art nouveau motifs, made popular in France, gradually came to our shores. Some people feel that the period from 1895 to 1920 was gaudy; others say it was sterile, and some feel it was an era when the most grotesque styles were perpetrated on the public. Glass felt the design changes more than anything else. Louis Comfort Tiffany helped to popularize iridescent-colored glass, and his name is attributed to many items, which may or may not be the product of his factory. His stained glass windows for churches and breakfast rooms in fancy homes are overshadowed only by the magnificent Tiffany glass curtain at the Palace of Fine Arts in Mexico City. To see this creation, you must go there on a Sunday morning, since this is the only time it is lowered. It is made up of over two million pieces of glass fused together to show the two volcanoes, Popocateptel and Ixtaccihuatl, at

Tiffany vase, gold iridescent with heavy pearl.

Tiffany vase, lipstick.

Tiffany stem lamps.

Tiffany vase c. 1896.

different seasons of the year and at different times of day as lights are changed behind it. It is one of the most artistic creations of all times by an American glassmaker. Tiffany's European counterparts were very busy making and sending their iridescent and cameo carved wares to America, where they found great favor with the wealthy.

Greentown

Whatever you call it, Greentown glass or "chocolate glass," much of it was made at the Indiana Tumbler and Goblet Company in Greentown, Indiana. Our historians tell us that Jacob Rosenthal perfected the formula for it about 1900. Prior to that time, the company was making the usual lines of dinner and decorative wares. At the Pan American Exposition in Buffalo in 1901, examples were shown to the public for the first time.

One will notice that examples found today will vary in the shading of brown to tan and even streaks of caramel white, which indicates that stabilizing the colors must have been difficult. The makers of cobalt and ruby glass experienced similar difficulties in their wares. Another factor in determining provenance is that some makers in the Pittsburgh area created their own versions of the colors, so one must be a student of form, design, and decoration to be sure of origination.

James Measell, in his book *Greentown Glass* (Grand Rapids Public Museum), indicates such patterns as Austrian, Brazen Shield, Beaded Panel, Cord Drapery, Cupid, Dewey, and others. Perhaps the most famous and valuable is the holly amber, some pieces of which have advanced into the five figures for particular sets. Chocolate glass reusable food containers were popular for mustard, peanut butter, and other items. One motif used extensively was the bird with a berry in its beak (Robin with Berry). Animals and birds were subjects of decoration and one will find these on steins and mugs.

The factory burned to the ground in 1903 and the company went out of business, so this glass is not plentiful. Not all chocolate glass is Greentown, so be sure to read the Measell book before you start collecting.

Steuben

Various forms of glass with iridized gilt surfaces were made by the Steuben Glass Works in Corning,

New York. The company name, since 1903, has been associated with fine glass and still operates today. Steuben gained a great reputation for its cut and engraved products, much of which has landed in fine collections both museum and private.

The plant was managed by Frederick Carder and financed by another great name in glass, T.G. Hawkes. Carder's art nouveau aurene and other colored glasses made Steuben famous. In the book, *Cut and Engraved Glass of Corning* (Corning Museum of Glass) we are told that Carder disliked cut glass, but he made it as well as his contemporaries.

In 1918, the Corning Glass Works bought the Steuben Glass Works from Hawkes and used the

Corning, NY, Steuben aurene vase in iridescent green with gold leaves and weaving. This is a product of the Art Noveau period. Value: $800-$1,200

factory to increase its manufacture of electric light bulbs. Very little fine glass was made there during this period. There is one interesting note: During prohibition, wine and cocktail glasses were still made in great quantity at Corning, which is a commentary on social life at the time.

In 1933 at the beginning of the depression, after many other glass works had gone out of business, Steuben embarked on an unlikely project for the future, the manufacture of the finest crystal in the world. John Monteith Gates was hired as Steuben's director of design, and sculptor Sidney Waugh designed all the glass for the first three years. Winning of World's Fair awards in 1937, 1939, and 1940 established the factory as one of the finest in the world. One may see great examples of the work at the Corning Museum of Glass in Corning, New York.

Lalique

The Art Nouveau period, which dates from about 1895 to 1920, brought with it a radical change in the style and colors of glass. Louis Comfort Tiffany of New York is the acknowledged leader of this work in America, but he was merely following in the footsteps of his teachers in France. Today, one will find pieces of Lalique glass in most fine gift shops. This is the product of a company, which as founded by a former jeweler, René Lalique of Paris. His designs in jewelry gave him international attention and his experimentation in glass accorded him additional acclaim.

He worked with rock crystal and this fired him to create his own forms in glass with his first commission coming from the noted perfumer Cote, to make bottles for the scents.

It was not until 1920 that he formed his glass company in the province of Alsace-Lorraine, which was annexed by France after World War I, after many years of dispute concerning ownership of the territory, which lies between France and Germany. He began making regular tablewares, bottles, fruit dishes, and stemware. He worked in blown and blown molded techniques and was soon creating forms of birds, people, animals, trees, and flowers. Most of his statues and figures are in a satin finish, though clear glass is often used to highlight them. It would be almost safe to say that all pieces are signed.

René Lalique modeled this view of Susan au Bain, an exotic dancer who performed early in the 20th century. She shocked those who came to her performances by dancing in the buff. Value: $450-$600

René Lalique died in 1945, but his son Marc is still directing the operations of the factory. During the war years, 1939-1945, the plant was demolished, but was rebuilt.

One of the finest collections of Lalique glass is at the Brighton Museum in Brighton, England. Here, one will see a full-sized glass table, as well as a full range of the decorative glass.

Depression Glass

A relatively new phenomenon in the collecting world is "Depression Glass," so called because it was popular during the 1930s. In the past, most Depression Glass ended up in the dump or at summer cottages, since no one thought it would ever be worth anything. It languished in the shadow of more exotic glass, and was being sold by auctioneers for 25 or 50 cents a boxful simply to get rid of it. The mania for collecting anything brought prominence to Depression Glass, and the prices for it are now off and running. The high prices reached by the finer older glass have created the demand for Depression Glass by those with limited funds. This glass was made by the Jeanette

Glass Company, Indiana Glass Company, Hazel Atlas Glass Company, Imperial Glass Company, MacBeth Evans Glass Company, Anchor-Hocking Glass Company, United States Glass Company, and Federal Glass Company. Production was centered in the Pennsylvania, Ohio, and West Virginia areas, as it was with carnival glass.

Depression Glass was everyday dinnerware. Pieces that were heavily used and therefore, prone to breakage (butter dishes, handled pitchers, cookie jars, and even ashtrays) are not found in abundance today. American Sweetheart is the most desired pattern as more was made. Red is best, blue second, and pink least desired. Blue Madrid made by the Federal Glass Company is in short supply because they were not able to produce the exact blue wanted. Most Depression glass was made in the "mold etched" process which was unique to the period. However, some was made by the "chip mod," paste mold, or even handmade process. The latter techniques were a holdover from the carnival glass period in which some of the finer pieces of relatively inexpensive glass were produced. Many glass patterns were given names, such as Old Café, Lace Edge, Miss America, Queen Mary, Colonial, Coronation, Roulette, Hobnail, Oyster and Pearl, and the like. A good reference book for this type of glass is listed in the bibliography.

Contemporary Glass

Many are concerned about the advisability of collecting contemporary glass. This is fine as long as proper documentation of artists and makers is provided. Experience has shown that most antiques change hands at far greater value if the name of the maker is known. The hours spent on research to document old unrecorded items could be spent in other pursuits, so the information should be recorded now for future generations. Some concerns do not mark their pieces, and I do not recommend collecting their output. Some companies may sign them with their name, but not with the name of the artist—again, the artist's name is most important. Several people may be involved in the making of one glass piece—be sure you get the names of all those who worked on the piece, or do not buy it. You will realize the wisdom of this if you are concerned with the future interest in and value of the piece. If value is of no concern to you, buy what you please, but realize that you have

actually done the piece an injustice by not permitting future owner to know its origin.

If paper labels are provided, keep them on the piece since they are valuable for documentation. Do not put your glass in the dishwasher, just clean it with a damp rag and dry it carefully. Not long ago, a broken Tiffany bowl with the paper label intact sold for $45 at an auction. The label will undoubtedly find its way to the bottom of an unmarked bowl (which may or may not be Tiffany) in order to raise its value. As with most antiques, those items, which are American made, will have the most value in the future, so it is best to collect contemporary American glass. Buy rejects, samples, and closeout pieces from concerns where handwork is still in process. The oddity and small flaws, which caused rejection, will often command more interest and value as time goes on.

Areas of Collecting Interest

Bottles

It is recorded that the bottle made its appearance about 250 B.C. when the first blowpipes appeared in the Mediterranean area. They, along with window glass, were the main product of our early glass works. They were a quickly made, inexpensive container, which could handle the commerce of liquids and foods. They were free blown. Then, early in the eighteenth century, blown into wooden and then metal molds. When the pressing of glass began in the 1820s, the hand-blown bottle was still a necessity. It was not until the early twentieth century that machines took over the process of bottle making and handwork almost totally disappeared. Much philosophical glass was still made by hand, on order, such as test tubes, beakers, piping and the like which was used in laboratories. Custom glass houses still made glass items by hand, on order, to satisfy those who wanted them. This is why a bottle made by Tiffany craftsmen as late as the 1920s may be worth much more than a bottle dug from Roman ruins. The desirability of the piece sets the price.

Color in glass most often will heighten value; so one must learn which is most desired in the type of bottle you choose to collect. Cobalt blue glass was made with radioactive cobalt, but I learned at a seminar that there is no danger from handling old glass made with it. This color is much desired in most glass collecting categories.

Bottles were made as early as 1608 (when Jamestown was settled), and many interesting ones are being made today. Pre-revolutionary American-made bottles are rare. Most American bottles of that era came from overseas, primarily from England and France. During the seventeenth century, bottle and window glass houses were set up in many places in this country, but no documented pieces have been found. Some eighteenth century pieces have been located, with enough documentation to land them in museums and great collections. After the Revolutionary War, the American glass industry expanded quickly, and there are many examples which have survived and are available to collectors. Bottles are divided into categories—there are historical flasks, bitters, medicines, and figurals. Early flasks were free blown, but by the early part of the nineteenth century most were being blown into wooden or iron molds so that designs would appear, and uniform sizes would result. The early blown mold bottles are quite plentiful which is amazing when you realize how fragile and brittle the old glass is. As the settlement of the country moved rapidly west, the glassworkers went with it, and as a result, there is much good glass in bottle form made throughout the nineteenth century. This is quite desirable today, and a directory of early glassmakers appears on pages 132-133.

Design, color, and condition are also important. Foreign bottles are not of great importance in American collecting, unless they are extremely old. Recent digs have uncovered seventeenth and eighteenth century English and French bottles, which have considerable value as they were used by the Indians and our first settlers. Wrecks of old ships off the coasts here and in the Caribbean have long held old bottles, which are being brought up by divers every year. Bottle auctions are held throughout the country and help set the prices by which bottles are bought and sold today.

Bottles are of great interest as a collectible, since you can dig them from the ground at no charge. Diggers will spend weekends tracking down old dumps behind farms in the country, and even hunting in old town dumps. The bottles have lain buried for years, so all you have to do is arm yourself with a shovel, pick, and hoe and you are in business. A first aid kit, gloves, and high boots are also necessary. Snakes are common around old dumps, so be sure your legs and hands are covered. Poison ivy is a hazard, so you must protect against it. Above all, obtain permission to hunt from the landowners, as some are quite touchy about having their ground dug up. Some bottle collectors attend building wreckings and ask permission to search the foundations, cellars, and walls for hidden bottles. Many good bottles are found while a backhoe or bulldozer is digging a cellar for a new building or cleaning up the debris from one just torn down. A cement layer and his crew, while laying a sidewalk for me, once reinforced the concrete with the many beer bottles, which they emptied on a hot day and threw into the mix. These will undoubtedly be the subject of much conjecture when they are dug up someday.

Log cabin bottle, which sold for $11,100 at auction the mid 1970s. It is one of only three which have turned up. It has Tippecanoe molded in the side. At the time of the presidential election, Tippecanoe and Tyler Too, was the slogan, c. 1845.

Bitters, Figurals, and Flasks

Bitters bottles are quite rare, as they were not made in quantity. Those with original labels are of most interest, as they promised cures for diseases,

> **Collecting Tip**
>
> Bottle collecting has had its ups and downs. It reached a peak in the early 1970s, but since then has tapered off. The rarities are still bringing good money, but the lesser bottles have declined in value. The rush of collecting Jim Beam bourbon figurals has diminished considerably. There is no question but, that some years hence, many of the early and scarce examples will ascent to high prices again. When a new generation of collectors appears, demand can grow for just about anything.

which are unheard of today. Most contained rather potent drugs such as cocaine, which lulled a person into a sense of well-being. Contrary to popular opinion, America experienced its greatest drug culture in the 19th century when many drugs were legal. The Food and Drug Act of 1906 put an end to this and an end to the sale of bitters.

Figurals (bottles shaped in the form of bodies, heads, animals, houses, buildings, etc.) have always been with us. Today's output is confined mostly to ceramic figurals, but since these are in the bottle category, they are collected as well as the glass. The early medicines are interesting because some were molded with identifying characteristics so the blind, or those searching for medicine at night (before the days of electric lights), could just feel the ridges, or in the case of poison, a skull and crossbones to warn them of the contents.

Perhaps the most desirable bottles are early nineteenth century historical flasks with good color. Many of the early flasks were blown into wooden molds and feature historic motifs of important people, places, and events. Early flasks, very often, were made in olive amber as much silica melted to that color, so one will find examples from many parts of the country. Beware of the Persian saddle flask. They appeared in abundance in the early 1960s when they were made by hand and aged quickly in the desert.

Booz Bottles

An interesting bottle to collect resembles a cabin and was made at the Whitney Glass Works in Glassboro, New Jersey. One will note the molded roof which reads "E.G. Booz's Old Cabin Whiskey." On the side is the address "120 Walnut Street, Philadelphia." On the reverse roof is the date 1840. Because of this, early collectors were led to believe that these bottles were made in that year during the campaign of William Henry Harrison.

However, in the book *American Glass* by George and Helen McKearin (Crown) we are told that Booz was not located at the Walnut Street address until 1860. Prior to that time he was listed as Edmund G. Booz, importer and dealer in wines, brandies and liquors, 54 South Front Street. From 1860 to 1870 he was listed at the Walnut Street address.

About 1931, a reproduction of the bottle was made with a straight roof ridge and a period missing after the word whisky on one end. Original

Original cabin bottle in which whiskey was marketed by J.A. Booz of Philadelphia. Mold blown, it was made in New Jersey, mid 19th century. These have been reproduced extensively. Original: $10,000

Booze News

One can easily see where the slang name for liquor originated as Booz was quite a famous dealer of liquors. In the book American Glass by George and Helen Mc-Kearin we are told that the word booze actually is derived from the seventeenth century French word bouse, and it came into common usage primarily due to this bottle.

colors were shades of amber and olive green, but later reproductions can be found in light blue and green. Reproductions have been made since World War II and can be found on the shelves of gift shops, so one must be alert and know what he is buying.

There were other bottles made to resemble log cabins and the term log cabin whiskey might be applied to many more. Whitney is known to have made others in this style. Also, Booz perhaps wanted to capitalize on this appellation in marketing his liquor, hence the name on this bottle, which lacks the molded log sides, which can be seen in others.

Caster Sets

There are still many farm tables that sport caster sets, right in the same place mother and grandmother used them. It is a handy holder of spices, condiments, and sauces and is making a comeback in the contemporary home. Caster sets take up little space and can be passed around the table easily. Anything so functional was bound to be revived for use today.

Most caster sets one will find consist of a silver-plated frame holding five or six bottles or

❧ Collecting Tip ❧

When buying a caster set, it is important that all the bottles or shakers match. Pressed design, engraving, and stoppers must all be alike. Check these carefully.

shakers. One would use them for salt and pepper or other spices, and oil, vinegar, pepper sauce, catsup, or other dressings. They originated in the days when most families made their own sauces and grew their own spices. They did not come in the handy bottles and shaker tins one finds in the supermarket today. They would be filled for each meal to complement whatever food was being served.

Those with colored bottles are quite desirable, but all the examples of these I have seen came from England or France. Clear bottles seem to be the choice of American makers. I have seen only one sterling frame with cut glass bottles, which was made in America, though these too are common in England and France.

Most often, the glass and metal work were done by separate factories, but in one case, two such manufacturers joined together to turn out the work in one building—the Mount Washington Glass Company and the Pairpoint Silver Company in New Bedford, Massachusetts.

Enamel

The art of enameling reached its peak many centuries ago in Byzantium and Georgia. There are three ways it was done. The first, called champleve is probably a lost art today. Cavities are punched, ground, or chiseled into the surface of a material, often gold, and then filled with colored smalt. Smalt is made of powdered glass that is colored and then mixed with an adhesive that binds it to the surface. Colors are put into the cavities to form a picture or design, and then the entire work is fired, and then polished to remove the excess material, leaving behind a true work of art. When you consider that much of this work was done on gold, often on items as tiny as beads and hanging pendants, it is little wonder that artisans today marvel at it.

The second technique, called cloisonné, involves raising a wall of material on a surface. The early work was done by soldering fine gold wire to a gold surface in the desired design. This was done by the cold solder method, using mercury as a flux, since mercury is a solvent of gold. The outlined areas were filled with smalt and then polished. Cloisonné was used extensively not only in the Georgian area, but also in the Orient and in France. It is mostly cloisonné from China and France that we collect today, since their output during the 19th century must have been tremendous. Cloisonné was done in a less expensive manner, using brass or bronze as the metals and is quite desirable, as it is demanding on the artist. The production coming out of the People's Republic of China today is very good. A simple new eight- to ten-inch vase will command over a hundred dollars.

The third technique is simply called enameling. Materials such as those used to beautify porcelain and glass are merely painted on the surface, with lines of gilding detailing the design between the colors. This line can be mistaken for the raised brass wall in cloisonné, so you must examine it carefully to determine what you are buying. The value of enameled metal pieces is not as high as that of those made with the raised walls and smalt. Much imitation cloisonné has been made and is still being made today, so be careful when you buy.

Glass Hats

Glass hats have been made extensively from the last century into this one and have many collectors. One will find glass hats in many colors, designs and sizes. They were made in New England as well as in the Midwest region around Pittsburgh. There is much conjecture as to their original use. Years ago most identified them as toothpick holders. Some felt they were for after-dinner candies or nuts. Years ago, one found them holding stick matches alongside ashtrays.

However, some years ago at a seminar, Kenneth Wilson, former curator at the Corning Museum of Glass and director of collections at the Henry Ford Museum, stated that they originated as master salts. This caused a minor stir in the crowd. In discussion, some have argued that if they were made as master salts, where were the individual salts to match them? All the glass books I have do not even mention glass hats. None is pictured in Mr. Wilson's book, *New England Glass and Glassmaking,* or in *Pittsburgh Glass* by Lowell Innes, or the 1874 reprint of the Boston and Sandwich Company's catalog, by Ruth Webb Lee. One opinion is that they were mere whimsies originally, then mass manufactured to take care of those who found specific uses for them, such as toothpick holders.

Many are found pressed in the popular daisy and button pattern. After World War II, the glass houses in Murano shipped thousands in millifiori, opalescent, Burmese, and other exotic glasses to capitalize on the American craze of collecting them. Whatever your opinion, they are functional and inexpensive to collect. Do not invest heavily in them—there is no shortage, nor does it seem there will be one to stimulate higher prices. Just have fun with them.

Oddities

Many whimsies were made from glass, since this was an easily worked material and colors could be used at little extra cost. Canes, penny banks, pipes, toys, candy holders, darning balls, animals, birds, floral displays, and the like poured from the factories. Some say this was the result of extra glass being used up at the close of the day by workmen who made such trinkets as gifts for families and friends. You must judge these items on their interest and workmanship, and on whether they are pleasing and desirable. It is not necessary to spend huge sums of money for them—you should enjoy them for the artistic artifacts they are.

Paperweights

Paperweights are an important facet of glass collecting, since they represent an art form, which demands good workmanship, and are usually pretty and functional. Many fine weights were made overseas, especially at Baccarat, Clichy, and St. Cloud in France, but some weights on a par with these were made in America. Most of the large glass factories employed paperweight makers, but this effort must have been concentrated in New England. Both the Boston and Sandwich Glass Company and the New England Glass Company were well known for this work. The Pairpoint works in New Bedford and some works in New Jersey (such as the works at Millville) contributed some elegant pieces.

Many private makers have been at work, and some of the contemporary pieces are commanding more money than the old ones. Domenick Labino of Grand Rapids, Ohio; Charles Kasiun of Brockton, Massachusetts; Ronald Hansen of Mackinac City, Michigan; and Johnny Gentile of Star City,

Morgantown, West Virginia are among the contemporary makers whose works are being studiously collected at this time. There are a lot of handmade weights coming to America from the Orient and Europe—some quite good, but all must be judged on the quality of the design and workmanship.

Some weights are referred to as having sulphide interior decoration. This is merely a porcelain design or figure of some sort imbedded in the glass. The difficulty of molding the decoration into hot glass without destroying it is what gives these weights interest and value.

Paperweight base goblets made by Nicholas Lutz at the Boston and Sandwich Glass Factory, c. 1876. These were made for his wife.

EARLY GLASS MANUFACTORIES

Amelung, John Frederick—See New Bremen Glass Manufactory.

Bakewell & Ensell—Pittsburgh, Pennsylvania, 1808-1882; operated under various partnership names; *Bakewell & Pages: Bakewell, Pears & Bakewell; Bakewell, Pears & Co.*, etc.; glass of all kinds including art and pressed.

Boston and Sandwich Glass Company—Sandwich, Massachusetts, 1825-1888; Deming Jarves; all types of glass, including early pressed glass.

Boston Crown Glass Company—Boston, Massachusetts, 1793-1829; Robert Hewes and others; window glass, bottles.

Owl and Possum goblet made at the Portland Glass Company in Maine, which operated between 1863 and 1873. It seems to be a pattern native only to this company. Value: $250-$350

Boston Porcelain & Glass Manufacturing Company—Cambridge, Massachusetts, 1814-1888; George Blake, Thomas Curtis, and Jesse Putnam; glass, stoneware, porcelain. In 1817, became the *New England Glass Company*. Originated amberina, pomona. Prolific in the art glass period. Moved by final owner, Edward Libbey, to Toledo, Ohio, in 1888.

Brooklyn Glass Works—Brooklyn, New York, 1823-1868; full range of glass items. John Gilliland. Moved in 1868 to Corning, New York, to become the Corning Glass Company.

Cape Cod Glass Company—Sandwich, Massachusetts, 1858-1869; under direction of Deming Jarves. Operated 1869-1881 by a Dr. Flowers. Cut, pressed, and decorative glass.

Chelmsford Glass Works—Chelmsford, Massachusetts, 1802-1839; Jonathan Hunnewell and Samuel Gore. Window glass and bottles. Moved to Suncook, New Hampshire, in 1839 and operated there until 1850.

Cincinnati Glass Manufacturing Company—Cincinnati, Ohio, 1814-1822; Isaac Craig. Bottles, window glass.

Dorflinger Glass Works—Greenpoint, Long Island, New York, 1858-1865; Christian and Christopher Dorflinger. Also, White Mills, Pennsylvania, 1865-1918. Cut and colored glass; table and decorative wares.

Glassboro—New Jersey, 1781-1824; started by members of the Stanger family.

Granite Glass Works—Philadelphia, Pennsylvania, 1771; advertised with the name of Thomas Dyott after 1824. Changed to Dyottville Glass Works in 1833. Operated under various ownerships into the twentieth century. Noted for historical flasks and bottles under Dyott's ownership.

Hewes, Robert—Temple, New Hampshire, 1780-1782; bottles and flasks.

Jersey Glass Company—Jersey City, New Jersey, 1824-1860; established by George Dummer. All types of glass.

Kensington Glass Works—Philadelphia, Pennsylvania, 1771; advertised with the name of Thomas Dyott after 1824. Changed to *Dyottville Glass Works* in 1833. Operated under various ownerships into the twentieth century. Noted for historical flasks and bottles under Dyott's ownership.

LaBelle Glass Works—Bridgeport, Ohio, 1872-1900; pressed and flint glass.

Mantua Glass Works—Mantua, Ohio, 1821-1829; bottles, flint glassware.

Marlboro Street Works—Keene, New Hampshire, 1815-1850; J. & F. McKee; all types of glass.

Millville, New Jersey, Glass Works—founded 1806 and still in business. Originated by James Lee. Originally produced window glass and bottles. Acquired by Whitall Brothers in 1844 and became *Whitall-Tatum Company.*

Mount Vernon Glass Company—Mount Vernon, New York, 1810-1844; bottles, flasks, flint glass, historical flasks, etc.

Mount Washington Glass Company—South Boston, Massachusetts, 1837-1869. Moved in 1869 to New Bedford, joined with Pairpoint Silver Company. Closed in 1958. Reopened by Robert Bryden as *Pairpoint Glass Company,* 1970, Sagamore, Massachusetts. Glass of all kinds. Originated Burmese, peachblow, rose amber.

New Bremen Glass Manufactory—Frederick, Maryland, 1784-1795; started by John Frederick Amelung. Noted for engraved glass.

New Geneva Glass Works—New Geneva, Pennsylvania, 1797-1807; Albert Gallatin and others. Window glass, bottles, tableware. Later moved to Greensboro.

New Hampshire Glass Factory—Keene, New Hampshire (North Works), 1814-1855; window glass.

Pitkin Glass Works—Manchester, Connecticut, 1783-1830; Elisha Pitkin and Samuel Bishop. Originators of Pitkin type flask; also made bottles and tableware.

Pittsburgh Glassworks—Pittsburgh, Pennsylvania, 1797-1886; James O-Hara and Isaac Craig. Window glass, bottles hollowware.

Portland Glass Works—Portland, Maine, 1863-1873; lamps, tableware, colored glass.

South Stoddard Glass Works—South Stoddard, New Hampshire, 1850-1873; bottles and historical flasks.

South Wheeling Glass Works—Wheeling, West Virginia, 1835-1880; flint and colored glass.

Stiegel, Henry William—Manheim, Pennsylvania, 1764-1774; noted for enameled, decorated, and colored wares.

Stoddard Glass Works—South Stoddard, New Hampshire, 1842-1850; Joseph Foster. Mostly bottles and flasks.

Suncook Glass Works—Suncook, New Hampshire, 1839-1850; moved from Chelmsford. Window glass, tableware.

Vermont Glass Factory—Salisbury, Vermont, 1813-1842; in 1842, became the *Lake Dunmore Glass Company.* Bottles, flasks, and hollowware.

Willington Glass Company—West Willington, Connecticut, 1815-1872; bottles, flasks, and hollowware.

Wistar, Caspar—Salem County, New Jersey, 1739-1780; window glass, bottles, and hollowware.

Zanesville Glass Manufacturing Company—Zanesville, Ohio, 1815-1851; hollowware, bottles, and historical flasks.

GLASS GALLERY

Bluish green small-footed bowl or master salt, c. 1840, knopped stem; wide cylindrical base, Stoddard, New Hampshire. Value: $600

The Mt. Washington Glass Company joined with the Pairpoint Silver Company in the 1880s to create some of the best items to collect. Pairpoint lamps, with interior painted shades, are commanding big dollars. Generally, shades which are molded are worth more. Value: $2,500-$3,000

Bennington Museum.

Three hand-blown bowls, that probably originated at the Lake Dunmore Glass Works near Burlington, c. 1813-1817.

There are over 5,000 designs in pressed glass. This display of goblets exhibits some of them, made mid 19th century.

Sandwich Glass Museum.

Case containing early blown candleholders, lamps and serving dishes. All Sandwich, made after 1830.

Peony table lamp, another of Tiffany's creations. Most lamps of this type were used for decoration and night lighting, not for reading. Value: $22,000-$25,000

Tiffany favrile glass and bronze hydrangea floor lamp c. 1899-1910. Butterfields in Los Angeles sold it at auction on March 20, 1994, for $71,800.

Leaded shades of this type can be suspect as many are being brought from Mexico. If you pay a lot of money, be sure of provenance when you are buying. Value: $60-$80

Galle Mont Blanc Elephant Vase, made by Emile Galle, Paris, early 20th century. This is an example of cameo cutting, for which Galle was famous. Value: $2,800-$3,200

Steuben aurene vase with flared mouth, 4-1/2" h.

Two Argy-Rousseau pate de verre vases; lions and les loups dans le neige, made c. 1926. Either piece is worth over $20,000.

Blown glass flytrap, Pittsburgh area, c. 1840s. Flies could get in, but not out. Value: $450

Slag glass is a product of the art period, c. 1880-1990. Slag from local steel mills, was introduced into the glass metal to create the design. This has been reproduced. Value: $125-$150

Vases by Baccarat of France, made during the 1920s in the height of the Art Deco period, green. Value: $250-$450

Brilliant cut glass was made between c. 1890 and 1915. The pressed glassmakers took up the challenge by creating deep molded glass to compete. Many had such words as NEARCUT, NEWCUT, or DEEPCUT, molded in the bottoms to heighten a relationship to the more expensive cut glass. Value: $75-$85

Late 19th century covered bowl made by Portiault in France. Much of their glass is identified by a rosette molded in the bottom. Many repros of this. Value: $250-$325

Ruby-flashed glass. Color at top was applied by flashing, or dipping the finished product into a ruby-colored stain. Value: $75-$125

Diamond banded goblet, in maiden's blush cranberry. Portland Glass Factory, Maine, 1863-1873. The diamond banding design was popular in Portland. The cranberry tint is native only to this factory. Value: $225-$250

Pressed, clear glass cake stand, John Adams, c. 1851. Adams must be credited with the revival of the use of lime and soda as fluxes to make inexpensive glass. The switch away from the lead flux doomed the New England glass companies, who continued to use it and could not compete in price. Value: $125-$175

Valentine glass sugar and creamer, molded, Midwest. Named after the donors to the Bennington Museum.

Ruby-stained glass, c. 1900. Since it was pressed, color could be applied only by staining it with a brush, while hot. Value: $75-$125

Early 19th century, amber glass stoppers, shown here being made in a single mold. They were broken off for use.

The Mason's Patent canning jar; an original, dating 1858 has some value. One will find many reproductions with this date on them. Value: $18-$20

Snuff bottles made of glass. Most came from the Orient. Value: $150-$350

Carnival glass tumbler, peacock at fountain pattern, 4" h.

Carnival glass Jack-in-pulpit vase, 8" high, marigold color.

Durand art glass vase, floral decor on bulbous shape, 6" h.

Durand art glass vase, peach w/blue leaf design on bulbous shape, 6-1/4" h.

GLOSSARY

Agata: A mottled effect obtained by spraying alcohol or other chemicals onto the bodies of colored glass.

Amber: Amber colored, very popular during the last part of the nineteenth century into the twentieth.

Amber (Rose): Basically an amberina made by the Mount Washington Glass Company.

Amberina: An art glass, most popular during the last part of the nineteenth century, believed to have originated at the New England Glass Company. Shaded from ruby to amber by including gold in the glass metal, which would turn amber first and then to varying hues of red as more heat was applied.

Amberina (Cased or Plated): An inner core of glass, which is most often fiery opalescent creamy white, covered with an amberina exterior. Most glass in this style is ribbed.

Art: A general term used to describe the many various colored fancy glasswares of the late nineteenth century.

Art Deco: The period between 1920 and 1940. Artistic work was done as well as the inexpensive work now called carnival and Depression glass.

Art Nouveau: The period between about 1895 and 1915, characterized by the iridescent colorings and Oriental shapes. Leading makers were Tiffany, Lalique, Gallé, etc.

Aurene: A product of the Corning Glass Works, attributed to Frederick Carder, most often in a blue shade with gold iridescence; twentieth century.

Baccarat: High quality French glass manufacturer, still in business since early in the nineteenth century. Well known for its paperweights.

Blown Three Mold: Glass hand blown into a tri-divided mold, found in vertical ribbed patterns; diamond quilting, gothic, sunburst, and fluted. Some geometric. Early nineteenth century.

Bryden: Robert Bryden, last manager of the original Mount Washington-Pairpoint Glass Works in New Bedford, closed in 1958. Reopened the Pairpoint Glass Works at Sagamore, Massachusetts, 1970.

Burmese: Shaded pink to a lemon yellow. First made in the 1880s at the Mount Washington Glass Works, New Bedford, by Frederick Shirley. Most often found in a satin finish.

Cameo: Glass which has been dipped into another colored glass (or "flashed") then cut in cameo relief.

Carnival: An inexpensive iridescent glass first produced by Frank Fenton in Newark, Ohio in 1907. None was made in New England. It received its name as a result of being used as prizes at carnivals and fairs.

Clichy: A French glassworks at Clichy, dating from the early nineteenth century. A maker of fine paperweights.

Coralene: Art glass with frosted crystal decoration.

Crown Milano: Made by Frederick Shirley at Mount Washington Glass Works. A satin finish ecru colored glass, decorated with flowers and gilding. 1880s.

Cut Glass: usually heavy lead crystal with designs cut into it by a spinning abrasive wheel. The Mount Washington Glass Company is considered by many to have made the best in the world. The most brilliant period for this product is 1890-1915, when it was the height of fashion.

Daum: During the last half of the nineteenth century, Antonin and Auguste Daum worked at Nancy, France, with Emile Gallé. Their pieces are usually signed "Daum-Nancy."

Depression: A name given to the inexpensive colorful glass made during the Depression, and often given away at theaters as an incentive to go to the movies on slow nights. It was used as premiums, and also sold at the five and dime stores.

Durand: Victor Durand worked 1925-1932 in Vineland, New Jersey, and produced colorful glass in both art nouveau and art deco styles.

Etched: A reference to inexpensive glass, which was decorated by lightly etching it with a spinning copper wheel.

Favrile: Made by Louis Comfort Tiffany in the first quarter of this century. The word is taken from the German word "faber," which means color. It can be any color, with iridescent tints and highlights.

Flashed: Flashed glass is made by dipping a clear body of glass into a liquid mixture of colored glass. This is bonded by heat to create a coating, which may be cut or etched to reveal the clear glass beneath.

Gallé: The master French glassmaker of Nancy, France, Emile Gallé is noted for his art nouveau glass and cameo glass.

Gunderson: Robert Gunderson was plant manager of the Pairpoint Works in New Bedford from 1939-1952. Glass made there during this period is often referred to as Gunderson glass.

Iridescent: A name applied to any glass, which has an iridescent shine, created by chemical processes. It was made in imitation of early Roman glass, which had absorbed minerals from the soil while lying buried for hundreds of years.

Kew Blas: Gold iridescent glass made at the Union Glass Company in Somerville, Massachusetts. Late nineteenth century.

Lalique: René Lalique, France, first quarter of this century. Worked in art nouveau styles; with pressing, cutting, frosting, cameo, etc.

Lutz: Best known for his threaded glass and other art glass work at the Boston and Sandwich Glass Company. Worked also for Dorflinger and the Mount Washington Glass Works, mostly during the third quarter of the nineteenth century.

Mother of Pearl: A satin finish glass with design worked into it, created by Joseph Webb in 1885 in Beaver Falls, Pennsylvania.

Mount Washington: The Mount Washington Glass Company was formed by Deming Jarves in 1837 for his son. It was later moved to New Bedford. The name has been synonymous with the name Pairpoint since 1894, when the two companies merged, the latter originally being the Pairpoint Silver Company.

Pattern-Glass, which is pressed mechanically into a mold, is called pattern glass. This was first done by Benjamin Bakewell in Pittsburgh in 1825, and was improved at the Boston and Sandwich Glass Company in 1827.

Peachblow: That made by Hobbs and Brockunier in Wheeling shades from rose to yellow. That made at the New England Glass Works shades from a rose-red at the top to white at the base. The latter is also called "Wild Rose" and was first made in the 1880s.

Pigeonblood: Known to have been made by Hobbs and Brockunier. It looks ruby in color until it is held to the light, which causes the color to change to an orange-yellow.

Pomona: Made by Joseph Locke at the New England Glass Company. It is a clear glass with etched pattern, having amber staining and often, blue cornflowers for decoration.

Portiault: A noted concern of the nineteenth century at Portiault, France. Identified by imprint of name and later by a rosette design, generally at the base of the piece.

Quezal: Named after the exotic Quetzal bird of South America whose brilliant plumage it resembles. Made in 1916-1918 by the Quezal Art Glass and Decorating Company in Brooklyn. It features deep colorings and iridescence, much in the manner of Tiffany. Most is Art Nouveau in style.

Rubena Crystal: First made by Hobbs and Brockunier. A ware that shades from red to clear.

Rubena Verde: A ware which shades from red to yellow.

Sandwich: Common name given to items made at the Boston and Sandwich Glass Company, Sandwich, Massachusetts, 1825-1888.

Satin: Glass which has been bathed in hydrofluoric acid to give it a soft, satin finish.

Spangled: Generally, a cased glass, which has been colored with design and fragments of metals such as gold to make it sparkle.

Spatter: Made by rolling hot glass over broken bits of colored glass to incorporate them into the body of the piece.

St. Louis: A firm which had its beginnings in the seventeenth century in France. Noted for its pressed glass and paperweights.

Stained: Glass is often colored by staining it while hot. Much pressed glass is colored this way.

Steuben: The famous works still operating at Corning, New York. Well known for its handmade clear glass.

Threaded: The best-known artisan of this style is Nicholas Lutz, who worked at the Boston and Sandwich Glass Factory. The glass is threaded and striped in the Venetian style.

Tiffany: Louis Comfort Tiffany was an American pioneer of Art Nouveau designs and iridescent glass. He worked beginning in 1878, and his plant continued working until 1933, the year of his death.

Vasa Murrhina: The Vasa Murrhina Art Glass Company operated in Hartford, Connecticut, during the art glass period. This glass sparkled with imbedded mica colored with gold.

Venetian: A term given to the delicate styled glass, which has been made in that region of Italy since the fourteenth century.

Waterford: Originally operated at Waterford, Ireland, between 1794 and 1851. It was reopened in 1951 as the Waterford Glassworks.

Chapter Three

CERAMICS

Introduction

Historical Overview

One of the most useful elements to mankind has been common clay, which is found everywhere in the world. We find mention of it in Genesis, X1.3: "The early descendants of Noah found on the plain in the land of Shinar, the clay for their construction and said to one another, 'Let us make brick and

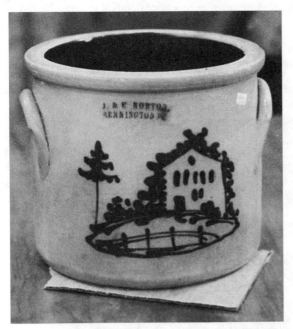

The Norton Pottery was founded in 1793, in Bennington, to make jugs in which to market cider. It was in business until 1894. There are various Norton partnership names used during this period. One son went to Worcester, Massachusetts, to set up a business which is still operating. Stoneware pieces with buildings are the rarest to find. Value: $7,500

burn them thoroughly, and they had brick for stone and slime for mortar'." The slime was probably the semi-fluid bitumen used in early periods of Egypt and Palestine as a cement. We learned this from an 1858 encyclopedia.

There has always been conjecture on how the pyramids were built: How were such large stones raised to such heights? The only quarries with stone large enough were near Aswan and this would have required a boat trip on boats not big enough to carry them. In a patent issued in 1984 to a Frenchman, Joseph Davidovits, one learns his theory that wooden molds were created where the blocks would lie and then were filled with a cement, which may have contained clay and other ingredients. He disputed the theory that blocks of stone were hauled long distances. Lone Star Industries of Greenwich CT makes Pyrament from the formula he created. It is felt the heat of the sun for thousands of years has hardened the mixture into what is mistaken for stone today—Pyrament does not need this long exposure.

Discussions on clay began as early as the time the pyramids were built at Howara, 10 leagues from Cairo. A translation of a writing by Herodutus, states, "Do not undervalue me by comparing me with the pyramids of stone, for I am better than they, as Jove exceeds the other deities. I am made of bricks from clay brought up from the bottom of the lake, adhering to the poles." Davidovits must have read this information while doing his research. Perhaps his interpretation was that the size of the "bricks" could be as massive as they could create.

Red clay is the most common and is found all over the world. The ancients found that if they molded and heated it, it would harden into useful vessels. Later, they learned to glaze the pieces to waterproof them. Gradually, decorations became important and we see excellent examples in early Greek and Turkish wares. In the Orient, better clays seem to have been discovered and the secret of making the thin brittle opalescent porcelains lay locked there for centuries. It is reputed that Marco Polo returned from his trip with examples of the "China" ware, which started potters and chemists on the search for a formula to duplicate this work.

In the 17th century, the Dutch East India Company was formed to trade in the known world, and soon, their ships were bringing back loads of this china for sale in Europe. The art of decoration had flourished, and colorful pieces, all hand done, are sought by today's collectors.

Looking back in our history, we find that the first pottery was made at Jamestown early in the 17th century. Andre Duche was a potter who was born in Philadelphia and later settled in Windsor, South Carolina, c. 1735. In 1738, he returned to Savannah and opened a pottery where he was successful in making good pottery. We learn from Arthur Clement in his book, *Our Pioneer Potters*, (500 published privately in 1947), that in March of 1739 he proposed to the trustees of the Colony of Georgia, in London, to provide him with necessary machinery and pots to set up a large pottery, as the clay in the area was excellent. It seems that the English were not keen about creating any competition with their Staffordshire County potters and they refused his requests.

However, the secret of unaker clay was out—most of it was owned by the Cherokee Nation. On May 30, 1745, William Cookworthy, who founded a pottery at Plymouth, England, purchased the entire area of clay from the American Indians and began shipping it to the mother country. Other potteries purchased it from him. Much of the fine china made in England during the 18th century may have been made with American clay. According to Clement, no one can ascertain that Duche ever made porcelain, though he had the clay to do it.

Surely the earliest collectibles—as notable for their artistic merit as for their functional value—are ceramic objects. The art of fashioning clay into usable vessels is as old as civilization. In ancient times, people learned to shape readily available clay into useful objects, and then harden them in the sun. They learned to make them hard enough to withstand heat, and also that such heat hardened them even more. They learned later that with the addition of crushed flint or other stone they could make a very strong body that would withstand rough usage. The final step in early ceramics was the discovery that after glazing, the clay vessels would no longer soak up water and that liquids could then be stored in them for indefinite periods.

The simplest glaze was that of a clay with a lower firing temperature than the body clay. This would be mixed with water and then slipped (or poured) over the vessel and fired, leaving a clear, hard coating that was bonded to the surface by the intense heat. In the late eighteenth century, metal glazes were perfected, with lead being the most preferred and the most dangerous. Lead was mixed with a liquid clay mixture, and after firing provided a very luminescent surface, though dangerous if food or edible liquids were stored against it for any length of time. The lives of our ancestors were undoubtedly shortened immeasurably by the amount of lead used in household ceramics, plates, and other cooking utensils. Tin was often used in glazes, as were iron filings, zinc, copper, and other minerals and metals that would contribute a hard surface or color to the piece.

A later technique involved the use of common table salt, which was thrown into a kiln during the last minutes of firing. As it vaporized, it was deposited on the clay bodies, providing a hard sheen, rough with imperfections.

The art of ceramic making in Europe was confined to the most basic work in earthenware when the Pilgrims settled this country. It was not until the later seventeenth century in France that porcelain was made with much success. The first porcelains that bore any resemblance to those from China were turned out at Rouen and St. Cloud in France. However, it was not until 1708 that Johann Freiderich Bottger perfected a true porcelain body by the use of kaolin and the petuntse clays, which had been an oriental secret for so many centuries. It was not long before potteries copying Bottger's formula and techniques were set up both on the continent and in England, and the vast ceramics industry was born. To attempt to discuss the industry before that time would hardly be worthwhile as little of that production can be found today, either here or overseas. It is enough of a project to concentrate on what can be found and collected today.

There are actually many more fine types of ceramics from all over the world in America today than there were at the turn of the century. The importation of such antique ceramic pieces did not reach great heights until after World War I, when American affluence climbed. Before then, most homes were equipped with relatively inexpensive dinnerware made by some concern in this country and little interest in these wares was noted in antiques collecting. Lucky was the bride who received a complete service of French, English, or German dinnerware, as this was the ultimate gift. Much of this dinnerware has survived, but hardly enough to satisfy the demand on the part of collectors who want something old and of good quality. We were fortunate that the makers continued to turn out the same patterns in open stock for many years so that the replacements were easy to obtain. Today, you must most often scrounge about in antiques shops and shows looking for needed items to fill out a set, since many patterns have been discontinued in favor of more contemporary designs.

Types of Ceramic Ware

The most delicate ware to collect is *porcelain*—a fine, thin-bodied ceramic that is translucent and beautiful when decorated. Next in importance is *bone china*, which originated in England. Instead of the expensive kaolin clay used for porcelain, it is made from ground-calcined bone ash, which gives a good thin body, but is opaque.

The term *earthenware* is used to describe most pieces found as common china in the home. Earthenware is also opaque. Just hold any piece to the light. If you can see light through it, it is porcelain. If not, it is earthenware.

Another type of china is *vitreous ware*. This is quite hard, most often very thick, and is used extensively for commercial chinas for hotels, trains, ships, etc. It has better quality and is stronger than earthenware, but does not possess the fragility or beauty of porcelain.

Beneath earthenware is *stoneware*, made from various colored clays. Stoneware clay pieces must be made with thick walls to prevent their collapse in the kiln. This is why stoneware crocks, butter pots, jugs, etc., are so thick and heavy. There is no stoneware clay in New England; all of it had to be hauled by wagon or ship until the railroads were in operation. One potter, Jeremiah Burpee (c. 1805) died with his secret of making thin bodied stoneware pieces. Whatever he added to the clay is not known. Where he obtained his clay is not known either, as he was a native of Boscawen, New Hampshire, and there is no stoneware clay in the area.

At the bottom is *redware*, made from common red clay out of which bricks, tiles, flower pots, etc., are made. Americans are inclined to collect simple redware and stoneware, which is most often made of light-colored clays reinforced with flint or other hardening material. Both products are still made today, some by kilns operating in the same way they did in the nineteenth century, and some by craft potters working in both traditional and contemporary motifs.

Manufacturing Techniques

It is interesting to note the technique of making simple stoneware. The following recipe is from *Mackezies 5,000 Receipts* (sic) published in 1828:

Tobacco-pipe clay is beaten much in water; by this process, the finer parts of the clay remain suspended in the water, while the coarser sand and other impurities fall to the bottom. The thick liquid consisting of water and finer parts of the clay is further purified by passing it through hair and lawn sieves of different degrees of fineness. After this, the liquor is mixed in various proportions for various ware with another liquid of the same density, and consisting of flints calcined, ground, and suspended in water. The mixture is then dried in a kiln and afterwards beaten to a proper temper, it becomes fit for being formed at the wheel into dishes, plates, bowls, etc. When this ware is to be put into the furnace to be baked, the several pieces of it are placed in the cases made of clay, called saggars, which are piled one upon another, in the dome of the furnace. A fire is lighted; when the ware is brought to a proper temper, which happens in about 48 hours, it is glazed by common salt. The salt is thrown into the furnace through holes in the upper part of it, by the heat of which it is instantly converted into a thick vapour; which, circulating through the furnace, enters the saggar through the holes made in its side (the top being covered to prevent the salt from falling on the ware) and attaching itself to the surface of the ware, it forms that vitreous coat upon the surface, which is called its glaze.

Stoneware from Vermont

John Norton established a pottery at Bennington, Vermont, to make jugs in which he could sell his cider. His stoneware business soon outdid his cider business and he expanded to take care of the demand for his wares. The pottery continued to operate in the hands of his family through most of the century, turning out a variety of functional and decorative pieces. His son-in-law, Christopher Weber Fenton, opened the United States Pottery Company in 1847 and continued in business until 1858. Fenton hired the great English modeler Daniel Greatback, who turned out designs for many animal figures and other decorative pieces, which were made in both the brown-colored Rockinghamware and the pure white parian. Rockinghamware is reputed to have originated at the estates of the Earl of Rockingham in England, and found much favor in England and America. Many American concerns turned it out, but that from Bennington seems to be the most desired.

Bennington Museum.

Bennington, Vermont was the home to two famous potteries, Norton and the US Pottery Company. Illustrated are some of the output, such as the pair of scroddled vases; white graniteware, Rockingham ware and parian.

The formulas for the more sophisticated wares, such as porcelain, bone china, soft and hard paste, Queensware, and the like, are much more complicated, but all ceramics begin with the basics noted above. A once popular glaze was a shining black which was made up of 100 parts of lead, 18 parts of crushed flint, and 40 parts of manganese. With such ingredients, the glaze must have helped spoil the food. Most manufacturers today used fritted, body sheen, or soft glazes which are made up of basic clays with nothing to affect any food stored next to them. You must be careful in purchasing clay artifacts from underdeveloped nations as some may be coated with the dangerous lead glaze. It was not until the 1820s that experimentation resulted in glazes made with no lead, but they were expensive at the time and did not come into general use on stoneware until a decade or two later.

Determining Age and Authenticity

There are no set rules for determining the age and authenticity of early ceramics, but the following pointers are offered as an aid. No one rule can guarantee authenticity—you must inspect many features before attribution can be made. A simple clue is the wear on the bottom of any piece that must rest on a table or shelf. If the piece is old, this wear will show as roughness, wear of the glaze, or small chips and cracks. Many early ceramics become crazed with age, and this crazing is difficult to reproduce. Items fired in kilns before the middle of the nineteenth century often show the marks of the tripod on which they rested in the saggar so that the heat could flow evenly around them. These are called tripod marks, and there are usually three, which pierce the glaze on the underside of the dish out toward the rim. They will show up as three dots. There may be a triple dot at each point—this is almost always a guarantee of age. Contemporary pieces are still being fired on tripods, so this clue is not always constant. I have seen tripod marks on Doulton pieces whose other markings put them as being made after 1892. However, a piece without tripod marks should not be evaluated as being made before 1850.

Painting designs on the clay bodies, then glazing and firing, was the most popular technique used in all countries back to the eighteenth century. However, some pottery was painted over the first glaze, then reglazed and fired. A good general rule

There were many fine potteries in New Jersey because clay was plentiful. The Jersey City Pottery Company was one. This pitcher is one of series of twelve made during the centennial to commemorate the presidents. This piece depicts William Henry Harrison at the 1840 presidential campaign. Value: $450

to early handmade pottery value is that the more colors used, the higher the value. In the early days, each color had to be painted on, glazed, and then fired, which was a time consuming process. Some plants used the technique of painting with colored glazes, which would then be fired, doing away with the extra steps color usually demanded. Such glazes used at the Fenton works in Bennington are still brilliant today.

Some people feel that a piece must look old to be old, but on the surface many Chinese porcelains several hundred years old look as if they were made just a few days ago. This is a tribute to the superior formulas and ingenuity used by the Chinese artisans. However, most ceramics will show their age up to a point; it is up to you to evaluate how old a piece is if there are no markings or other identification to help you. If you are concerned about age, and are not satisfied with the determination of age either from the person from whom you are buying or from your own analysis, leave the item alone. A "lost" treasure can sometimes be a headache you really don't need.

Clay

Inventories of estates in eighteenth century America reveal little or no fine china, except in the homes of the wealthy. Tea drinking was not really popular until the time of Queen Anne, although tea is known to have been imported as early as the 1660s. Ceramic tea sets were in demand after her time, and most wealthy homes were equipped with at least one. The poorer people were still eating from wooden or pewter plates and vessels.

Perhaps our first recognized potter was John Pride of Salem, Massachusetts, who was registered as early as 1641. A brickworks was established in nearby Danvers as early as 1629, but there is no evidence that eating vessels or plates were made. I could provide a relatively good list of seventeenth and eighteenth-century potters, but it would do little good to collectors, as little or none of the production can be documented today.

Fortunately, some stoneware bears the imprint of maker's names and often bears the name of a commercial concern for which they might have made it. Most noted among these are the Remmy and Crolius families of New York City, who imprinted their names, as well as that of Manhattan Wells, which was near the site where they worked. The wells were the water supply for the city. If you find marked stoneware, you can document it from books listed in the bibliography, as space does not permit a complete listing.

Needless to say, any eighteenth century work is very desirable. Of course, the best area in which to look would be the thirteen original colonies. However, the area that includes New Jersey, Pennsylvania, New York, and New England is the prime place to look, as their output was the greatest during those times. Unmarked redware and stoneware has value if the shapes and workmanship are good. The decorated slipware made of red clay and then hand painted throughout the northern colonies has now become highly collectible. Some of these pieces have reached the high three-figure price range and have no place to go but up.

Types of Ceramics

Delft-Type Ware

There is evidence that a Delft-type ware was made in this country in the latter part of the seventeenth century and well into the eighteenth, but none has survived. Inventories of the period tell of the blue and white ware copied after the fashion of its European counterpart. This type of decorated earthenware originated in Ireland. Dutch traders hauled clay from there for the makers in their own country and brought with them some gaily decorated tin glazed ware that caught the fancy of those on the continent. The Dutch copied the style and are generally credited with originating it due to the large output from Delft, whose name was eventually attached to it. Delft was made in other countries, including the Lowlands, Germany, France, and England.

Group of blue and white Delft plates, made in Holland. Oriental motifs were popular as much of this was sold in the Orient as part of the trade with the Dutch East Indies Company in the 18th century, Historic Deerfield.

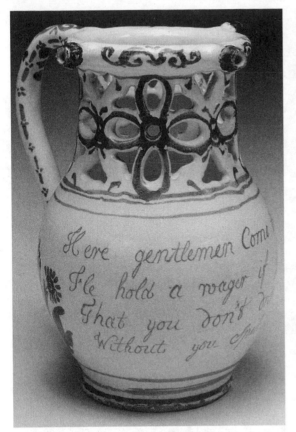

Delft puzzle jug, c. 1765. Some were made so that fingertips had to be held over holes so that one might pour or drink from a piece, Historic Deerfield.

Few redware makers marked their pieces. This is the only known example marked by Abner S. Wright of Marlboro, New Hampshire, 19th century. Value: $450

Redware

The first American redware was unmarked, but as the eighteenth century progressed, the Pennsylvania Germans began coloring their pieces with designs and sayings and some were well signed by their makers. Added to this was the technique of sgraffito—the scratch carving believed to have originated in the Commonwealth of Pennsylvania. Artisans created these designs by carving the original clay body before firing, filling the indentations with a coloring agent, and then glazing and firing it. The carving might also be done after the glaze was applied, with the coloring added using a colored glaze. For protection, painting was done under a glaze, which was later fired. Tin glazes were popular at the time, since they could be colored themselves, lending a better look to the piece. Though most of this work seems to have turned up in Pennsylvania, it is known that this technique was copied throughout the colo-

nies. Perhaps you can trace the origins of such pieces through design, as the Pennsylvania motifs are quite regional in their look.

However, you must be careful in your attribution, since much simple ware was shipped in from other countries, notably England, during these years. Fragments have been found at many historic sites in this country and their documentation has led back across the ocean, even though most people would think that such simple wares were most likely made in the colonies.

As clay refining methods improved, potters grew more sophisticated in their work, and much thinner and very functional wares appeared including shaving mugs, drinking mugs, milk pitchers, and batter jugs. The bean pot made its appearance early in the nineteenth century in both redware and stoneware. This type of work is being reproduced today. With the knowledge of old recipes and methods of firing, all of us are exposed to the possibility of buying a recently made piece, which has been aged quite quickly through the use of chemicals. There is no known easy way to tell the old from the new, but science can prove the age of an item if a fragment is examined.

Most of you will not want to go through the expense of this, so you must familiarize yourself with the "look" of old redware by searching it out in museums and collections and doing a lot of studying. There is no formula that I can put into print to help you. As far as collecting is concerned, you should look for pieces documented with dates and makers' names. Next of importance are those pieces with good folk art decoration, with animals, birds, and people being the most popular. Color must be good and condition is very important. Many a cat, dog, or chicken has been fed from old redware as it fell from popularity, and many pieces have suffered as a result.

Stoneware

The American stoneware industry did not take hold until after the Revolutionary War. Eighteenth century production is noted and some of it is cataloged, but there is not much chance of finding examples today, except in the better shops, which specialize in ferreting out such pieces for the discriminating customers. Most pieces are preserved in museums or historical societies, as well they should be. After the turn of the century, production was increased to the point that much ware was exported to other countries. Accounts of American manufacturing in 1828 reveal that stoneware was one of our greatest exports. Rarely would a piece be discarded if it were still usable, so if you are a traveler, you may look for it in antiques shops in Europe as well as South America.

Switchel jug in redware. This was a rum drink hung on a horse's harness and taken out into the field so the farmer could refresh himself from time to time. Value: $150-$250

Redware plate of Pennsylvania origin, 11-3/4" d.

Much fine redware to collect was made in Pennsylvania. There are lots of decorated pieces. This cupboard fully illustrates some of the forms and decorations.

Unusual stoneware pitcher by Jeremiah Burpee, Boscawen, New Hampshire, c. 1804-1805. It is thin-bodied stoneware, which is unusual because most stoneware is made with thick walls to withstand firing. Also, there is no stoneware clay in New Hampshire. Value: $600

Stoneware butter pot made by the Ottman Brothers in Ft. Edward, NY, 1881-1882. These are the years they were in business together. The bird decoration is a beauty with good blue color and dimension. Value: $600

Designs were created by sgraffito (scratch carving) and by direct painting under the glaze. You can easily determine the most valuable pieces by following simple rules, which, of course, must have their exceptions. *Shapes* and *forms* are important as well as good workmanship. *Decorations* are graded for importance, as follows: at the top of the list are buildings, most often farmhouses and the like; next in rarity are those of animals and fish, followed by birds, floral designs, and finally those with unidentifiable designs or no decoration at all. Some feature the names of concerns that marketed them. Drawn in cobalt blue or stamped in various colors. Age is helpful, regardless of decoration, but most collect these pieces only as examples of early folk art.

Rare pieces such as large water coolers, foot warmers, batter and switchel jugs, and funerary urns command much interest regardless of decoration, since they are difficult forms to find. (One used a switchel jug to carry a rugged rum drink out into the fields. Hung from a horse's harness, the potion was well mixed in time for enjoyment at the noontime meal.)

You must realize that stoneware items were made well into this century and that as recently as the 1920s, concerns were still using them in marketing products such as molasses, vinegar, tea, jams and jellies, and chemicals and other liquid products. By today's standards, they look quite old and most acquire a good patina after lying unused in cellars and barns for many years.

The kiln needed to mass produce such items had to be quite large and this limited the number that were used for salt glazing, no other glaze could be fired in it, as the residue of salt from past firings would make it impossible for other glazes to stick to the bodies. Fuel for kilns and availability of clay were important and often dictated the location of a business. Richard Carter Barret relates that farmers from the Bennington area traveling to sell their produce in Troy or Albany were encouraged to return loaded with clay from any cellar hole being dug along the way, since they could sell the clay to the potteries in Bennington. The clays of New Jersey are world famous, and were shipped just about everywhere—at first by boat and ox cart, and later by rail and ferry. Colored clays will not necessarily remain the same hue after firing. Some blue clays are known to turn red and some green clays turn black. Tobacco pipe clay was favored for delicate pieces and was much in demand.

Naturally, the first fuel was wood. Coal was adapted for this purpose after the Revolutionary War. As early as 1827, a railroad was built in Carbon County, Pennsylvania, to haul coal down to the ferryboats, which plied the Delaware River to Philadelphia. After the discovery of oil wells in Pennsylvania at mid-century, oil was successfully used as a fuel for kilns. Mary Chase Perry Stratton first used electricity for firing during the late 1800s at her Pewabic Pottery in Detroit. Gas was employed where available, and to this day natural gas is very much accepted.

Ceramic makers are still experimenting with glazes in an effort to come up with something new. One potter frequents a local junkyard to retrieve ashes after the dealers have burned the tarred coatings from old electric and telephone wire. Mixed with a clear glaze, these ashes create an unusual effect on his pottery. Other potters use manganese and manganese oxide, and still others work with tin, zinc, copper, and other minerals, which create an illuminating effect. The greatest artisans are those who combine a talent for design with skill in painting on their pieces. Perhaps the most noted craftsman in this field is left-handed Russell Henry of Birdsboro, Pennsylvania, whose artwork is as compelling as the shapes and forms he spins on his wheel.

Spongeware

Spongeware is one of the hottest collectibles today. It is stoneware on which a mottled decoration has been applied by use of a sponge. Artisans dip the flat edge of a sponge in cobalt blue and apply the design. The earliest examples of spongeware date from about 1840 in this country. It can be found on most forms of stoneware and was made practically all over the country where suitable clays could be found.

There are some who question whether sponges were really used on some pieces we call spongeware. But contemporary artisans are still using this method, not only demonstrating that it is possible, but also proving without doubt that it was the manner in which the cobalt was applied. One of the most noted contemporary potters who makes spongeware is Nancy Sampson of Westminster, Massachusetts. She has demonstrated the tech-

Early 20th century spongeware that might have been anywhere in the country. Colored with a sponge dipped in cobalt blue. Today's potters prove this was the way it was done. If colored green, this is greenware and piece for piece it is most often more valuable. Value: $150-$250

nique and her work is a true reproduction of the old we collect. She feels there is no other way it could have been done as conveniently and quickly.

Only twenty years ago, simple milk pitchers with spongeware decoration were selling at but a dollar or two as they were considered country pieces and the demand was not great. However, the rising interest in folk art has prompted a reexamination of techniques used and the product has risen so that some pieces are in the three figures today.

A companion to spongeware is greenware, which is a green mottled decoration on a buff or beige body of clay. This is rarer than the blue, so commands better prices in equivalent form. Spongeware can be found all over the country, though the best place to locate it is at farm auctions out in the countryside.

Porcelain

America was quite late in developing good porcelain for sale to the public in any quantity. The first firm on record is that of Bonnin and Morris of Philadelphia. Some of their output has survived, but there was very little made, which accounts for the fact that it is not regarded as collectible. The next successful effort was that of Dr. Daniel Mead in New York City about 1812. His work was on a par with that of the Europeans, but again little was made. The first really successful porcelain maker was William Ellis Tucker, who produced ware as early as 1825, and though perhaps not on a par with its European counterparts, Tucker's work survives today as the most collectible of the early work in this area. The plant survived under various partnerships until 1838, and produced much ware that has survived. Tucker imported workers from France; hence the French look to his work. You might mistake his pieces for the contemporary Sèvres in color, shape, and decoration.

Not much Tucker china has turned up on the open market in recent years. The Hammerslough collection of Tucker china at the William Penn Memorial Museum in Harrisburg was acquired piece by piece in Pennsylvania, New Jersey, and Delaware years ago. Very little of it was marked, as many companies during that era were willing to let the public think they might be buying a foreign-made product, since most buyers felt that the best work was not done in America. For identification: Tucker bodies have a greenish tint to the white; the gilding has a purplish tint; the pedestals on vases and urns are never fully painted and often turn up at the corners, and the top surface of the pedestal is always white, but some decoration or gilding may be on it. Some of the Tucker workers also signed their pieces with their initials. Edwin Attlee Barber's book *Marks of American Potters* (listed in the bibliography) will provide you with the complete listing, as well as that of other potters and potteries in this country.

Another maker of porcelain was Smith, Fife & Co., of Philadelphia, who was in business about 1830. Some pieces bear a marked resemblance to Tucker's work, and it has been learned that one molding concern supplied both potteries. It is also known that professional modelers sold their designs to more than one company. Other modelers might have worked for several different concerns, causing a great similarity in the work produced.

David Henderson was involved in the creation of the Jersey City Pottery Company in 1829 and

The Sèvres pottery in France was world-renowned as much was made there for royalty and gifts to rulers and important people from other nations. Much porcelain was made here for Napoleon. This figural ewer is an example of the classic work done there in the 19th century. Value: $1,200

Ott and Brewer of Trenton NJ is known as a maker of fine porcelains, such as this gilded Belleek pitcher. This is quite a rarity to collect. Much of the pottery's work is just marked O&B. The pottery operated between 1863 and 1892. Value: $3,500

the American Pottery Company in 1833. The American Pottery Company was operated under different ownerships until 1892. It created a prodigious amount of good pottery and porcelain, which is prized by collectors today. The company pioneered the use of transfer painting in America and did much commemorative work.

It was not until the 1880s, when Lenox set up shop in New Jersey and Castleton went into business just above Pittsburgh, that Americans enjoyed any long-lived production of fine porcelains. Most collectors will agree their output is on a par with that of the rest of the world as far as quality is concerned. Both concerns are still in business and are engaged to do many custom presentation pieces by the White House, as well as making dinner services for the president's home. However, collectors have not yet taken to collecting these porcelains as antiques, perhaps because most of the patterns are still being made and do not possess any aura of age and early workmanship.

There are many other American potteries that made their mark with very good production, most of which is well marked, which makes identification easy. You must approach ceramic collecting with a definite set of rules to follow. Since much of the collectible American production was made during the period of industrial growth, you are faced with the problem of determining if you will be content with machine-made items, or if you will zero in on only those items that were handmade or custom modeled and hand decorated.

Lotus Ware

If you have any ceramics with the initials K.T. & K. stamped on the bottom, you will know that this is the mark of Knowles, Taylor and Knowles, which was incorporated in 1854 in East Liverpool, Ohio. In its early years, the pottery specialized in making ceramic food canning jars. Also under production were brown Rockinghamware, creamware, and eventually whitewares. By 1891, it was the country's largest pottery, with twenty-nine kilns in operation.

In the 1880s the company hired Joshua Poole, a former manager of the Belleek Factory in Ireland, and brought him to this country to supervise the making of similar translucent porcelain. Production continued until the plant burned. After the plant was rebuilt, the company introduced its now

Rare pastel-colored lotus ware by Knowles, Taylor and Knowles in East Liverpool, Ohio. Many feel it is the finest Belleek porcelain made anywhere. Jabe Tarter. Value: $7,500

famous Lotus Ware in 1890, which was made until about 1897. Lotus Ware rivaled the best of fine porcelains made anywhere in the world. Paper thin, its survival rate was very low—hence the scarcity today. It was decorated with under glazed painting, as well as applied figures in flowers, leaves, lacy patterns, and filigree. All the decoration was done by hand and is perhaps as fine as any found on American porcelain. However, the cost of production exceeded what the public could pay, and it went off the market.

Little Lotus Ware is found in the East. Perhaps it was too fragile to ship any great distance. One can see excellent examples of Lotus at the Museum of Ceramics in East Liverpool, which is administered by the Ohio Historical Society.

Hound-Handled Pitchers

East Liverpool, Ohio is known as the Crockery City as it is the center of an area where over two-dozen potteries were located. Many English potters from the Staffordshire County region emigrated there, as there was plenty of clay, natural gas to fire their kilns and good transportation both by water and rail. Many immigrants found their way there because of the many job opportunities. Benjamin Harker came to Ohio in 1839 and purchased 50 acres of land. There was plenty of clay—enough to sell to others who could not manage the business, so he had his sons trained to take over. James Taylor entered the firm in 1846 and the name was changed to Harker and Taylor and Company. In later years, others entered partnership in the firm under various names. However, as early as 1848, they manufactured the brown Rockinghamware, perhaps some of the best made in this country throughout the century.

An early example is the hound-handled pitcher. These had been made in England during the 18th century and the tradition carried here with the incoming potters. Daniel Greatback is known to have modeled them in Trenton and later moved to the United States Pottery Company in Bennington, Vermont during the 1840s. Here, he varied the design, which aids collectors today. Those made in New Jersey featured the hound with his muzzle closed down over his paws. The Bennington versions exhibit a dog with a space under his chin—the muzzle looking more like a duck's bill—a chain link collar, and also ribs which must be seen or felt. Some which came later in Ohio looked more like those from New Jersey, but are judged more on the color of the clay and Rockinghamware

Rockingham-type hound-handled pitcher.

finish. Harker and Taylor was the exception, with a stylized hound with head raised high above his paws—and all I have seen bear the pottery's mark. I have never seen another hound-handled type with any mark—including those from Bennington. They went out of favor by the 1890s, but we have a small one in blue, with 1926 Minton mark—it came from the Bermondsey Market in England. This is the latest I can identify.

Imports

Europe and the Orient represent the other sources for most of the ceramics to be found here. Though America lagged in porcelain manufacture, we were not hesitant in importing it from countries that made it well. The Winterthur Conference Report of 1972 reveals how limited such trade was before the Revolutionary War, in that very little china appears in the inventory of estates through the seventeenth and eighteenth centuries. Archaeological digs along the coast from Virginia to Massachusetts have unearthed fragments of all kinds of pottery and porcelain, which reveal a great deal about their origins. As would be expected, china from England predominates, but it was limited to those who were wealthy. Researchers have been able to pinpoint the area in England from which some sherds came. In one dig at Plymouth, Massachusetts (which reflected the period between 1760 and 1835), they uncovered eight plates, eight chamber pots, and three bowls in delftware; three mugs, a bowl, a teacup, teapot lid, saucer and plate in white salt-glazed stoneware; an agateware bowl; a slip decorated redware pitcher; four slip decorated redware chamber pots; three redware crocks; five smaller redware bowls; and one Whieldon-type teapot. The predominance of chamber pots is puzzling, but they must have been considered more essential than dinnerware through those years.

In the September, 1891 edition of *Scribners* magazine, Alice Morse Earle wrote of her experiences as a "China Hunter in New England." She bemoaned the fact there was little early work to be found. She stated that Bow, Chelsea, and Derby wares were seldom seen in old New England homes, "nor have we found specimens of the better class of Wedgwood's manufacturers in any great numbers." The demand for the better Wedgwood ware was great in England, so little of it was sent to America.

Chinese export famille rose porcelain, c. 1770-1780. A very desirable period for Oriental porcelains, which may have come to this country aboard a clipper ship. Value: $750-$1,200

Pickard China

The information about Pickard china comes from a booklet called "Secrets of Correct Table Service," which was published by the Pickard Studios in Chicago in 1911. This concern imported porcelain and china blanks from foreign manufacturers in Japan and Europe, decorating them and marking them with the Pickard name. Skilled decorators from Germany, France, England, Russia, Italy, and America worked their own ideas into the decorations, most of them including applied gold, and then signed their work. They created some of the most beautiful pottery ever to be sold in this country; there is great interest in collecting it today. The Pickard China Company was formed in 1898 and continues working to this day making commemorative and limited-edition items.

The booklet "Secrets of Correct Table Service" is priceless in its instructions, which include the following: "A 'silence' cloth should always be used under a tablecloth to protect the surface of the table and to lessen noise. Twenty five to thirty inches should be allowed from plate to plate. The advantage of passing a dish first to the hostess is that it enables her to see if it is properly prepared and provided with the necessary fork and spoon. Before dessert is brought in, everything not pertaining discreetly to it should be removed and the table crumbed." There is much more.

Designs pictured in the booklet are the Hyacinthus Bordue Antique, Dahlia Rubra, Lily Ornatum, Orange Tree Decoration, Enamel Chrysanthemums, and the Modern Conventional. The value of a complete set of any of these would be astronomical today. The work is elegant, the gold is real, the beauty unsurpassed. Collect your Pickard before it is totally gone. Many of the gilt pieces still appear on the market.

Art Pottery

The art pottery era began shortly after the Civil War. Located mostly in Pennsylvania, Ohio,

Indiana, and West Virginia, the art pottery concerns developed lines of specialty and decorative pieces, glazing them in many colors. Flowers and fruits were popular, with most designs molded in relief. Much of the production was good and much was shoddy, yet this type of production continues to this day, with many lesser quality pieces commanding attention as collectibles. Most of these items were made in earthenware, but some of the better companies turned out porcelains.

Buffalo

Deldare Ware

Deldare ware, made by the Buffalo Pottery in Buffalo, New York, early in this century, was given as premiums for the purchase of Larkin Soap. This is an earthenware that is decorated with decals or by means of transfer printing. The scenes are taken from an eighteenth century English book on the travels of fictitious Dr. Syntax. The book was lavishly illustrated with hand-tinted prints. In the nineteenth century, Royal Doulton made a series of Dr. Syntax plates in England, and these are good collectibles as well. Sensing this great interest in the Doulton plates, Larkin decided to capitalize on the popularity of them as well. Because they started out literally worth nothing, people who owned them often relegated them to summer cottages or just threw them away outright, as they did carnival and Depression glass.

There are some variations in Deldare ware design, but the most wanted pieces involve Dr. Syntax. Unusual forms command a premium. The body of the pieces is olive drab with white, black, and various colors creating the scene. Deldare just seems to keep going up in price. Copies of the Dr. Syntax book have appeared at auction, as well.

Dedham

Perhaps the most innovative artist in American pottery was Hugh Cornwall Robertson of Chelsea, Massachusetts. In 1868, he and his brother, James, opened the famed Chelsea Keramic Art Works, specializing in making terra cotta and redware pieces. From this, they branched out into decorative art pottery and some of the forms and colors they created met with instant appreciation. At the Philadelphia Centennial Exhibition, their wares

Deldare ware made by the Buffalo Pottery Company to be given away as premiums by the Larkin Soap Company. The scenes depict the travels of Dr. Syntax in England during the 18th century. Made c. 1922-1923. Value: $50-$350

won prizes and attention. In 1880, James Robertson died, and Hugh took over control of the company, which continued production until 1948, when it closed its doors.

Perhaps his greatest achievement was making crackleware, which looks like it sounds, with a spider web appearance over the surface. In a contest for a trademark, a local teacher submitted a design featuring a rabbit, and this was chosen as the identifying mark. The company moved to Dedham, Massachusetts, in 1895, and the words "Dedham Pottery" appeared with the rabbit. Perhaps the most collected Dedham pottery today is in the crackle glaze with a blue border, hand painted with designs of flowers, animals, and other forms of nature. The rabbit border was most popular and featured the bunnies heading in a clockwise direction. Some plates were made with them facing counterclockwise, however. These are rarities and are called "reverse rabbit" plates and are worth much more than the clockwise facing bunnies.

Robertson uncovered the secret of the oxblood color, which until late in the last century was known only in the Orient. He made but three hundred pieces in stoneware with the oxblood glaze. Two fine examples of these, the Twin Stars of Chelsea, are at the Museum of Fine Arts in Boston. Much Dedham pottery goes unnoticed in many homes. It is quite valuable today. Look for the rabbit mark with the words "Dedham Pottery," or the CKAC mark, or, in some rare instances, the initials HR for Hugh Robertson.

Dorchester

The Dorchester Pottery, located just off the Southeast Expressway, south of the center of Boston, was founded by George Henderson in 1894. All the pottery was made and decorated by hand. Much work was done for business clients, such as the Mug and Muffin which uses their wares at their tables. Many foot warmers were made and these are well marked. The company made a wide range of table and decorative wares, much of which is still used in homes.

Practically all the late output in the 1960s and 1970s was cobalt blue decoration on white stoneware. Floral patterns such as dahlia, chrysanthemum, and lilies were featured. The blueberry and scroll patterns were popular as well. In 1967, regular drinking mugs were selling for $3.85 at the pottery. Today, most fetch between fifty and a hundred dollars. Dinner plates were eight to ten dollars—today, most are over fifty dollars.

Some pieces are initialed with NR, indicating Nando Ricci as the potter. CAH are the initials of Charles A. Hill, who did the decorating in the later years. Ethel Henderson, the daughter-in-law of the founder, ran the pottery with the help of her sister, Lily Yeaton, and Charles Hill, her brother. She passed on in the 1970s and a few years later, the pottery closed.

Majolica

Majolica was and still is quite popular. Majorcan potters are generally credited with making the first majolica ware. This is an earthenware that has been highly decorated and is most often quite colorful. Colored tin glazes were used as early as the twelfth century. They were applied over a white glaze, which gave good background to the decoration. In 1743, the Majolika Geschirrfabrik went into business at Holitsch to serve the nobility in Austria and Hungary. Some pieces from this factory are marked with an HF or often an H alone. During this period there were many makers in practically every European country, but such wares do not seem to have been made in this country until after the Civil War, when there was a boom in art pottery.

Dedham Pottery plate, rabbit border.

The saber leg was popular in this period. It was influenced from the Egyptian furniture being uncovered in excavations by the French early in the 19th century. If all four legs are alike, such as exhibited, it is not American furniture.

Superb Queen Anne breakfast table, mahogany, most likely from the Portsmouth, New Hampshire area. It differs from the tea tables in that it does not have a gallery, tray, or drop leaves. Value: $3,500

Dunlap Circle of Cabinetmakers, 18th century, New Hampshire six-drawer chest. The bandy legs have sharp ankles and pointed knees. C scrolls and spoon handle carvings are marks of their work.

Drop-leaf table made in Portsmouth, New Hampshire, with cabriole legs, and Chippendale period, ball and talon feet, from the third quarter of the 18th century. If the ball is carved with bird's talons, it is named as above. If carved with animal claws, ball claw would apply. Value: $2,500

Transitional side chair with Queen Anne base and Chippendale back, c. 1750. Chairs in the Queen Anne and Chippendale periods, in American furniture, must have slip seats. This is a ribband back chair, with protrusions at the top of the chair posts—a mark of Chippendale. Value: $1,000-$1,250

Webb House, Wethersfield, Connecticut.

In cased furniture dating prior to 1830, before the machines took over, it is important that all four legs are alike. In this cherry chest, we see bandy legs with ball and talon feet in front and bracket legs in the rear.

During the 18th and 19th centuries, tavern tables of this type were made most often with wide pine board tops and breadboard ends to keep them from splitting. Some have a drawer, as pictured. Keep these in old, original condition. Refinishing will harm their value. Value: $1,200-$1,500

Currier Gallery of Art, Manchester, New Hampshire.

Ball and talon feet with the undercut talon, a mark of the Newport cabinetmakers. The Townsend and Goddard families of cabinetmakers are known to have used this design.

Game table, c. 1790-1800, in mahogany with figured birch veneers and tapered legs of the Hepplewhite period. Most likely Portsmouth, New Hampshire, area, c. 1790-1800.

Currier Gallery, Manchester, New Hampshire.

Drop-panel chest, of the type made extensively in the Portsmouth/Salem, Massachusetts' area. This is the first piece identified as to maker, Joseph Clark, who had a cabinet shop in Greenland, New Hampshire. He made it as a wedding present for his daughter, married in 1813. All recorded on the bottom of the top drawer.

Clark House, Strawberry Banke, Portsmouth, New Hampshire.

Transitional chest with bow front and rope corner posts, turned legs. A fine example made by Samuel Dockum, 1821.

Legs can aid in provenance. This worktable evidences them both turned and square. This is not a characteristic of New England furniture. One can judge New York State with fairly good accuracy. The design turned up in Canada in the hands of cabinetmakers who emigrated there, as well as in Pennsylvania and Ohio. Value: $400-$500

Game table with Sheraton-styled legs, turned and reeded. The demi-lune, or half moon, inlay across the top is generally credited to John and Thomas Seymour who worked in Boston, early in the 19th century. The wood is mahogany with a figured birch panel. Value: $7,500-$12,000

There were various legs used in the Empire period. The scroll leg at the right is the least popular. Note the corner posts and overhanging top drawers.

This pine chest sold for $700 in Porter Corner, Maine, during 1972. The features that made it desirable are the three graduated drawers, not common in pine chests. The third feature is the French legs, which normally were not used on pine chests. This is a mark of the Shaker work, originating at the Niskayuna, New York colony.

Through the 19th century, fine furniture was made in Canada. The carved diamond design is a French influence. On old country pieces, one will find them shaded with blue cobalt.

Excellent Victorian couch made in the period, c. 1840-1870. Walnut with inverted heart cameo. Best design incorporates thin wood, cameo or mirror, or in this case, heart back; cabriole legs; serpentine front with carvings atop the arches and on the front. A minimum of upholstery is desired. This fills the bill as the finest your writer has ever seen. It is in a farmhouse in Gorham, Maine. Value: $3,750

Pictured is a table with a Roycrofters mark. This was the heart of the oak period. Value of pair: $1,600-$1,800

Oak ladies' desk made by Larkin in Buffalo, early in the 20th century. Larkin Soap Company gave away furniture, ceramics, and other prizes in return for soap wrappers. Most were labeled on the back. Value: $400-$600

Tightly woven "wicker" chairs of this type are generally made of paper wrapped around a wire and woven. This is identified as the Cape Cod weave. Value: $250-$300

The cylinder-top desk is not as popular as the roll top, but still desirable. The originals appeared late in the 19th century. Most that we see are in oak, made in the 1890-1930 period.

Currier Gallery of Art, Manchester, New Hampshire.

Form in glass can help identify provenance. The pear-shape, pedestal base and stringing at the top mark this as South Jersey glass—the design originating with Casper Wistar late in the 18th century. Value: $600-$800

Casper Wistar's glass factory closed and workers left to take up their trade elsewhere. The pear-shape form went with them to Redford, New York; Burlington, Vermont, and even Stoddard, New Hampshire. Color helps determine provenance. This example must have come from Redford, New York, featuring the lily pad design. It is the largest example of lily pad in the country. Value: $800-$1,000

Boston and Sandwich Glass Co., Joan E. Kaiser Collection.

Pressed pedestal lamp, canary; three dolphin standard with hexagonal base, blown clear lamp glass and blown clear unpatterned lamp with whale oil burner, c. 1850-1860.

Boston and Sandwich Glass Co., Joar E. Kaiser Collection.

*Pressed covered dish. Translucent green hen. 8",
c. 1850-1870.*

*Painted glass handed
down in Emma
Gregory's family. This
type of decoration was
painted by Mary, as well.*

*The Boston and Sandwich
Glass Company ceased
operations in 1888. The plant
was opened on two occasions
to make glass, but both failed.
We note the pictured "Trevais"
glass in Art Noveau style, made
by the last company to operate
there until 1910.*

Sandwich Glass Museum.

*At left is a tall vase by Louis Comfort Tiffany, and
at right, a bowl made by Emil Galle in France.
Both exhibit cameo cutting. One color of glass
had to be layered above another, so the design
could be cut in relief.*

*Inexpensive glass made between about the 1920 and
1940 period is identified as Depression Glass. None
was made in New England. Factories in the
Pennsylvania, West Virginia, and Ohio areas are
responsible for just about all of it. Shown is a rare
orange squeezer. Value: $65*

Carnival glass was so named, because during the early days of the depression, glass factories emptied their warehouses by selling products to carnival promoters to be used as prizes for their games of chance. The first of it was made in 1907. None was made in New England—it came from the Midwest region. Value: $75

There are some fine contemporary glass workers, whose classic pieces are much in demand. Pictured is a vase by Domenic Labino of Grand Rapids, Ohio. The piece shown was exhibited at the Victoria and Albert Museum in London. Labino's work may be seen at the Toledo Museum of Art. Value: $2,250-$2,500

No bronze in the world can match this life-size horse and rider, which is exhibited at the art museum in Athens. It was rescued from a shipwreck occurring about 50 AD. The Nubian features of the rider would suggest it was made in Africa. Most bronzes are judged by the motion they display. This is the most spectacular example I have ever seen.

Rene Lalique of France started his glass works late in the 19th century. The company is well known for its cologne and perfume bottles as well as a wide range of Art Noveau and Art Deco glass.

Early English silver is in much demand in America. In a Massachusetts home is this teapot by Peter Bateman, a member of a family of silversmiths, some of whom were women artisans. They worked late in the 18th century. Value: $2,500

18th century silver tankard by Benjamin Burt of Boston. Three members of this family, Benjamin, John, and Samuel, were all accomplished silversmiths.

During the 18th century, most every community has a resident pewterer who fashioned out household items in a metal that was a mixture of tin and antimony. Most are signed with names and touch marks on the bottom. One will note the heart cutouts on the handle of the porringer on the left. Richard Lee and a son worked in New Hampshire, Massachusetts, and Vermont, and are known to have used this design on their work. Value: $600-$800

Cloisonné is made by applying colored enamels or smalt to bronze which has designs created by wire walls which are soldered to make the design.

Napkin rings with figures, are most desirable. Despite their plain condition, they would range in price from $300 to $550.

Kitchenware of all kinds are acquired for collections, as well as to be used. This teakettle may be described as graniteware, porcelain ware, or enamelware, depending on the collector. They are colorful, and many pieces are still used today. Value: $125-$175

Most electroplated silver has little value. Pieces which feature figures, such as animals, birds, butterflies, turtles, etc., are collected as figural silver. This has opened the door to a whole new field of collecting. Most unusual is this set of steak knives on a stand with griffon head at the top. Germany. Value: $125

Children's toys are popular. Witness these steam-powered boats made in Germany. Condition is important. Many were destroyed by rust. Value: $75-$175

Another fine artist was Benjamin Champney, who roamed the mountains of New England and New York State. Pictured is his view of Mt. Mansfield in Vermont, a favorite area for skiers from all over the world. Value: $6,000

Many stories are told about artists. This is a still life by Benjamin Champney, painted in his later years. It is said he no longer could roam the countryside, and took up still life painting. He did not do too well with this example as the pot does not rest on the table. Value: $4,000

Marine paintings evoke the nostalgia of a distant era. Ships with American flags are most desired. Some were painted in the harbors in China for the clipper ship captains who went there. Value: $2,500-$3,500

Contemporary watercolor by Mildred Sands Kratz, AWS, of Akron, Ohio. It is a view of the Portsmouth, New Hampshire, harbor with the historic Wentworth Gardner House at the center. This was once owned by Wallace Nutting, who photographed indoor scenes for his print series. Also, from this home, he sold antiques to museums and collectors. Value: $8,000

Pickard vase, Antioch, IL. Wilder Pickard decorated for Rookwood before leaving to set up his own decorating studio. Ceramic blanks were purchased from some of the finest potteries in Europe and the Orient, then glided and painted by local artisans. Seen at Irish Acres Antiques, Versailles, Kentucky, $2,250.

At left is a vase made by Fulper in Flemington, New Jersey, and at right, Rookwood, with under-glaze decoration, made in Cincinnati. The Fulper has a dull, matte finish and is usually marked with the name on the bottom. Value from left: $450-$600; $350-$500

Covered porcelain jar, Japan, with double "T" mark, (maker unknown). Unusual decoration of American Indian in a canoe. Value: $50-$65

Colorful decorations are what make stoneware crocks valuable. At the top of the heap are those with houses or other buildings on them. Note this one, on which the decorator put the pottery buildings. Ft. Edward, New York.

At right is vinegar bottle sold at the A&P, made by Weller in Ohio. At left is an early 20th century bowl in Indian design marked by Roseville, with the large blue "R."

Simon Willard, who worked in the
Boston area, is regarded by many as the
dean of our early American
clockmakers. He liked to make unusual
timepieces, such as this wall clock, with
the hands and dial on the pendulum.

Tall clock by Nathaniel Munroe,
Philadelphia, c. 1825-1850. The
Sheraton-styled case was most popular
with American clock makers early in the
19th century.

Banjo-styled clock by Elnathan
Taber, a Willard apprentice who
bought Willard out when he
retired in 1839. He acquired the
rights to Willard's patents, so
when one sees Willard Patent on
a clock, you know it is a Taber.

Bata Shoe Museum, Toronto, Ontario.

Tenth Anniversary shoes, American, 1873, silver.

Inuit carving from Canada's Hudson Bay region. It is in greenstone. These carvings are very desirable to collectors all over the world. Similar work is done in Alaska.

Fine Art Deco cigarette lighter, Ballet, Paris, c. 1920s. The ball held lighter fluid, and a metal striker with flint and a wick were used to create flame. Value: $350-$450

A unique collectible, this pair of aluminum mittens was made early in the 20th century. They prevented a child from scratching sores by smallpox and other childhood diseases. Value: $125

Bennington Museum.

In stoneware, more important decoration is that of buildings. Next in line are animals, such as the Bennington deer (pictured); then birds, eagles are preferred; then floral, followed by abstract blue decorations and sgraffitoed ware.

The best known is that made by Griffin, Smith, and Hill in Phoenixville, Pennsylvania. This company began making it in 1878. The native clay and glazes gave it color and beauty that is unmatched either in this country or abroad. Pieces were hand decorated by local girls and women and the pastel shades they used make this majolica the most desired in this country today. GSH entered two vases and a jug in an exhibition in New Orleans during 1884 and won the gold medal, its highest honor. A colorful catalog was prepared and soon the product, named Etruscan Majolica, spread all over the country. Most pieces bear this name as well as the initials G.S. and H. superimposed on one another. Many pieces are identified only by number and decoration, so a pottery-making book must be employed to authenticate them.

Decorations were drawn from nature, and among the most popular are shell and even cauliflower. There may be variations in color on identical pieces as each painter decorated as she saw fit. An original catalog with color illustrations and number code was printed by Brooke Weidner in Phoenixville.

Niloak

Niloak pottery is native to Benton, Arkansas, which is the only area that contains the special clay that makes it up. C.D. Hyten discovered the unique clay as far back as 1868 and began making the distinctive ware, which is characterized by the wavy graining of various colored clays. Between 1868 and 1898 there were as many as a dozen potteries in Benton turning out Niloak, which is a clay name kaolin, spelled backwards. At the turn of the century, however, Hyten's was the sole operating concern and was pretty much out of business by 1950.

Jardiniere and stand, majolica, Ohio, 20th century. Sold at auction in New Hampshire for $180 in 2001.

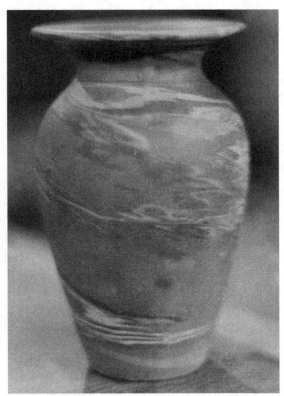

Niloak vase from Benton, Arkansas. About a dozen potteries turned out decorative pieces from the unique clay found there. The name is kaolin, spelled in reverse. Most pieces are marked. Value: $65-$75

Niloak features a satiny unglazed finish with colors of blue, tan, red, white, and cream. Potters today, attempting to imitate the original, are having little luck, as it seems the secret in blending the colors came in the firing.

Some experimental pieces of Niloak were glazed; these would be quite valuable today if located. The product most collected today was perfected about 1912. An additive had to be used to keep the blue a true color, and other chemicals were present to assure color and even shrinkage of the clays in firing. Vases and bowls should be sought in this color.

Though most Niloak was sold in the Arkansas area, it was nationally advertised. Hyten toured the country putting on demonstrations with his pottery wheel. Buyers are collecting it today, as no more is being made, and it is unlikely that anyone will unlock the secret of reproducing it. Niloak is most likely unmarked.

Ohio Ceramics

James Bennet, who was born in Newhall, South Derbyshire, England, opened the first pottery in East Liverpool, Ohio, in 1839. Early in the 1840s, three brothers joined him. At first, they made yellow ware, then the popular Rockinghamware, often miscalled Bennington by the unknowing. Though much was made in Bennington, the greatest production was in Ohio and nearby West Virginia. During the late nineteenth century, East Liverpool earned the title of "Crockery City." In 1877, twenty-three potteries were listed as being in business in the town, with their output going all over the country.

Naturally, much of the work showed the influence of potters who emigrated there from Europe. One has but to visit the Museum of Ceramics in East Liverpool to see the wide range of forms and designs, much of which could be mistaken for European production. One wonders if this were some intent to suggest foreign manufacture at a time when most felt the best goods came from overseas. In 1887, the Laughlin Brothers Pottery declared its superiority over English ceramics by introducing a mark showing the American eagle standing over a prostrate British lion.

By 1930, East Liverpool was at its zenith, with about seven thousand employed in its area potteries. However, the Depression took its toll, and some firms also moved to new locations. Collectors are now learning that at East Liverpool, ceramic ware was made as well as anywhere in the world.

Rookwood

The Rookwood Pottery was founded in 1880 by Mrs. Maria Longworth Storer, who named it after her father's country estate near Cincinnati, Ohio. In 1883, Mr. W.W. Taylor became a partner and director of the works. In 1890, Mr. Taylor acquired the interests of Mrs. Storer when she retired. He enlarged the facility in 1892 and again in 1899 and 1904. The pottery closed in 1960. The site now houses a fine restaurant overlooking the city.

Rookwood is best known for its Art Nouveau and Deco forms with under glazed painted decoration. However, the pottery made tiles, mantels, architectural faience, and garden pottery as well. The top maker, Rookwood 1882, was used until 1886, when the R in reverse and P were conjoined. A flame added above this RP mark indicates 1887. A flame mark was added for every year thereafter, which makes the pieces quite easy to date. On the bottom of each is a shape number with a letter indicating size and another referring to the color of

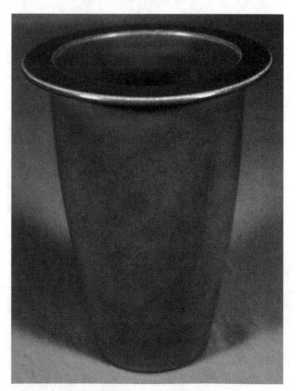

Example of a Rookwood vase.

clay used in the body. It was customary, but not necessary, for the decorators to cut their initials on the bottoms of pieces they decorated. Quite often, owners of such pieces do not realize what they have, as no name is mentioned.

Roseville

As interest in American art pottery grew, so did interest in pieces made by the Roseville Pottery Company in Zanesville, Ohio. Years ago it was a

Roseville Pottery has only recently come in to vogue, some selling for big money. Made in Ohio, it is simple earthenware, but the floral and other designs have great appeal. Value: $75-$125

Roseville Pottery in a popular art deco design. This is one of a pair of vases. One is advised that many items are to be only looked at, not used. Value of pair: $250

common gift to newlyweds, most of whom could not wait to dispose of it as many considered it gaudy and not of very good quality. New appreciation has grown for work of this type, however, and today the name "Roseville" guarantees an immediate sale, as the collectors are numerous all over the country.

The factory was begun in 1890 in Roseville, Ohio, in a plant once owned by the Owens Pottery. In 1898, the owners bought the Midland Pottery in Roseville and then the Mosaic Tile Company. In 1910, all production was at Zanesville, which had become an important pottery center in Ohio.

In addition to the mass-produced wares, the pottery made some art pieces, which sell for much money today. Patterns such as Rozanne, Mara, Egypto, Woodland, Crystallis, and Azurean made their appearance. The competition with other potteries was keen, and the best designers and decorators that could be found were employed. Fortunately, the pieces were well marked, often with the artist's signature or initials. Many of the production pieces came only with a paper label, but in later years the name "Roseville" was molded on the bottom.

Weller

Zanesville, Ohio, was the location of several fine potteries. Among them was one owned by Samuel A. Weller, who founded it in 1872. He made pottery with such strange names as Louwelsa, Eocean, and Sicardo. The company continued in business until 1948.

In the manner of other Ohio potters, flowers were a mainstay of decoration at Weller. He used metallic tints to highlight his work. In 1901, a French potter, Jacques Sicard, joined the firm and gave his name to one of his creations. Dickensware featured characters from the famous writer's books. Since the pottery operated during the period when both Art Nouveau and Art Deco styles were in vogue, one may collect a wide range of forms.

Van Briggle

The Van Briggle Pottery is located in Colorado Springs, Colorado. Artus Van Briggle worked both for the Avon Pottery and Rookwood in Cincinnati before heading west due to his health. He went to Colorado Springs in 1899, and by 1901, was in business turning out work that won him awards and immediate fame. His wife, Anne, was his model for some of the Art-Deco-type nudes, which appeared on his decorative wares. The mark, two A's joined together, was derived from their names. Mr. Van Briggle died in 1904, leaving his wife president of the firm.

In the early 1970s, the company moved to larger quarters where it continues to make fine pottery. The company achieved fame with its unusual glazes, some applied by means of a spray unit. Much decorative art ware was made as well as flower holders, tiles, and garden ornaments. The company continues today, turning out well-molded handmade items, which are being collected by those who know that such items will be much in demand if production ever ceases. This *can* happen—witness the demise of the Pennsbury Pottery in Morrisville, Pennsylvania, which closed its doors in 1971 after having been in business about twenty years. Its story is typical of the many small enterprises which are set up to provide an interesting quality product, but which surrender slowly to competition from within this country as well as from overseas. Since Pennsbury is a current collectible which has not yet entirely disappeared, and one about which little is known, I feel it is of enough importance to devote space to it. (See page 202.)

England and the Continent

Problems in Attribution

Even pieces that are well marked are subject to suspicion because of imitators and fakers of the nineteenth century. Quite notable in this respect was the firm of Mssrs. Samson and Company of Paris, which went into business in 1845 and worked late into the century. The company usually produced wares in the style of the eighteenth century and marked them with original marks, and this can confuse the average student of ceramics today. In the eighteenth century, most potters in England were still working with soft paste bodies, using a mixture of powdered glass and clays. Samson reproduced porcelain, and this might have been made from the oriental formula of china clay and kaolin, or from the Spode formula, which included bone ash and good china clay. You must arm yourself with

Weller vase with under glaze decoration, 1872-1948, Zanesville, Ohio. This piece made early in the 20th century, was made in the manner of the Rookwood pottery at that time, with the under glaze decoration. Value: $350

Van Briggle Pottery shell-shaped vase.

information on how to tell the two apart. Hard paste does not warm quickly to the touch. If there is a chip on a soft paste piece, its open surface will appear glassy. A glaze on soft paste can wear away, whereas a glaze on hard paste will survive almost intact over many years. An enameled decoration on soft paste will sink into the ceramic, but on hard paste, it will remain on the surface.

Nicholas Sprimont, a French silversmith, brought the Chelsea Works to the attention of the ceramics world in the 1740s by copying the oriental porcelains. You will have to do your homework to learn to differentiate the Bow, Meissen, St. Clous, and Chantilly blanc de chine from that made in the Orient during the eighteenth century, as they all look alike to the untrained eye. Samson's work in the nineteenth century just adds more confusion. Fortunately, by the nineteenth century most firms in England were well established, and were contemporary enough so that others did not attempt to imitate them or copy them in later years. By the middle of the century, each company's work and markings were so distinctive that we have little trouble in accurate attribution.

During the eighteenth century, English makers copied the best Chinese designs, as these were popular, and also copied the Chinese porcelain bodies. Thus, determining the country of origin can be quite difficult even for experienced students. Some of the early Bow, Worcester, Newhall, and Caughley pieces are easily mistaken for Chinese work. A concern at Lowestoft gave its name to a great deal of what must have been Chinese export porcelain. History records that some potteries acted as importers and exporters as well as makers, and sold both native and export chinas. It seems likely that Lowestoft was one of these, attaching its name to both, and this has helped to cause this confusion.

The ceramics factory at Bow is considered to be the oldest in England. It was located in the eastern section of London. Some of its product was stamped "New Canton" because the buildings were in the Chinese style. Bow is thought to have been founded as early as 1730, but its first patents for making porcelain using Virginia unaker clay were taken out in 1744. Bow led in the production of the first bone china, made with the addition of powdered bone ash, and is also credited with turning out the first china with transfer prints done under the glaze.

A factory was established in Chelsea about 1742 which made fine porcelain—the counterpart of the best from Europe. A Huguenot refugee brought his knowledge to this plant, thus enabling it to copy the best French work. William Duesbury (owner of the Derby Works, also in London) purchased the Chelsea enterprise, and at one time owned the Bow Works as well. This creates a real problem in identifying the output from these plants, as molds were interchanged and workers might work in one or more of the plants, taking their designs with them. You must rely on the markings of these pieces to aid in identification. The bibliography lists books that will help.

China was made to order in both the Orient and England, and it is likely that much was made for the wealthy in America. Alice Morse Earle tells the story of a Miss Leslie, the sister of a great painter, who ordered a dinner service made and decorated for her in China. She directed that a coat of arms be placed in the center of each plate, and made a drawing, which she pasted in the center of a specimen she had drawn. She wrote "Put this in the middle" under the coat of arms. When the service arrived, she found on every piece not only the coat of arms, but also, carefully written and fired in, the words "Put this in the middle." I wonder at the whereabouts of this set today.

Collectors are fortunate the English provided a good marking system for their nineteenth century ceramics. Until 1842, pieces were often identified by the name of the pattern or design, and either the name or initials of the maker, and, at times, the location of the factory. Between 1842 and 1883, the "diamond" mark, which enables us to pinpoint the day the piece was made, came into use. In the corners of the diamond are numbers or letters, which, according to established charts, reveal the day, month, and year, as well as the class of ceramic, and the lot number from which it came. In 1867, this was modified with a clue that can be helpful. If one sees a letter of the alphabet at the top point of the diamond, he knows the piece was made before 1867; if there is a number at the point, it came after 1867. Beginning in 1884, a numerical marking system was used, with a combination of numerals following the prefix (Rd. or Rd. No.). The number is the clue to the year the item was made, up to 1892. In that year, a U.S. law was passed which required the country of origin to be stamped on items imported here. However, one must examine each piece for other clues as to age. Between 1892 and 1908 one might find England and the Rd. or registry number. The number disappeared about 1908, leaving only "England" until about 1920, when items for export were marked "Made in England." Much has been brought here by immigrants or imported by dealers, which does not have the country of origin marked because this was not required in Great Britain.

England

Blue Willow China

One type of china that seems to hold its value despite changing tastes is Blue Willow. Made in great quantities years ago, it was used not only in the home, but in restaurants and hotels as well. Most people are familiar with the pattern: willow trees, a pagoda, bridge, and fences—all in oriental motif. Though the subject matter is from the Far East and was used in porcelains made there, the blue Willow, as we know it originated in England about 1780.

The design is credited to Thomas Minton, who worked at the Caughley Works owned by Thomas Turner. Turner is best known for his Salopian ware, which was the first really successful transfer printed china made in complete sets. The Willow ware was but another pattern he popularized. Soon it was being made by other potters in Staffordshire County, so unless a piece is marked, it is difficult to attribute it to any particular pottery. Other names one might find on a piece are Standard Willow, Old Willow, Real Willow, Caughley Willow, and English Willow.

Blue Willow was made in the United States by several concerns; the most noted being the Buffalo Pottery Company in Buffalo, New York. This company was created by the Larkin Soap Company to make premiums, which were given away for soap wrappers. Most of the Buffalo output was commercial, for hotels and restaurants, and examples of this china keep turning up at auctions and marketplaces. Willow ware was also made in Germany, France, and Holland.

There is a legend that the design depicts an event of unrequited love between a mandarin's daughter and one of his accountants. According to this sad story, both met an untimely death and turned into doves, which are depicted on the china.

Commemorative and Historical Ware

After the Revolutionary War, English potters were quick to forgive political differences in return for American business, and a lively trade was begun, with commemorative and historical wares shipped here in great quantities. The art of transfer printing had been perfected in the 1770s by Thomas Turner, who was the first to turn out complete dinner services in this manner. Artists were sent to America to paint or sketch scenes of prominent buildings, landmarks, or landscapes. These scenes were immediately transformed into transfer prints for china. Famous military and naval engagements were also portrayed, along with portraits of famous men and ships that did the British in during the war. These rose in popularity until the War of 1812. Interest was renewed in them after this war, and between 1820 and 1840 a great amount of historic china entered the country. Blue was the most popular color, but much was also done in other colors. Items with a lot of detail, such as ships and rigging, were most often done in black against a cream or off white background. Most of the black and white transfers are referred to as "Liverpool transfers," as they came from this port.

The blue pieces are commonly referred to as "historical blues" since most portray a place, event, or person of American historical importance. Another series of the blues was done as a revival

Blue commemorative plates made at the end of the 19th century and even today, are collectable as most were made limited editions. Witness this example from Lookout Mountain near Chattanooga, Tennessee. Most are made in England. Value: $75-$125

during the 1890s, but these blues are clearly marked to document their age. Even these later blues are assuming some importance now. You might do well to collect the blues being made today by such firms as Wedgwood for historic homes, churches, and the like, as these will be among the collectibles someday. Some that sold as souvenirs as recently as fifteen years ago for $2 or $3 are commanding up to $50 now, because they are made in limited edition.

Creamware and Pearlware

Creamware (or Queensware, as it was called later in the eighteenth century) is simply a yellow lead glazed ware popular from about 1750 to 1820. Wedgwood is commonly referred to as the originator, but this is an uncertain attribution because others were making it at the same time. Ivor Noel Hume tells us that nine out of ten creamware pieces were unmarked and probably no more than one out of a thousand was dated. Pearlware is a whiter composition that came into favor at the turn of the century, and is often decorated in oriental motifs.

Lustered China

Applying metallic oxides to decorate china is a practice that has been with us a long time. The technique of lustering pieces seems to have originated in Mesopotamia, and then spread to Syria, Egypt, and Spain. It is the art of applying a metallic overglaze to clay, sometimes lustrous and

Pearlware coffeepot, made c. 1800-1815 by a maker in Staffordshire County, England. No more sophisticated a pot has been turned out since, by any maker, Historic Deerfield.

sometimes almost iridescent. Though this was done in about the ninth century, it was not until the latter part of the eighteenth century that it became a popular decorating technique. The reincarnation is attributed to Josiah Wedgwood in the 1790s, and it was not long before many potteries in England were turning out the same product.

Lustering china pieces dates back a couple thousand years, but it was revived about 1790 by Staffordshire potters. Illustrated is the copper luster which is most plentiful. It is still being made today. Repros have hurt interest in this type of china. Value: $25-$75

We are most familiar with the copper luster as this was the least expensive to make then and the least expensive now. There are lusters in silver, gold, platinum, bronze, and even brass. The production prior to 1842 is not marked, so it is difficult to know which pottery made particular pieces. The pottery at Sunderland is known to have employed this luster in the decoration of the transfer printed bowls and pitchers, which are often called "Liverpool transfer ware." The luster would be in addition to a picture of some scene, perhaps patriotic or historic.

The silver resist pieces of the early nineteenth century are much desired and quite rare in good condition, as they can tarnish. However, the production of the copper lusters has never stopped, and the reproductions coming in from overseas are hurting the value of the older pieces. Those not skilled in distinguishing new from the old can make mistakes in buying—hence the declining interest. Also, it is almost impossible to tell old from new at an auction because of the distance from the auctioneer. There are better ceramics in which to invest as the future of the value of copper luster items is in doubt.

Mocha

In 1981, C. John Smith, lecturer at the College of Technology at Stourbridge, England, came to the Shelburne Museum in Vermont to conduct a seminar on mocha ware, as it is called in this country. Mr. Smith informed us that in England it is referred to as industrial slipware as it was inexpensive earthenware, colorfully decorated to appeal to those who could not afford the more expensive porcelain and bone chinas. The museum had received a large collection of almost a hundred pieces, which were out for examination by all who attended.

Henceforth, we shall refer to it as mocha, as it is best known by that name here.

We were told that the years of manufacture were between about 1825 and 1925. Some credit Wedgwood with the creation of the first "yelloware" as it is often called, as early as the 1790s. The inexpensive buff-colored clay came from Ireland and little was done to refine it before making the utilitarian pieces, which we enjoy collecting, today. In his book, *A History of World Pottery,* Emmanuel Cooper tells us the name most likely came from clay with "dendritic patterns resembling an ornamental quartz called mocha stone. Backgrounds of brown, cream, orange, and green were usually decorated with brown or black designs." Eventually, some production was decorated with transfer prints, which may confuse buyers into thinking the product is something else. Most of the decorations were "trailed on" by a slip pot and this resulted in many variations.

Stories crept in that the popular seaweed pattern resulted from an early potter who expectorated his tobacco juice onto the green clay and the pattern spread in the treelike design that is called seaweed. However, Mr. Smith brought with him a movie made by the Victoria and Albert Museum. They had located a potter who had worked in Staffordshire County in the 1920s, making the mocha. This was a fascinating 15 minutes, showing him at a horizontal wheel turning out pot after pot. Seaweed? He used an eyedropper to touch a spot of steroid to the clay and the liquid spread out in this fashion. Evidently, the tobacco had gone the way of many legends. Other designs were painted on, mostly by women, and various names were attached. One that interested most was the change in name from earthworm, to cable, which Mr. Smith insisted was the correct name for the design.

Mr. Smith revealed another name which I had never heard used by a dealer or collector—this is in

Mocha ware pitcher with applied handle.

Mocha ware jug with cat's eye and snail pattern.

reference to those pieces having geometric or abstract designs—he referred to the decoration as "dicing," so, dicing it is. Mr. Smith was gathering information for a planned book and was on his way to East Liverpool, Ohio to do research there. Much mocha was made in this country, but it was most often called yellowware by the American potters.

Little decoration seems to have been done on the Ohio pieces—most are familiar with the "banded mocha" which is sold extensively, which is a simple decoration of a band or two of various colors around the pot, mug, or bowl. The Ohio Historical Society maintains perhaps the finest ceramics museum in this country. Located in an abandoned post office in downtown East Liverpool, it is loaded with the finest of wares, which were made in the area, and are the equal of much of the best made in England. One will see many examples of mocha and yellowares that most collect on a routine basis, today, but with variations rarely seen in the marketplace.

Parian

In 1842 at the Copeland Spode works at Stoke-on-Trent, England, a new porcelain—white and unglazed—was developed. It was named Parian

because it resembled the Parian marble, which was used extensively for busts, and classic figures on the islands of Crete and Paros. By 1843, it was a well-accepted product on both sides of the Atlantic. It was made that same year in Bennington, Vermont, at the Norton Works, which employed the services of an English modeler, John Harrison. It is only natural that porcelain was eventually made in Vermont as the state has some of finest kaolin clay available in the country. This, mixed with other clays, gives the body a hard, translucent quality. The pieces were glazed on the interior, leaving the outer surface with a marble-like, satin finish.

Much was made at the United States Pottery, which was run by Christopher Webber Fenton along with the various associates, between 1847 and 1858. I have never seen a marked piece. Richard Carter Barret gives us clues on how to identify the Vermont parian. There was much iron pyrite in the soil and clay, which made screening the particles quite difficult, so one will find black specks in the Bennington pieces, whereas those from England or other potteries will be clear white. Parian was made in the heart of the Victorian period, in which grapes were a popular decorative motif. Look for large, crude grapes in the Bennington pieces and smaller, refined examples in the English. Some parian from England and America is decorated with a cobalt blue glaze. Some pieces have pictures fired on them, as well.

Royal Doulton, Minton and Royal Crown Derby

Space does not permit an examination of all the English concerns that contributed so much to the development of the industry. However, I will examine the history of one concern that is still operating in order to show the numerous changes it has undergone. Sir Henry Doulton was the second son of John, founder of Doulton and Company in the late eighteenth century. Sir Henry was a creative Victorian potter, and during his lifetime outstripped his competitors in the production of such industrial wares as airtight jars for storing food and tobacco; screwed topped food warmers and bottles; and architectural terra-cotta statuary and tiles used by many London architects. An example of this work is the lion outside Waterloo Station. Doulton concentrated on industrial ware until 1862, with the exception of some stoneware

Toby jugs and mugs, which were shown at the International Exhibition of 1862. Following this was an association with the Lambeth School of Art, which designed salt-glazed vases and jars with simple incised and colored decorations along with terra-cotta statues, portrait heads, and medallions. In 1877, Sir Henry purchased a works at Burslem, Staffordshire, and began to manufacture decorated earthenware and bone china. Most of the china collected today stems from this late nineteenth century production.

Another important potter was Thomas Minton, who began his career as an engraver apprenticed to Thomas Turner. Minton supplied Josiah Spode with printed designs for his wares for a short time, and then opened his own plant in 1796. It was not until 1824 that he made his reputation in the field by turning his production to forms influenced by the then popular Sèvres factory in France. One of the most important techniques developed by Minton was the Pate-sur-pate, brought from France by Marc Louis Solon, acknowledged master of this art form. Pate-sur-pate, meaning body on body, is an expensive and frustrating method of decoration developed from the original Chinese technique. Solon went to work for Minton in 1870, and, though it was imitated, this art product was turned out only by Minton. Spectacular models were

Royal Doulton made many series of transfer-printed pieces, which are a challenge to collect. Most done in a series of twelve, have been broken up over the years. Getting them back together can be fun. Value: $125

produced showing the prevailing influence of interest in Sèvres china of the Louis XV style, Grecian influence parian figures, chinoiserie designs, and an overriding opulence of decoration. The Minton concern was later purchased by Doulton as the second member of the triumvirate that makes up Doulton today.

The third member of the Doulton triumvirate is the oldest. Royal Crown Derby has been in continuous operation since 1756, when an agreement between Andre Planche, William Duesbury, and John Hatch made them partners. Duesbury insisted on thinner potting than was prevalent at the time. This work, along with the finer enameling used, attracted the attention of George III, who conferred the right to use the crown as a factory mark. The ware then became known as Crown Derby, and by the end of the eighteenth century, Crown Derby was the leader in the English fine china industry. Early in the nineteenth century, the factory passed into the hands of Robert Bloor, a former clerk. He introduced the highly colored Japanese or Imari decorations for which Crown Derby became famous. Much of the production of this period was actually of inferior quality and could be listed as seconds.

By 1877 a new company was formed, and the management of the Derby Crown Porcelain Company set about recovering its reputation. By 1890, the excellence of the wares and the favored Japanese decorations had come to the attention of Queen Victoria, who permitted the pottery to change its name to the Royal Crown Derby Porcelain Company. It was the only pottery permitted the honor of using the Royal and Crown designations in its name. Also in 1890, a decorator by the name of Desire Leroy left Minton. His raised gilding, white enamel painting on colored grounds, and delicate floral and bird studies are uniquely beautiful.

The three great potteries, Royal Doulton, Minton, and Royal Crown Derby are now all part of Doulton and Company. It is currently engaged in producing a collector's series of many types of modeled human and animal figures, some of which are selling in the four-figure price range. Fine modeling and fine coloring are featured in these collectibles for tomorrow. The tradition of great work done by three separate concerns is obviously still very much alive in the consolidated company of today.

*From the Watertown, New York, area came this milk
pitcher with molded name of the Schmitt's Dairy, which
marketed Guernsey milk. This mottled or spatterware
decoration in the green/yellow color, with marking,
makes this quite special. Value: $85*

Spatterware

Spatterware looks like it sounds. The colors in
the border are applied in spotted fashion to form a
design much finer than that of spongeware. It was
most popular during the first half of the nineteenth
century, with much supposedly made for the Pennsylvania German trade. Those pieces that picture
the peafowl are among the most desired and most
valuable today. Some came with various floral
designs such as the Adams rose pattern. Others
feature what is thought to be a schoolhouse.

Various colors were used in the borders, the
most common being blue. Green and yellow were
used, but the latter is so scarce one might never find
one for sale. Plates and platters are the forms that
seem to have survived best. One can occasionally
find a sugar bowl and creamer, but the larger hollowware pieces such as teapots and chocolate pots
are rare. Cups and saucers were made in abundance
in sets, so these are more readily available. Spatterware cup plates are not as common; one might
judge that few were made as the less expensive
glass plates were heavily in production after 1827.

Not all spatterware was made in England; some
was made in Ohio. Though not the same weight
and quality as the English, it is being collected
because of its lower prices, which collectors feel
will eventually rise. There are more recent
reproductions, but anyone who can judge old china
will have no difficulty in identifying it. Excellent

spatterware can be seen in the permanent
collections at the William Penn Memorial Museum
in Harrisburg.

Wedgwood

Josiah Wedgwood, who lived from 1730 to
1795, started his pottery business with only twenty
English pounds in the 1750s. An apprentice of
Thomas Whieldon, he founded a concern that is
still quite active in making ceramics at Barlaston,
Staffordshire County, England. During tours of the
factory, I have always been told, "If the name
Wedgwood is not on a piece of ceramic, it is not
one of ours." Thus one should not be enticed into
buying "unmarked" Wedgwood, for, according to
those in the factory, it does not exist. They even
mark their seconds, which are sold from a shop
there, and have always done so. This may disturb
some dealers and collectors, but I can only repeat
what I have always been told at the factory, as I
have taken tour groups through there on six occasions.

Most noted of the Wedgwood wares are those
identified as jasperware, which is made of basalt.
Made in many colors, the most common are those
in dark and light blue and green featuring figures in
white relief. I have watched them make the figures
by hand pressing the white clay into a continuous
mold. It is elastic enough that they can pick up the
entire piece, which will surround a plate or pot,
and by moistening the clay, make it stick to the
piece being decorated. The potters have time to
arrange the figures perfectly, and then they are
fired on permanently.

Remember, there is no middle E in the name
Wedgwood. This is a much-imitated form of decorative ware.

Wedgwood and Spode

Names like Wedgwood and Spode are known
even to the casual observer, as a lot has been written about these two famous concerns, both of
which are still operating. The Wedgwoods were
involved in pottery making by the end of the seventeenth century, but it was not until Josiah took
command in the mid-eighteenth century that
Wedgwood developed into a respected manufacturer responsible for much of the best ceramics
available. Both Josiah Wedgwood and Josiah
Spode served as apprentices to Thomas Whieldon,

Wedgwood basalt or jasperware is known around the world. It was made in several colors, some not in vogue today. This 19th century Barlaston, England, piece is colored black, which is not common to find.

A range of Spode ceramics made by one of England's most famous potteries. It is now joined with Wedgwood.

Jones Museum of Glass and Ceramics, Sebago Lake, Maine.

who is credited with making the popular tortoiseshell ware.

Spode is located at Stoke-on-Trent. Both are in Staffordshire County, which had 150 potteries at work within its borders after 1800. Today, Wedgwood and Spode are one and the same concern, joining other pottery firms who have found that consolidation is necessary for survival in this competitive business. Staffordshire was occupied by the Romans at the time of Christ, as there was abundant clay and plenty of firewood available. Also, the fog and dampness that plague southern England are not as evident in Staffordshire. This is quite important in manufacturing ceramics because humidity affects glazing and firing. The term "Staffordshire" is generic when referring to chinas made in that county—it could have been used by any or all of the potters. The term is now used by collectors and dealers as a quick reference to the area of a piece of china's origin.

France

Another country that competed for American business was France, whose famous factories at Rouen and St. Cloud date back into the seventeenth century. Very little of the Rouen production has survived, although it is known that a reasonably good European porcelain was first made at Rouen. This porcelain was soft paste, and most was decorated in blue. The St. Cloud production is documented by pieces marked as early as 1697, decorated in Japanese and other oriental styles, with gilding featured. Another factory, founded at Chantilly in 1725, produced wares that imitated currently favored oriental designs.

Sèvres

One of the most prominent works—Sèvres—had its humble beginnings in Vincennes. It was in operation there from 1738 to 1756, when King Louis XV took it under his patronage. He allowed the formation of a new company, which was moved to Sèvres to make soft paste porcelain. Most of the Sèvres production from 1753 to 1756 carries the same markings as that of Vincennes. In 1761, the formula for making hard paste porcelain was acquired, and this made up the bulk of the company's production thereafter. The concern used the double L as a mark from 1740 on. From 1753 to the time of the revolution (1789) a date letter was inserted. After 1802, the Sèvres markings were done in red, with a date abbreviation used between 1818 and 1834. After 1834, the full date was used. By order of the Nazis, a special edition of eighty small plates was turned out in 1943 to commemorate the reuniting of the French and German lands by Hitler. I wonder about the location of these today. Sèvres was one of the most imitated potteries, and it trained some fine craftsmen who later joined other concerns, bringing with them skills unsurpassed anywhere.

Faience

About 2,000 B.C., potters learned they must glaze works of clay so that liquids put in a piece would not be absorbed. Early glazes were made of a clay that would fire at a lower temperature than the pottery. Later, the use of minerals and even metals was introduced into glaze mixtures. Among them was tin, which is traced back to a Babylonian pottery dating about 1,000 B.C. It seems to have disappeared between about 500 B.C. and the eighth century, when Persian potters used the mixture. The Moors carried the formula to the Mediterranean, where it was used on the island of Majorca, which is usually credited as the location where majolica originated. In France, majolica pieces, made at that time, highly decorated and given a tin oxide glaze, were called faience.

Quimper plate made in Northern France. Very popular with many collectors of old pottery. It is still being made. Value: $125

Example of Faience plate, 9" d.

Limoges game platter, partridge décor, artist signed, Haviland.

The term "faience" is still used to describe very early pottery that has been hand decorated and glazed with tin. Pieces turn up from time to time, but most are chipped, as it is brittle.

One of the best-known contemporary makers of similar ware is Quimper, which is in Brittany, France, and was founded in 1690. Scenes on the pottery are of peasant life. Many people collect the new as well as the old; one must learn the marks and colors to tell them apart. I have seen it used as everyday china in homes in New England.

Limoges

Another famous name in French porcelain is Limoges. A pottery was formed in this town as early as 1771, and as many as thirty-five concerns were eventually located there. You will see such markings as Elite, JP or J. Pouyat, Guerin, JPL, Aron and Valin, Pierre Tharoud, and, perhaps the most famous of all, Haviland. David Haviland, an importer from New York, established a plant at Limoges in the 1840s and provided his own outlet for the product in America. This high-quality porcelain caught the fancy of the American public, so much so that Haviland Limoges was once considered a necessary wedding gift for the well-to-do bride.

Two sons of David Haviland became owners of separate porcelain works at Limoges. They included Charles Field Haviland, identified by name or by CFH underlined with an L below to denote the town. Theodore Haviland identified his pieces by name or by TH with an L beneath. In 1908, the two companies became Haviland and Company, identified by H & Co with an L beneath.

Germany

Americans have always held ceramics from the Germanic regions of Europe in high esteem. After Bottger perfected the porcelain body recipe in Dresden and the famed Meissen works opened there, the secret for making porcelain soon spread throughout the area, so that by 1718, it was quite well known. The names Meissen and Dresden are synonymous with respect to ceramics and both are similarly marked. The work was greatly imitated by other concerns in Germany in the nineteenth

There are almost a hundred varied patterns in Old Ivory, all similar, but numbered to differentiate them. The plant was bombed in Germany during World War I. Value: $450

century, and Samson imitated it in Paris. Although he was required to mark his pieces to show they were reproductions, he got around this nicely by stamping the original marks beneath the glaze, and putting his mark on the glaze where it could be rubbed off at will, in the same manner that paper labels used today to identify country of origin fall off so easily. There were many other great porcelain manufactories in Germany, but none captured the fancy of the American buyer as much as Dresden. As a result, little of their production is found in America.

Although very good work was done, the production from potteries elsewhere in Europe had little impact in America. People have a fetish for collecting not only good but good names as well, and if the supply of items is not sufficient, they will lose interest in trying to locate it. Scarcity can hurt collecting by lowering the price, quite contrary to the idea that if something is rare it is more valuable.

Meissen Figures

Since the earliest days of ceramics, figures, both human and animal, have been subjects of the potters' art. At first, simple clay was used, but when porcelain was perfected in the Orient, this became the favored material.

One of the early great modelers of the famed Meissen works was Johann Kaendler, who worked between 1731 and 1775. A former court sculptor, he brought new vigor to the art and became the source of inspiration for all European porcelain artists. One series of figures of musicians has been attributed to him. They are whimsical and charming at the same time and date back to the second quarter of the eighteenth century. He is known for his crinoline figures, shepherdesses, and ladies and gentlemen of most walks of life. He was a student of mythology and created many allegorical groups.

Many other fine modelers were at work as well at this famous plant, among them Horoldt, Meyer, and Acier. From about 1774 to 1814, Kaendler was dominated by Count Marcolini, who introduced an academic, classical taste into the figures made.

The famed crossed swords as a factory mark were used early in the century. This mark was changed to swords with a point added from 1763 to 1774, and this was referred to as the point period. Not all crossed swords are Meissen, however. It is one of the most copied symbols, used in England, France, and the Orient as well. The true student can identify the Meissen work easily; generally the work was much superior to that from other potteries. Early Meissen figures are quite rare. Most fine museums have good collections.

Meissen in Germany is credited with making some of the finest porcelains. This 19th century tea set is a good example displaying fine form and decoration. Value: $650

Royal Bayreuth

Sunbonnet Babies—There has always been a pottery in Bayreuth, Germany, since the sixteenth century. The pieces made late in the last century and into this one are the most available and collectible. One type, labeled "Royal Bayreuth," is generally a fine porcelain, often made into forms of people and animals, colored and decorated. Among the most desirable Royal Bayreuth to collect are the pieces with decorations of the Sunbonnet Babies. Bertha L. Corbett is known as the mother of the Sunbonnet Babies. She studied art in Philadelphia and later moved to Chicago, where she was employed to design picture postcards. A fellow employee once told her that no figure could show expression if the face was not shown, but Bertha managed to achieve immortality by creating such figures with their faces hidden by large white bonnets.

The days of the week series, which portrays the Sunbonnet Babies in various household chores,

Sunbonnet Babies plate, "Ironing."

were done on postcards made of paper and leather, as well as china by Royal Bayreuth, who purchased the rights to Bertha's designs. This series

Queen Louise

Louise Augusta Wilhelmina was born March 10, 1776, in Hanover, Germany. Her mother died when she was six, and she went to live with her grandmother. To escape advancing French troops a few years later, she sought refuge with her eldest sister, the Duchess of Hildburghausen. While there, she was presented to the king and was seen by Crown Prince Frederich Wilhem III, who fell madly in love with her. On Christmas Eve, 1793, they were married, going eventually to Potsdam to live.

Being of royalty, it is natural that Queen Louise was painted many times. A story has been told that she had a goiter on her neck and always wore a scarf to conceal it. The interest in collecting Queen Louise decorated objects today centers around the scarf. One will find portraits of beautiful women on dishes, cups and saucers, framed porcelains, miniatures, jewelry, and the like and it is customary to refer to all of them as Queen Louise if the scarf is there to hide the real or imaginary goiter. I have a painted ivory Queen Louise, framed, about 4 by 6 inches; the star on her hair band is jeweled, and her hair is done in long curls. The value of it is considerably higher than it would be if the scarf were missing, as then it would not be as easy to identify as Queen Louise. Those who grade these pieces suggest that the scarf must always be white; hair in long curls; dress white trimmed in gold; and cloak, if worn, scarlet, trimmed with brown-tailed white ermine. As best we know, Queen Louise died in 1810 from heart spasms.

She left us a legend of beauty—one that inspired porcelain makers to extol her face and form so that she might be seen and appreciated around the world. Most of the porcelains were made in the Germanic countries such as Austria, Bavaria, and Germany. They represent fine collectibles, and investments for the future, as it is unlikely they will ever be duplicated.

was quite popular as gifts for children because they taught the Puritan ethic of keeping gainfully employed every day of the week. Some pieces, however, portray the babies visiting a circus, taking a balloon ride, or even having parties as rewards for their work.

The porcelain Bayreuth pieces have not yet been reproduced, so they have maintained high value. Collecting these Sunbonnet Babies on both the porcelain and the postcards is a rewarding challenge.

Villeroy and Boch

The Abbey of Mettlach was built in the second half of the sixteenth century on the banks of the Saar River. More buildings were added in the eighteenth century, only to fall prey to the architects of the French Revolution, who plundered religious orders and laid waste to many buildings. The French laid claim to the Saar region at this time and stole all the wealth from it, with no respect for churches and monasteries. Jean Francois Boch bought the ravaged premises in 1809 and turned it into a pottery. Part of his deal with the state was that he would have to burn the plentiful coal in the area to fire his kilns. Since wood firing was the order of the day, he had to devise a way to make coal heat compatible to the process. He succeeded. The old abbey is represented by the castle, a trademark of Mettlach, which is imprinted on the steins. Later, Boch joined forces with Nicholas Villeroy,

Villeroy & Boch marked, small Dresden teapot with lid.

who ran a pottery near Saarlouis, and the firm became known as Villeroy and Boch.

The concern studied methods of old stoneware construction and decoration and turned out the many items we like to collect today, as perhaps the best examples of that period. The chromolith method of ornamentation—a process of inlaying various colored clays to create beautiful designs, in much the same manner as enameling—reached new heights at the hands of Mettlach workers. This method won the concern new fame and established it as one of the outstanding potteries in the world—hence the interest from collectors everywhere.

Perhaps the artistry was inspired by management-worker relations, which were second to none. Workers were given retirement pay at a time when it was unheard of elsewhere. If they lived outside the town, they were given free transportation via rail. At noon, specially heated wagons came to the homes of workers and brought their noontime meals back to them, straight from their own kitchens. There were amusement parks and recreational plans that made it quite bearable to work for this concern. The attrition rate of workers was low.

Along with inlaid and decorated stoneware, Mettlach produced dinner sets, jardinières and pedestals, steins, tea sets, toilet sets, and the like. Like the steins, these pieces are marked with the castle imprint, most often with an interlaced VB in a circle. Numerals were used to indicate the year a piece was made, for instance 07 for 1907. Roman numerals indicate that the piece comes in more than one size. If you see a combination of numerals, such as 1077/880, the first refers to the shape, and the second, the style of decoration. A later mark, which appeared in 1874, was the winged head of Mercury, most often printed in green under the glaze. Those with Mercury, which read "Reg. U.S. Pat. Off." are products of post 1900, when the pieces were imported for sale in this country.

There are several other less common marks, including the initials VB or V&B, which were used mostly at the end of the last century.

Steins—The lids on steins were designed primarily for health reasons, to keep away flies and other insects attracted to the lip of mugs at outdoor beer gardens. Some steins have lithophane bottoms, which held to the light, show damsels in various stages of undress, to encourage the imbiber to

Stoneware steins, Germany, 20th century. Both of these are of the type which were brought back as souvenirs from some beer hall, not much value. Value: $25-$45

down his drink hurriedly, so he could enjoy the sights.

The Mettlach stein is the most desired. There are steins made by other manufacturers, some of which are of good quality, but one must judge them on this quality before buying. There are regimental steins, popular at the turn of the century, which list the officers and men who belonged to a particular military group. Atop the lid is a metal figure that signifies the branch of the service in which they served. There were several makers of regimental steins.

Many production steins were brought to this country by servicemen after both world wars and by tourists as well. This is the type made for beer halls, which used them as advertising pieces. These are not very good in quality, so are not bought by the serious collector. As with other items, quality is the most important factor—the Mettlach will not let you down. The unique designs, inscriptions, and handwork in their creation, decoration, and coloring set them apart from all others.

Central and Eastern Europe

Porcelain making began in Germany, where many potteries operated in the eighteenth and nineteenth centuries. Notable is the first, the Meissen works at Dresden. At a visit to the art museum in Hamburg, I noted many potteries not heard of in this century—so many, in fact, it would take a book just to list them. The work of these potteries is very similar—fine, fragile porcelain with all types of floral and gilt decoration. This tradition spilled over into all the adjoining countries. The ready availability of kaolin clay, which is a necessary ingredient to porcelain, was the key to the development of these industries.

There is a tradition of porcelain manufacture in Russia, as well, with potteries at St. Petersburg, Moscow, and Minsk. Today several are operating to make the collector plates of Russian scenery, which are marketed around the world. Some years ago, we noted in the commission shops in Moscow and St. Petersburg lots of small porcelain items that

Lipizzaner horses for which Castle Augarten is famous. The horses are quartered in Vienna. These porcelain figures are found all over the world. Value: $450

had been consigned to them for sale. Many pieces came from continental Europe as well as the Orient. There were maker's names I've never seen in books in this country and that have not appeared in any markets or shops I have visited.

There is a problem in buying dinnerware services made in countries other than England—there is practically no available open stock for replacement of broken items.

Castle Augarten Porcelain

The Vienna Porcelain Manufactory was founded by a Dutchman, Claudius Du Parquier, in 1717. Two professional potters hired away from Meissen destroyed many of the Meissen models made for future manufacture. Du Parquier learned the location of a good supply of kaolin clay, which is necessary to the making of porcelain, near Passau, Germany, which ensured that the finest work

Workman at Castle Augarten in Vienna, assembling a statue of the Marly Horses, after Guilliaume Costeau. Statuary like this was molded in many sections.

could be accomplished. Between 1744 and 1781, under the reign of Maria Theresa, the pottery prospered. Its work was acknowledged as the best in the world at that time. In 1749, a better clay was found at Schmolmitz in Hungary. Products made with this clay are marked with a blue shield under the glaze. Workers came from Dresden to create new forms, which were gilded and hand decorated. The factory prospered under Baron Sorgenthal, between 1781 and 1805, in a period described as classical. Other influences on style were Joseph Niedermeyer (took over the factory at the time of Napoleon) and Franz Joseph I (1848 to the closing of the pottery in 1864). Wahliss in Karlsbad tried to copy the original shapes and forms.

In 1922, the pottery was revived as the Vienna Porcelain Manufactory Augarten. It is best known today for the figures of the Lippizaners, the horses that perform at the Spanish Court Riding School in Vienna and around the world. Fine porcelain dinnerware as well as decorative wares is made in the tradition of the original factories. Located in a wing of an old castle, its original site (which I visited in 1971) continues to produce as fine a porcelain as there is.

Delfts Blauw

The ceramic, generically known as "Delft," has an interesting history. In the Netherlands, it is known as "Delfts Blauw." Collectors are most familiar with the blue and white examples, which are found in almost every shop and marketplace, as well as that which is new in gift shops. Much is still being brought in to this country by tourists and other travelers who, while in Holland, are confronted with the product no matter where they turn. It is a pleasing ceramic to own and use, hence its popularity here as a gift to family and friends.

Years ago, historians taught us that this combination of white earthenware with cobalt blue decoration, was originally an Oriental product, which was carried by the Dutch East India traders to Europe in the 17th century. However, at a seminar in the 1980s at the headquarters of the SPNEA in Boston, John Austin, curator of ceramics at Colonial Williamsburg, informed us that the clay color and decoration originated in Ireland. Ireland is blessed with huge clay beds, from which potteries all over the British Isles and Europe obtained their supplies. Many potters set up shop in Staffordshire

All the decorating at Castle Augarten is done by highly trained artists.

County, which is Northwest of London, and near Liverpool, to which clay was shipped and from which much of the finished product was exported. Potteries in the lowlands of Holland and Belgium imported practically all of their clay from Ireland. Along with it, came samples of the blue and white ware, which was so popular in that country. The Dutch seized upon this as a product, which they could make and export, as it had great appeal. Their ships had command of the oceans at the time and soon they were hauling the "Delft" to the Orient as well as elsewhere in the civilized world. Hence, the feeling by Mr. Austin, that this influenced the Orientals into making blue and white wares in the style of the Delft to compete in the world trade.

Naturally, this opened the door to copies and soon potteries in Germany, Portugal, England, and Japan joined the Chinese in making such examples. The name "Delft" became generic, though the original appeared in Holland. The country excelled

Example of a blue & white Delft jug.

in the many potteries which turned out dinnerware sets and other dishware; tiles, both room and roof; lamps, boxes in all sizes, candleholders and various other objects and giftwares. Some made classic pieces and others concentrated on the tourist trade, hence the disparity of values when one goes collecting. Learn the pottery marks—they are your best friends.

Not all Delft is blue and white. Colored pieces keep turning up and these are referred to as Delft Color. Most of this work seems to have been done late in the 20th century and is still being done today. We visited a pottery there and watched the making of both the blue and white and color.

Delft ware was described as a kind of pottery of clay or clay mixed with sand and covered with a white enamel, which gives to it a look like porcelain. Though, in the opinion of many, the better Delft ware was made in England, one has but to go to the rail station in Delft to see walls and ceilings covered with the blue and white tile. In hotels, the bathrooms and other public rooms are covered with tile, as are the interiors and frames of fireplaces.

From the rail station, one can walk to De Porceleyne Fles, the royal Delft Ware Manufactory that dates back to 1653. At the end of the 17th century, there were at least 30 potteries in this area. The competition from the potteries in England gradually took its toll on the Dutch, and by 1840, only one pottery in Delft was still operating, De Porceleyne Fles. Signed pieces from the 17th and 18th centuries are rare. It is indicated that the mark IK refers to James Knotter who operated the plant between 1697 to the time of his death in 1701. PVD indicates the signature of Pieter van Doorne—this was registered in 1764, but no piece has turned up with this mark. An early mark is HL or IHL for Jacobus Harlees who owned the factory from 1771 to his death in 1786. One may see examples of much of this early work at Cinquantenaire Museum in Brussels at the Museum Bumans-van Buningen in Rotterdam and at the municipal museum in Leeuwarden. In 1876, Joost Thooft took control of the pottery and attempted to revive it with colored pieces as well as the blue and white, but this was not successful. However, the pottery remained in business and today is a showplace of fine work. There is a museum section, which exhibits the old work, as well as a room full of exquisite pieces, which will empty your pocketbook in a hurry. Throughout the pottery, walls are covered with blue and white and colored tiles. There is a chart with the marks used from 1871 through 1972 as well as the letters and symbols of the maker's initials.

In the 20th century, other potteries appeared on the scene, making rather inexpensive blue and white wares, which found their way into the hands of tourists who would patronize marketplaces all over the country. Most of these examples are not of really good quality, but collectors here either do not know how to identify the best, or don't care. We see Delft liquor bottles, lamps, ashtrays, lazy susans, wall plaques and a myriad of other items, which were not made by the better potteries. Years ago, collectors were taught to look for the crown mark which indicated the best quality.

In 1881, Leon Senf came to the factory as a designer and created what was called "New Delft," though it looked more like the work of Persian, Syrian, and Iznik potters. These are well marked and could be the highlight of any collection. The pottery survived two world wars and after the second, Cornelius Hartog and Henk J. Tieman came there to create monumental ceramics. Artists in this section were given free hand to create new forms and many unique items appeared. This is why collectors must alter their thinking that all Delft is blue and white dishes and related memorabilia.

China

There has been much speculation as to the feasibility of collecting Chinese porcelains. This country closed its doors to the western world for over twenty years, during which time the interest in oriental artifacts steadily increased. There has been some feeling that the market would be flooded with shipments of all kinds of antiques, as such, a large country must surely have antiques going back to its earliest civilization. Since the Chinese worker, under communism, is unable to amass the wealth needed to indulge in collecting, it would be logical to assume that many artifacts would find their way to western countries in search of dollars and other hard currency. If the markets were flooded with such merchandise, it would again be logical to assume that the law of supply and demand would drive down the prices of existing treasures outside China and provide an unsettling effect on collect-

ing them. However, in the opinion of those who deal in such antiquities, this is not going to happen. Years ago, the great capitals at Anyang and Loyang were stripped of their antiquities, most of which found their way into western museums, providing the basis for some of the world's finest collections of this art. When the railway system was expanded in China during the early part of the century, many lines were run through old cemeteries. When the graves were dug up for relocation, all sorts of worldly possessions were found with the bodies, having evidently been buried with them for their trip to the unknown. The easy sale of such items led to grave robbing everywhere, which has provided many antiques for the western world.

China developed the earliest porcelain industry, and until its wares were duplicated in Europe, much fine porcelain was sent there in trade. This trade continued throughout the rise of the porcelain industry elsewhere. Chinese trade with Europe began in earnest early in the seventeenth century, but it was not common in America until after the Revolutionary War. America began sending clipper ships directly to the Orient, bypassing the necessity of transshipment through England. You can assume that most of the oriental ware collected today came to America after 1800. This is the period when Canton blue earthenware and porcelains from Nanking, Fukien, and Canton first made their presence felt. The popular five color Chinese export porcelain, often called Rose Medallion, arrived in America as early as the 1790s, yet the bulk of it appears to have arrived after 1850 during the height of the Chinese American trade. Little or no green-colored celadon arrived in America until after the War of 1812. You must be careful in purchasing the pure white blanc de chine figures (whose history goes back many centuries) as they are being reproduced quite well today. Imari ware (first made in Japan in blue and orange with gilding) is now being reproduced in China with remarkable fidelity. It is still being handmade and hand decorated, which guarantees that quality pieces will rank high as collectibles in some future generation.

When Chiang Kai-shek left the mainland to occupy Taiwan, he took with him the palace treasures from Peking. Since then the People's Republic has been trying to replace them with similar items to restore the old palaces to their original dignity. There are agents from the People's

Republic buying items all over the world for return to China, and their buying offers keen competition to anyone interested in oriental artifacts. There is no indication that markets throughout the world will be flooded with Chinese antiques, since there really is little of fine quality or value left to export. No one looks for a drop in prices for such items. Some of the best will undoubtedly continue to rise in price despite the "open door."

Blanc De Chine

Perhaps some of the purest white in porcelain is blanc de chine (which means "white china"). Not much has been learned of the history and origination of blanc de chine in China. What we know about it today has been learned from records kept in Europe by collectors. Some feel that blanc de chine originated as early as the sixteenth century. This was a time when the royal kilns at Chintechen were not operating. Most of the early production came from Té-hua in Fukien Province. Much was exported to Europe in the late seventeenth and eighteenth centuries. Historians tell us that the pieces were fired only once, giving them a quality that cannot be matched by any other porcelain. The quality of the porcelain was never duplicated in Europe.

Most of the figures are Buddhist inspired, but there are decorative wares as well. The beauty of the early modeling in china lies in the delicate work done on the fingers, hair, and facial expression.

Reproductions of these white porcelain figures can be found in import shops today, so it is necessary to learn how to tell the old from the new, which is not easy for the novice collector. Potteries in Germany, England, and France attempted to duplicate the wares in the eighteenth century, but without much success. Some of the best early examples can be seen at Blenheim Palace at Woodstock, England, as well as at the Victoria and Albert Museum in London. The Danish Royal Cabinet of Curiosities began acquiring the figures in about 1690. I have seen the collection at Rosenberg Palace in Copenhagen as well as that at Hampton Court in England. Only three dated

Blanc de chine figures in white porcelain, 18th century. Seen at Blenheim Palace in Woodstock, England. Originally, these were made only for royalty.

pieces have turned up. There is a challenge in collecting good blanc de chine. The work is beautiful.

Areas of Collecting Interest

China Dogs

A favorite among collectors in America are the pairs of china dogs most often called Staffordshire dogs. They hailed from Staffordshire County in England, and most were made in the last century.

There are more than 130 potters in that region, many of who made such whimsies. I have never seen one marked by its maker, which makes attribution difficult. The quality of the pottery and its decoration and glaze help identify it.

In this country, for years these figures were called Staffordshire dogs. In England, they are called Sitting Spaniels, as tradition tells us that this breed was a favorite of Charles II in the seventeenth century. I am told Staffordshire dogs were popular gifts for newlyweds, who put them on either side of the fireplace to ward off the evil spirits who might descend there.

Early potters such as Thomas Whieldon, Ralph Woods, Astbury, and Walton called them pot dogs. More than 200 models have been identified, varying in height from 5 to 18 inches. Early forms had incised decorations, which make them more desirable than those simply molded. Dalmatians seem the first favored as models, but gradually the spaniel took over. Fancy models have molded chains, which are then gilded.

Actually, most of the work on these dogs is quite crude. They were made to appeal to people with lower incomes. Very little has been written about them, as most people do not consider them art objects. I might mention that some artisans are reproducing them, making them look very old. In 1972, I bought a 16-inch pair in England for $29, including delivery here. I couldn't tell them from the old ones.

Fish and Game Services

Since the advent of mass production of dinnerware, potters have created many forms just to make business good. Just as the silver makers created various spoons, forks, and knives for serving and eating different foods, so did the potters. Special dishes were created for serving all types of food, and they were promoted to create a complete service.

The French popularized this idea by making separate sets of twelve dishes to be used for dignified eating. For example, there were bowls with two handles for cream soups and fish platters for the fish course. The better sets, in porcelain, many made at Limoges, were hand painted with different

One of a pair of what most Americans call Staffordshire Dogs. In Britain, most are called sitting spaniels, or King Charles Spaniels, made as a tribute of his favorite dogs. They are made in Staffordshire at one of the many potteries; I have never seen one marked. These are being reproduced. Value of pair: $250

Limoges game plate, bird center, signed by artist.

Example of fish platter and plate set.

Why such great interest? Though the painting is over the glaze and will not stand up well under washing, some of the artwork is quite good. Patterns were copied from books or other china pieces, and each artisan tried to put some of herself or himself into the piece.

If you wish to collect this home-painted china, here are a few guidelines: Porcelain blanks are preferable to earthenware. The quality of work, design, and colors must be good. Look for pieces signed or initialed by the artisan. This is quite important, as the signed pieces generally command much more attention and price. You may see a factory stamp on the bottom, along with a name or initials in gilt or paint. Keep the pieces out of the dishwasher because the painting is not protected by the glaze. They are subject to wear for the same reason, so handle them as little as possible.

Occupied Japan

Items from Japan with the mark "Made in Occupied Japan" were made there during the occupation by American forces between 1945 and 1952. The *New York Times* reported that the first merchandise with this mark reached our shores in 1948.

fish on them. This painting was done before glazing, and most pieces were signed by the artists. Later, transfer printing was used for decoration, so these are of less value. The next course was the meat, so a meat platter with twelve dishes decorated with various animals was a must.

Similar services were made in this country, notably in Ohio. The Pennsbury Pottery Company in Pennsylvania made platters shaped like fish with scales. These are quite rare and are a good addition to any collection.

Hand Painted China

Late in the nineteenth century, nights were long and many looked for ways to busy themselves with crafts or other work. One of the favorite pastimes was painting china. White blanks of porcelain and earthenware were turned out by many of the major factories in Europe. Some of the finest in Limoges and Austrian porcelains were shipped here to be sold to enterprising home painters who did the work for the love of it and to occupy themselves in the days when there were few diversions to take one's mind off the chores of the day.

I have seen one hardcover book with instructions on how to paint china. It appeared at an auction and sold for well over $100.

Occupied Japan figurine.

Our country always enjoyed a big trade with Japan before the war, though the quality of much that was shipped here could be in question. Ceramics were perhaps the greatest export, but most items were channeled through our five and ten cent stores during the Depression. Figurines, lamps, animals, birds, wall plaques, vases, and planters, and the like continually turn up at auctions and flea markets. Unless they are of the paper-thin, hand-painted porcelain, there is little demand, even today. After the war, however, greater attention was given to quality, as reviving the postwar economy in that country was of prime concern.

Much was shipped here in ceramics, metals, papier-mâché, dolls, toys, and the like, stamped "Made in Occupied Japan." Collectors like ready identification as well as interesting objects to acquire, so it is natural that interest grew in this area. Books have been written on marks, markers, and what to collect. There are very few auctions where prices are not many times more today than they were when the items came here a scant 40 years ago.

Pennsbury Pottery

Pennsbury Pottery was started by Ernest Below, who had been a ceramics engineer at the Stangl Pottery in New Jersey. His mother served as the designer and was responsible for the Pennsylvania "Dutch" motifs, which were so

Pennsbury Pottery, 1950-1971, Morrisville, PA. Noted for its forms, brown-tone coloring and Pennsylvania "Dutch" decorations. The rooster was popular.

Photo of Pennsbury Pottery taken at the plant in October 1970. It reveals a lot of items not known to have been made there. They should be marked. (1950-1971)

successful. His father worked creating shapes in ceramics. Most of his work was cast in brown-tone background, which made the hand-painted artwork stand out. Local housewives and schoolgirls were trained to decorate the ceramics. The plant started with eight people and grew to employ between forty and fifty at the time of its demise. Clay came from Tennessee and Georgia and was mixed with flint and other ingredients. The plant originally used six different clays, and then narrowed it to two or three. Glazes were fritted, body sheen, and soft. Complete dinnerware sets and gift items were popular. The pottery started with sculptured birds, but found these hard to sell in the face of competition from Japan.

Pennsbury Pottery will be remembered best for its commemorative work. The pottery made ash-trays for Electrolux, dishes for railroads, plates for fraternal organizations and churches, mugs and ashtrays for nearby Washington Crossing State Park, and just about anything demanded by clubs or organizations for presentation at annual meet-ings and the like. The rarest item of all is a single plate made for presentation to Walt Disney when he attended the opening of the Walt Disney School in nearby Tullytown. It has never turned up, and its whereabouts are unknown, even to the Disney Archives in California. There are mugs for Historic Fallingston and another great rarity—scenic plates made for the last steam engine run on the Reading Railroad. The tray for this set had the engine pic-tured on it, and only 3,500 plates were made to be given to passengers. The rooster was a popular design as it symbolized happiness. Pennsylvania hex symbols and designs with Amish figures were popular with the tourists. The pottery burned down shortly after the auction was held to dispose of the remaining ceramic pieces. All the machinery and dies were destroyed.

There has been some reproduction of Pennsbury Pottery done at a kiln in the Pocono Mountains. However, the coloring is different and can easily be noted by those who collect the original.

Phoenix Bird and Flying Turkey China

The phoenix was a fabled bird in Greek mythology. It was supposed to have a life span of thousands of years. No one is sure when it first appeared on pottery made in Japan. Collectors feel most was made in this century judging from the marks of "Nippon," which would date it after 1892, and the mark "Made in Japan," which came after 1920. The flying turkey pattern is very similar, and some collectors feel there is no problem in mixing phoenix and flying turkey pieces in a collection.

The wings of the phoenix are always spread wide; it almost always has spots on its chest and its head is facing in the opposite direction from its body. Traditionally, the head is facing to the right, or back over its left wing, in what is called the "sinister" stance. With the head facing left and the body right, it is in the "dexter" stance. Some pieces feature both stances. The better grade designs depict the head perpendicular to the body with the head feathers pointing upward and carries mark #17 or #18, and indication of the fine quality. The

majority of heads are horizontal with the hint of a slant. There are four to eight spots on the chest. Some chrysanthemum's (a standard design motif) centers are blue and some are white, perhaps at the discretion of the decorator. Very rare is a green and white piece of phoenix and rarer still is a fluted piece.

Phoenix bird china was advertised as "HOWO ware," from the Japanese word for phoenix. Early in this century it was used as a premium to boost sales of other items, and even to boost attendance at Radio City Music Hall.

Rebekah at the Well

If you have a Rockinghamware teapot with a molded figure of a lady at a well with the words, "REBEKAH AT THE WELL" beneath, do not identify it as Bennington. Richard Carter Barret tells us that as many as thirty-five potteries could have made it late in the last century.

In his book *Early American Pottery and China* (Tuttle, 1926), John Spargo informs us that Charles Coxon, chief modeler at E&W Bennet in Baltimore, is the person who created Rebekah in this country. He copied the design from S. Alcock & Company in England, which featured the figure of Rebekah in white relief on a blue background. Potteries in New Jersey and Ohio made them as well, but in the brown ceramic. Some are modeled without the wording at the bottom. While director-curator at the Bennington (VT) Museum, Richard Carter Barret wrote the book, *How to Identify Bennington Pottery* in which he indicates that Rebekah was not made at Bennington.

Shaving Mugs

The development of the shaving mug follows closely the changing hairstyles of men throughout the world. Before the middle of the last century, the barber's basin was the common holder for soap and water used for shaving. During the time of the Civil War, beards became popular, so much so, that even President Lincoln grew one. Shortly after this time the shaving mug became popular as men suddenly decided it was time to rebel against the prevailing styles and be clean-shaven again.

Mugs were made to hold water and shaving cream, which was worked into a lather. Many shaving mugs were made in this country, but most of

Rebekah at the Well, Rockingham ware. In our text, Richard Carter Barret reveals these were never made in Bennington. Value: $75-$125

the better ones came from overseas. The latter are hand painted and made of porcelain. It was not unusual for men to have their names painted or gilded on their shaving mugs. Each barbershop had a line of shelves to hold their customer's mugs, and each would be used only by its owner. Most mugs look like drinking vessels with built-in holders for the brush. The scuttle type mugs seem to have been made only overseas; they do not appear in catalogs from this country. Some were made in silver plate and sterling; most of these were listed in the silver company catalogs and not in the barber books.

Mail order concerns such as Sears sold shaving mugs as well. The Lenox Company in New Jersey listed their mugs only in their own catalogs and sold them in fine china shops as well. Country of origin had to be marked after 1892, but many have no such mark, as the mugs were quite popular before that time.

Shaving mugs were still quite common on shelves in barbershops into the 1930s. The collapsible tube for creams and the electric shaver helped bring on their demise. They are interesting, colorful collectibles today.

Shaving mugs are popular collectibles. Though there are excellent examples from overseas, many were made in this country. Value: $50-$150

CERAMICS GALLERY

Attica black figure, lidded neck amphora and cover, c. 530-510 BC from the circle of the painter Antiminese. Sold for $41,250 in the June 13, 1990 auction at Butterfields in San Francisco.

Butterfield & Butterfield.

Greek red figure pottery bell krater by the Methyse painter, c. 450 BC. Embellished with finely detailed scenes including a seated woman playing a lyre.

Sotheby's.

Wedgwood basalt urn.

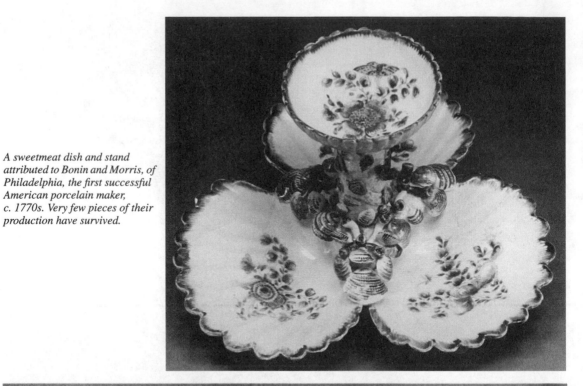

A sweetmeat dish and stand attributed to Bonin and Morris, of Philadelphia, the first successful American porcelain maker, c. 1770s. Very few pieces of their production have survived.

In ceramics, pots with the spouts at the top are called chocolate pots. These were made extensively in Europe and even in Japan. One must check markings to determine provenance. Value: $150-$250

Dutch crocus, blue enchantress, limited edition of 700. Made by Cybis Trenton, NJ, 20th century. One was presented to Princess Margaret, renamed the Snowdon Crocus.

Part of a large collection of Martin Brothers Stoneware; grotesque face jugs and vases, late 19th and early 20th centuries; sold by Butterfields in 1992.

Shelves at the Dorchester Pottery, located just south of Boston. The blue and white was popular. See text on the owners and operation. It started operations in 1894, and went out of business in the 1970s.

Moorcroft Pottery, England, 20th century. The finely proportioned bodies and bright colorings appeal to many collectors. Value: $220-$1,900

Unusual milk pitcher with dog's-head spout. Staffordshire, England, 19th century. One wonders at the design. Value: $350

Contemporary potters like the late Russell Henry of Birdsboro, PA, create a cult of collectors, because the interesting forms and decorations are done by the same potter. Pictured is a garlic pot used by my wife, made c. 1975. Value: $350

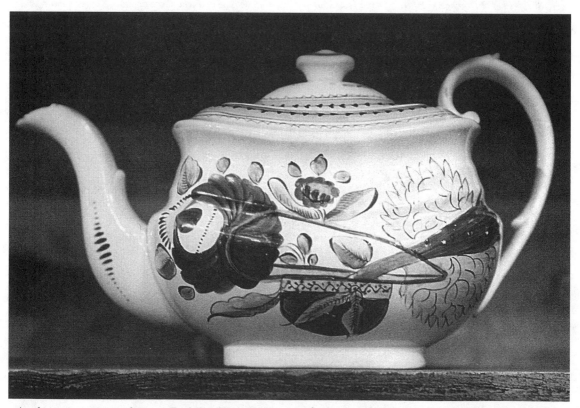

An elegant rose patterned teapot, English Staffordshire, early 19th century. There were various rose patterns, whose names might vary. Most refer to this as King's Rose. Value: $450

Van Briggle Pottery bowl.

Buffalo Pottery Blue Willow pitcher, c. 1905.

Buffalo Pottery sauceboat.

Rare urn by William Ellis Tucker of Philadelphia, c. 1830. Part of the Hammerslough Collection which is now at the William Penn Museum in Harrisburg. One learns that square pedestal bases were never colored on their tops. The design is French inspired as Tucker imported workmen from Sevres.

Blue and white Canton were exported to this country when the clipper ship trade with China became a reality early in the 19th century. Some felt it was shipped more as ballast, as it was inexpensive earthenware. Platter: $485.

Redware platter, Pennsylvania, 19th century. The decoration was made by trailing a finger through the glaze before firing. Value: $650

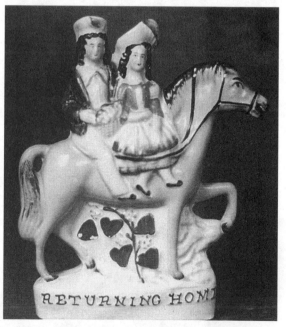

In this country, called a Cottage figure, in Britain, they are called fallbacks, as the backs are flat to rest on a narrow mantel. Most depict scenes of family and home life. This piece is from Staffordshire, England, dating to the 19th century. Value: $350

Staffordshire England, 19th century, Staffordshire stirrup cup. During foxhunts, riders had to completely quaff the drink served them, as they could not be put down. Value: $350

The last of the Pewabic Pottery in Detroit. Founded by Mary Chase Perry Stratton in 1903, the company made much art pottery, tiles, and decorative items. I photographed these last pieces early in the 1970s, shortly after the pottery closed.

Rare Turk's head bowl in redware, Pennsylvania, 19th century. This was used as a baking dish and mold. Sold at auction in New Hampshire during 2001 for $185.

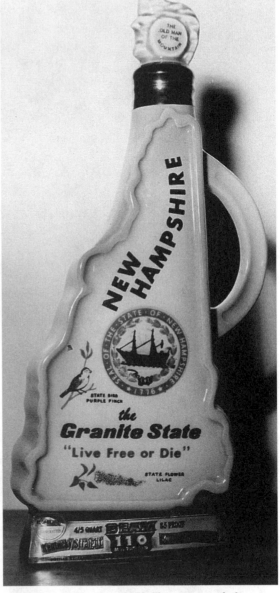

Beam bourbon bottle, c. 1970. These were made for many states and for organizations that used them as commemorative pieces. Right now, the market is down, but with a new generation starting to collect, they may experience a revival. Value: $10

Collection of George Ohr pottery, Biloxi, Mississippi, in Art Noveau styles. Value: $1,100-$7,000

Some of the decorators at potteries were quite artistic in what they put on jugs and crocks. Note the palm trees on this butter pot from Thompson Harrington, Lyons NY, mid 19th century. Value: $1,800

This jug with bullfrog atop is often called a spring jug, as food to be kept cold was stored in them and they were put in the springhouse to keep cool. Value: $650

Sleepy Eye pitcher made by the Red Wing Pottery Company in Red Wing, Minnesota, c. 1920s. The company started in 1876 under another name and after several name changes went out of business. Many items were made as premium giveaways. Value: $350

Collectors like marked pieces—witness this bean pot which states "It pays to trade at Lehman's Store, North Freedom, Wis." It was a great advertising item, most often used at least once a week. Value: $65

Minton teapot, grey with blossom decor in relief, 2-3/4" h x 7" l.

Canton creamer, c. 1810, 3" h.

Wedgwood Jasperware creamer, 3-3/4" h.

Wedgwood pitcher with salt glaze.

Weller "Hudson" vase, 6" h.

Weller green matte glazed vase, forest scene, 5-3/4" h.

Weller
Pottery vase,
Art Noveau
type.

Weller vase, floral decor, 14" h.

Shown clockwise are a spatterware rainbow cup and saucer; spatterware tulip pattern, blue cup and saucer; spongeware bowl, and spongeware pitcher. Observe the difference in the decorative texture between the two styles.

GLOSSARY

Basalt: A black stoneware made by mixing iron ore byproducts with basic clay.

Belleek: A delicate porcelain that originated in Ireland, characterized by its sheen and fragility.

Biscuit: A molded clay item fired only once.

Bone china: A clay mixture that includes powdered, calcined bone powder to strengthen it and give it a porcelain hard quality.

Caffette: A clay container that holds unfired bodies in a kiln.

Calcine: A technique for baking metals, stone, bone, or other materials to reduce them to powder before mixing with clay or glaze.

Ceramic: A generic term for items made from clay and fired to hardness.

China: A generic term used to describe tablewares and decorative items made from clay and other ingredients.

Chinese export: The ceramic wares that arrived in Europe and America from the Orient in the eighteenth and nineteenth centuries.

Clay: Fine-grained earth made up of hydrated silicates of aluminum, which forms a paste with water and can be molded and fired to hardness.

Creamware: A cream or ivory colored pottery, which originated in England in the eighteenth century.

Delft: Originated in Ireland as a tin-glazed blue and white decorated earthenware. Received its name from the city in Holland where it was made and popularized. Made also in England, Germany, and other countries.

Dresden: The home of the original porcelain in Germany, discovered by Johann Freiderich Bottger.

Earthenware: Simple opaque ware made of clay and requiring glazing to offset its porosity.

Enameling: Decoration of ceramic bodies before firing with paints made from various substances.

Flint enamel: A pottery enamel made by calcining flint stone into powder, then mixing it with liquid glaze.

Glaze: A transparent or colored coating put on ceramics before firing to offset their porosity.

Graniteware: A very hard earthenware toughened with calcine flint stone.

Ironstone: Patented by Mason in England in 1813. Usually a thicker, very tough earthenware; mostly in pure white with impressed or raised decoration.

Jasperware: Barium sulphate is added to clay to produce a nonporous hard body akin to porcelain. It is easily colored. Wedgwood is best known for working with it.

Ashtrays are an endangered species, as fewer are made for hotels, restaurants, and other places of business. This one advertises Bulldog Bottled Beer, England, 20th century. Marked, "Property of Robert Porter," probably the brewer. There is a place for matches as well as ashes. Value: $65

Kaolin: A fine clay used in making porcelain.

Kiln: An oven in which clay products are baked to hardness.

Lowestoft: A name often applied to Chinese export porcelains of the eighteenth and nineteenth centuries as late as the 1890s. It is believed that Lowestoft originally imported wares from China and reshipped them under its name from East Anglia, England.

Lusterware: Any ceramic body glazed with a metallic compound, which will give it luster and shine.

Majolica: Originally a Majorcan redware, which was colorfully fired with tin, glazes. It became a product of practically every country with minor variations.

Meissen: Synonymous with Dresden, as the wares were made at the Meissen plant in Dresden, Germany.

Parian: An unglazed porcelain originated early in the nineteenth century as a poor man's imitation of Parian marble.

Petuntse: A form of feldspar, which was mixed with clay to make various ceramics, including stoneware and porcelain.

Porcelain: A hard, translucent ceramic that originated in China.

Potter's wheel: A whirling device on which clay objects are formed by hand.

Queensware: Another name for creamware.

Redware: Made of red clay and glazed when needed to cancel its porosity.

Rockinghamware: A name given to the brown and mottled colored wares reputedly originating at the estate of the Earl of Rockingham in England in the eighteenth century. Much is referred to mistakenly as Benningtonware, a reference to the community in Vermont where a large number was produced.

Salt glaze: An inexpensive quick glazing achieved by throwing salt into the kiln during the final moments of firing—the vapors then depositing on the bodies.

Saggar: Clay holder inside a kiln, which holds the green clay for firing and protects it from direct heat.

Slip: A simple glaze made by mixing clay with water and slipping or trailing it on the piece to be protected.

Stoneware: A very strong earthenware which has the strength of porcelain and does not require an inside glaze to make it impervious to water.

Transferwares: Ceramic bodies with transfer printing done by the use of paper decals or transfers.

Under glaze: A reference to the painting or other decorating done on ceramics before glazing and firing.

Vitreous china: A strong earthenware body with an almost glass-like shiny glaze.

Chapter Four

METALWORK

Silver

Historical Overview

Silversmiths and metalworkers have always had a place in history, from the Egyptians of more than 3,000 years ago to the armorers of the Middle Ages, from Paul Revere to the present. Silversmithing, the cold working of metal, is both an art and a craft. The natural beauty of silver lends itself to the design of artists and craftsmen. It has been mined and worked into an endless variety of useful and decorative items that are highly sought after today.

Silversmithing in America goes back to the early seventeenth century. Silversmiths working in Boston were trained in England. Because of this, we owe much of our silver heritage to the British. Noted English craftsmen of the late eighteenth century include Matthew Boulton (1728-1809); Paul Storr, who began his work in 1792; and members of the Batemen family, including two women, Hester and Anne. Names like Philip Syng, Joseph Richardson, Johannis Nys, Ceasar Ghiselin, and William Vilant attest to the influence of European artisans on American silver.

The great silver-making centers of the eighteenth century were Boston, New York, and Philadelphia. The craft then spread into the smaller cities and towns and some very sophisticated country work has turned up to rival the urban centers.

Much of the early work by these and other makers is scarce, for several reasons. First, there was a limited output of eighteenth century American work because of a shortage of metal. The English withheld supplies of silver from the colonies in order to keep their own craftsmen busy, which held down production here. There was much melting down of coins and surreptitious buying of stolen metal from prize ships captured by pirates and others. A great deal of Spanish silver from mines in Mexico and South America found its way into the hands of American silversmiths as booty from battles at sea. Pieces were made to order and in most cases the buyer would bring his own metal to the silversmith who would be paid for his efforts by retaining a percentage of it.

Second, at the time of the revolution, many Tories still loyal to the Crown returned to England taking whatever they could, and if they owned silver it was first thing they took. Much silver was donated to be melted down to help pay for the war

Medieval helmets, swords, pole arms and the like, will turn up from time to time. Do not pay too much unless they are authenticated.

effort. In the course of the war, the English also besieged many cities along the American coast. When they received no cooperation from the colonists in supplying them with food or other needs, they would stand their battleships offshore and demolish the community. This resulted in the wholesale destruction of many of our native decorative arts. When the British captured a town, the first thing the solders stole was silver, since it was wealth that could be picked up and carried away.

Third, in 1793 and 1798, Philadelphia was scourged with serious epidemics of yellow fever,

and silversmiths either died along with everyone else or quickly relocated, draining the city of its talents. The capital was moved to Washington and the demand for fine silver in Philadelphia lessened. Naturally, after the turn of the century, as machines arrived to do the work, the quality of silver declined and gradually disappeared, hence the importance of early Philadelphia silver.

It was not until the twentieth century that much attention was paid to American handmade silver. Those who owned old silver thought most of it was made in England, since not much research had

Period suits of armor are rarely found in this country. There have been reproductions made, selling even in Sears Roebuck. These were used for decorations in restaurants, lounges, etc.

been done on early makers in this country, and names and touchmarks gave no apparent clues. Late in the nineteenth century Professor Woolsey of Yale suggested that more research should be done, and this was followed at the turn of the century by a book prepared by N.W. Elwell which had forty pages of photography of both American and English silver. In 1906, The Museum of Fine Arts in Boston mounted the first exhibition of American silver, featuring silver which had been identified as to maker. The Museum of Fine Arts held another display in 1911, at which over a thousand pieces were shown. Since then, many books have been written and much information has been assembled, and several large museums keep permanent collections on display.

Collecting Guidelines

America

The great interest in American silver has all but depleted the available supply for the common collector. Today, you must wait for the liquidation of an estate where there are no heirs, or where money is more desired than old silver. Until recently, nineteenth-century silver was not much in demand, but as the rarity of early work increased, so did the interest in later work. Actually, there were many silversmiths doing handwork until the Civil War, as this industry was not affected by the industrial revolution until the 1840s, when the method for electroplating was discovered.

Today, much nineteenth-century sterling is purchased for its scrap value. You will find if difficult to match pieces in a flatware set, and very few people wish to set a table unless the service is complete. There are some dealers who specialize in selling odd silver pieces, so if you have patience and get around to shows you may be able to select items you need.

The thin coin silver spoons which obviously were made in abundance during the early nineteenth century are still quite plentiful. Most are well marked, and a book such as Seymour Wyler's *Old Silver, English, American, Foreign* (Crown Publishers) is quite helpful in identifying makers. Collect spoons of native or regional interest to you. Spoon racks are handy for display. After polishing coin silver pieces, rub them with ordinary flour to remove the excess polish and to give them a sheen which will not tarnish quickly.

Commemorative and souvenir spoons in sterling are quite common and represent an interesting facet of collecting. Friends touring foreign countries can acquire some for you, and you can begin a collection on your own by purchasing them new or old from dealers. When such a collection comes up for sale it will reward the collector well for his efforts, as long as the pieces are varied and difficult to acquire unless one travels a lot.

Silversmiths were known to have done a great deal of work other than turning out pieces of church or tableware. Some smiths engraved the plates from which money was printed. Others turned out sword handles, belt buckles, coins,

Silver caster made by Paul Revere. Revere was the son of Appolos Rivoire, a Huguenot who emigrated here and worked with John Coney in Boston. Value: $7,500

buttons, card boxes, and other necessities of the day. Fortunately, since most American silversmiths were of English birth or descent, they marked their pieces well and because of this we know the pieces' origin and can note regional differences in style and workmanship.

Silver knives were used during the seventeenth century, but spoons did not make their appearance until the 1800s. Forks are rare, even in the eighteenth century, since the soft silver did not lend itself to rough usage. The English made Sheffield forks, but few or none of these were manufactured in America.

Covered sugar bowl made by George Aiken, c. 1787-1823, Baltimore. Early Baltimore silver is rare as it was not a large community. Value: $7,500

In the early part of the eighteenth century, American silversmiths did not copy the style of the tall English teapots, preferring the lower ones in the pigeon-breasted Queen Anne style. Even these went out of fashion during the third quarter of the eighteenth century, when tea urns became the standard. Most of these urns were built with warmers underneath, and some had a place where a piece of hot iron could be inserted to maintain the heat. The basic style was low pots for tea and tall pots for coffee and chocolate. Ceramics makers later evolved a pattern for the latter which had the spout at the top for easier pouring. It is not known why the silver makers retained the spout emerging from the center of the pot, as chocolate is a heavy liquid and can clog the spout. Chocolate arrived in England in the mid-seventeenth century, about the same time as tea and coffee. You can easily tell a chocolate pot from the early period, as most were made with a removable piece at the top where a stirring rod could be inserted. The English pots may have this device, but it does not appear in American colonial work.

Tea caddies were popular—the name coming from the Malaysian word meaning pound, with reference to the amount packed in a container of this size. Tobacco was another product which came into favor in the mid-seventeenth century, and boxes were made to hold it. Snuff became quite popular during the time of Queen Anne, and snuff boxes became fashionable. Silver spice boxes (or nutmeg boxes as they were often called) came into vogue in the eighteenth century, so one might season his food properly while traveling. Sugar was a very expensive luxury in England until the end of the seventeenth century, when the demand for it to sweeten hot drinks resulted in greater imports. It came in loaf or chunk form, so sugar boxes were made to house it with proper decorum for the fancy table. Tongs and cutters were added to the inventory of silver wares to handle the chunk sugar. One of the American colonial makers of sugar boxes was John Coney of Boston (1655-1722), who trained a very important Huguenot apprentice, Appolos Rivoire, the father of the noted Paul Revere. The Revere silver is cataloged *Revere I* and *Revere II* for identification.

Dish crosses, which served as trivets to raise heated dishes from the table, are rare in American silver. Marrow spoons were common in England,

Bennet Indian yacht Trophy, made by Tiffany's. Sold in 1993 by Sotheby's. It displays the flamboyant Art Noveau design of the early 20th century.

There is much contemporary silver being collected for investment purposes, and there is no doubt that most of it will increase in value. The price of the raw metal will rise with the economy and if the work is good, of artistic quality, or in a limited edition to make it rare, contemporary silver can represent a good investment. Many mints are turning out plates, coins, statues, and the like with a published assurance that only a limited number will be made. However, you must remember that any machine-made item can be reproduced at any time in the future and there can be no guarantee to protect you against reproductions. The best investment is in old handmade work which cannot be duplicated. Buy the contemporary silver if you like it, but remember that there is only a chance that it will acquire some importance in the future, and do not depend on it.

Plated Silver—The manufacture of less expensive silverware in America began when the electroplating technique was developed about 1840. A body of lesser metal such as copper, brass, Britannia or white metal was dipped into a silver solution. When electricity was short-circuited within the solution, it deposited the silver on the body. To provide the necessary thickness for wear, each piece was dipped several times and marked "triple

but not here. Chafing stands are rare in both countries; they were generally quite small in order to accommodate small silver pots. Ladles, wine siphons, andirons, chandeliers, scones, and frames for looking glasses were not common products by American silversmiths.

Early American Silversmiths

Many silversmiths worked in the seventeenth and eighteenth centuries, and to attempt to list them all would require a separate volume. However, it is well worth mentioning a few of the more notable.

Robert Sanderson (1608-1693) of Hampton, New Hampshire is credited with being the first American silversmith. With his partner, John Hull, he turned out work on a par with that made in England. Sanderson moved to Watertown, Massachusetts, in 1642, where he and Hull made the famous pine tree shillings which became coin of the commonwealth at that time. Sanderson's three sons (Joseph, Benjamin, and Robert) all followed their father's trade, and all worked in the making of church plates, much of which has survived.

Samuel Casey (1723-1773) of Kingston, Rhode Island, lived an interesting life. He was caught making counterfeit coins and was sentenced by the crown to hang. However, friends spirited him away from his jail cell and he was never seen again. Needless to say, his silver is a very premium collectible.

Philip Syng had a shop in Philadelphia on Front Street amid the docks and other busy shops. He made the beautiful inkstand, which was used to hold the pen at the signing of the Declaration of Independence and the Constitution.

plate" for three dippings or "quadruple plate" for four. This process continued until the 1890s, when the method of dipping was improved to the point where only one submersion was required to deposit the necessary coating on the metal base. The public has been conditioned to the designation "quadruple plate" as a term for the best in plated ware, and rather than risk loss of sales with reference to a single plate, the old designation was used up until World War I. In the 1920s, the phrase "silver on copper" was introduced and most plated ware is so marked today. If the letters EP appear, this indicates electroplate. NS is nickel silver plate; EPNS, electroplated nickel silver; EPBM, electroplated britannia metal.

After the Civil War, plated silver came into its own. The war industries were geared to making items out of metal and when peace came, they turned their efforts to everyday items. Victorian styling was still very much in vogue, and highly decorated work began to appear since machines made mass production possible. In the hand era (before 1840) decoration was applied by chasing or engraving the outside of the piece, or by repousse (hammering it from the inside against a mold). The highly figured pieces were stamped out in sections and then soldered together and plated. This type of work is popular to this day, although the designs have changed. Some experts feel that when these pieces are re-plated they do not have the look of the originals of years ago, but this is quite easily explained. After dipping, the early makers would have each piece polished ready for the trade, usually with a substance that would turn black with use. This was allowed to remain in the cracks and crevices in order to highlight the raised shiny surfaces. A man who had worked at a silver factory before the turn of the century gave me this information. It is unlikely this technique would be duplicated today, especially if the public knew how it was done.

There is a fad today for collecting old silver pieces and having them stripped to reveal the base, which can be copper, brass, white metal, or even steel. The pieces were often made of combinations of different metals, with copper forming the places where there is less stress, and other metals used for feet, handles, finials, and spouts. This rule also applies to those pieces which were plated in nickel and, later, chromium. You should look for interesting forms, as this is most important in determining the value of such items.

England

As mentioned, America owes its heritage in silvermaking to England. The early craftsmen who came from there were trained in the most progressive techniques. Silversmiths were regulated by the crown as early as the thirteenth century with stiff penalties levied on those who attempted to defraud the public. Until then, most work had been done in gold, primarily for royalty and the church. A goldsmith's guild had been formed to police its members and upgrade the quality of work by providing for an apprentice system in order to train craftsmen properly. Some of the great early work was done in monasteries since ecclesiastical gold and silver were in great demand for communion services, salvers, crosses, and candleholders.

Butterfield & Butterfield.

George III silver, six-section mirror plateau which is a table centerpiece. Made by Benjamin Smith, London, 1807. Sold at Butterfields in Los Angeles on Sept 21, 1993, for $18,400.

Coin silver was used between about 1790 and the middle of the 19th century, to make much in tablewares. Coin spoons are popular to collect as most were signed by the makers. Value: $20 ea.

A marking system instituted in 1477 required that a leopard's head, with or without a crown, had to be stamped on every piece that met the weight of 22 shillings to the pound. Two years later, the date letter was required on every piece, and this makes it possible to document the year it was smithed. Silversmiths began stamping their pieces with touchmarks for identification about 1479. Most people were illitcratc, so these marks were important for identifying the maker. The mark might be a flower, horse head, star, moon, or some other recognizable object, which was registered as the maker's mark. Silver had to be sent to the guild hall where it was tested for purity and marked—hence the term "hallmarked."

In 1560, the sterling standard 1000 indicated pure metal (sterling was 925 parts silver and 75 parts alloy). Coin, metal from which coins of the realm were made, had 875 parts silver and 125 parts alloy. Some continental silver will be marked 800, which indicates 800 parts of silver to 200 parts of alloy. This is frequently found on metal from Germany, Italy, and Holland.

In 1794, a new system of marking appeared in England which consisted of five cartouches impressed on the back sides of tableware and on the bottom of serving and decorative pieces. Most often, the first cartouche contained the initials of the marker or makers. The next will hold the touchmark, with the head of the reigning monarch beneath it, stamped to signify that the tax had been paid. The third is the lion passant (which holds the sterling mark), and the final cartouche bears the date letter indicating the year the piece was made. Marking books help interpret these. A span of years is indicated quickly by noting the head of the reigning monarch. Male profiles will appear from 1794 until Queen Victoria's ascension to the throne in 1837. In 1892, this marking system was discontinued, so one can figure approximate dates quickly.

In America, we follow the English standards. After the Civil War, a law was passed requiring that all items of sterling be so marked to guarantee its metal content. One will find the word sterling spelled out or a mark of 925, which indicates the silver content. Some concerns, such as Tiffany, used 925/1000. If a piece is not marked in this manner, one should not assume it is sterling.

Coin silver was used in the manufacture of many items in both America and England. The height of the period was between about 1790 and 1850. Most of the teaspoons and tablespoons—those which are very thin and bend easily—were made between about 1820 and 1840. Most are well marked, which helps in identification.

The Origin of "Sterling"

The term "sterling" was adopted from the name of a group of German craftsmen known as the Easterlings who migrated to England early in the fourteenth century. Their work in refining silver to its pure standards prompted a royal edict which set forth their formula as the law of the realm. However, it was not until after the Civil War that the term was much in use in America. If you see the word "sterling" stamped on a piece, you will know that it was most likely made after this time.

Sheffield Plate and Electroplating—It was not until the eighteenth century that much silver was made for those whose station was below royalty. As England's trade with the world increased, so did the affluency of her traders and they soon became patrons of the arts and crafts. At first, production was limited to functional items such as tankards, mugs, pieces for tea and coffee sets, and tableware. A later development in production that was to have a far-reaching effect was the creation of Sheffield plate. Two centers for its production were the cities of Sheffield and Birmingham. The process was discovered about 1743 by a Sheffield metal worker. Thomas Boulsover. Originally a sheet of silver was bonded to one side of a copper ingot by rolling or hammering. After 1765, the silver was introduced to both sides of the copper. These were rolled and pounded to remove any air between them. Then, the metals were heated until the silver began to melt and the unit was rolled into a thin sheet with the copper sandwiched between the silver layers. Pieces could then be fashioned from plated metal. Silver solder was used at the seams, which were hidden by burnishing and polishing.

Sheffield plate became very popular in both Europe and America, but there is no evidence that this type of plate was actually made in this country. One will find many examples here in the Georgian style, but since it is not sterling, none of it is marked. When Sheffield plate wears, the copper will shine through the edges of the repousse decoration. One should not electroplate Sheffield to hide this, as this destroys its value.

China

The Chinese-American trade brought with it a Chinese export silver of very good quality. A great deal of this silver came into America during the nineteenth century; yet it has been only recently that sufficient research has been done to make identification possible.

For some time, collectors and appraisers came upon pieces of "English" Georgian silver with silver marks that could not be found in marking books, hence the designation of "unrecorded maker." It was not until 1975, that this mystery was solved. The former Museum of the American China Trade, which was located in Milton, Massachusetts, published the book *Chinese Export Silver,* written by the director, Dr. H.A. Crosby Forbes, John Devereux, and Ruth S. Wilkins. In it, the authors document Georgian-style silver made in nineteenth-century China and stamped with phony British hallmarks. A coffeepot marked "SS" within a cartouche had been identified by a museum as being made by Silas Sawin, an eighteenth-century New York silvermaker. The mark proved to be that of Sunshing, who worked in the middle of the 19th century in Shanghai.

The collections of the Museum of the American China Trade are now at the Peabody Institute in Salem, Massachusetts. A copy of the book on Chinese silver is available there or you may order it (see the *Bibliography*).

Denmark

When one discusses Danish silver, the name Georg Jensen heads the list of those who are known to have been great craftsmen in that country. Jensen (1866-1935) opened his shop in Copenhagen in 1904. Originally a sculptor, he turned his talents toward designing and making silver items now considered to be some of the greatest examples of Art Nouveau and Art Deco styles. The Georg Jensen Company carries on the tradition of excellent design and production. From 1909, the majority of production was exported and sold in Jensen's own shops in Berlin, Stockholm, Paris, London, New York, and other major cities.

Other early twentieth-century designers include Johan Rohde, Harold Neilson, Sigvard Bernadotte, and Henning Koppel. Kay Bojesen was apprenticed to Jensen in 1907 and went on to establish his own company in 1958. His silver is much like Jensen's in style—undecorated and very functional. Great makers include Evald Nielsen (1879-1958), Frantz Hingelberg (who worked in Aarhus as early as 1897), Holger Kyster who worked c. 1898-1944, Hans Hansen (1884-1940), Morgins Ballin (1871-1914), and Peter Hertz (1811-1885). Some were appointed to the royal court.

Before World War II, much fine Danish silver was sent to a museum in the United States for safekeeping. Much of it is still here, the former owners having disappeared during the war. Makers' marks appear on all Danish silver made between 1490 and 1893. Since then, retailers have added their names to the makers' marks as well.

France

There is a new interest in early French silver today, but very little is available here. Actually, many of the styles popularized in England in the late seventeenth and early eighteenth centuries were created by Huguenot craftsmen who left their country after the Edict of Nantes was revoked in 1685, again denying them freedom from religious persecution. Among those who fled to England were the forebears of Paul Lamerie, who was destined to become England's most noted silversmith. Other Huguenots who had great influence were Peter Platel and Anthony Nelme. The workmen who were not affected by the Edict of Nantes continued to work in France, turning out the same quality of work as that made in England.

Japan

Collectors are well aware of a wide range of antique and contemporary works from Japan, including porcelains, paintings, prints, furniture, and the like. However, not much attention is being given to handmade silver by Dresser and Tiffany which is being sought today.

Christopher Dresser was born in Scotland. He was a silversmith who believed that items made of this metal should be functional. He traveled to Japan to seek new ideas in design and this resulted in a book, *Japan: Its Architecture, Art and Art Manufactures,* which was published in 1882. This set off a round of imitation of these designs by craftsmen throughout the world, which some feel gave birth to the Art Nouveau movement. Dresser's work at his plants in Sheffield and Birmingham resulted in pieces which often are mistaken for work in this century as it reflected the Art Nouveau influence which prevailed into the 1920s.

Louis Comfort Tiffany must have been inspired by Dresser's book, as he was a leader in the movement. One will note the resemblance to decorative ideas seen in the porcelain, paintings, prints, etc., in the form of animals, birds, fish, flowers and other inspirations taken from nature. Look for marks to determine provenance and quality of the silver. The few pieces I have seen at the Tokyo Museum do not seem to enjoy the quality of our sterling at 925/1000, but not being able to see the marks underneath, this is only an observation. If you travel to Japan, the elegant native silver work is something you should seek.

Identifying Reproductions

Most buyers of silver realize that any sort of marking system is not without its hazards, as fakers have been at work to turn it to their advantage. It is not too difficult to cast a die in the exact mold of an early touchmark, and then impress it on a later piece whose style and workmanship will not give it away. Another trick is to cut an authentic hallmark from a lesser piece and insert it in a more important one to increase its value. The marks from a spoon can be imbedded in the bottom of a teapot, as silver is quite malleable and this work can be done well enough to fool the naked eye. However, such fakery can be detected by the use of lights and close examination. Another method is to breathe on the piece—the moisture will reveal any reconstruction work. Experts who study shapes and forms can readily tell if there has been any tampering. Not long ago, a fine pair of candlesticks with marks of a mid-eighteenth century maker were sold as his work. However, he worked in a period when the style they represented could not have been made. Needless to say, the

Spoons by Paul Revere, who was not only a patriot, but also a fine silversmith, during the late 18th into the 19th century. These were made c. 1790 in the Old English pattern. Value: $2,500

smarter dealers offered no bids at the auction. You would not expect to find Federal period styling done by a maker quite prominent in the rococo period, which preceded it, especially when none of his known work reflects this design.

Design and Style

Decorating silver is an exacting art, and there are several ways in which it was done. Perhaps the first technique was engraving, which was done with a sharp tool to remove the metal where it is cut. The term "bright cut" is used so that there will be more brilliance as it reflects light. Chasing resembles engraved work, but it is done with a tool which impresses the design, thus removing no metal. Repousse is done by hammering a body of

Bennington Museum.

Silver caster by Benjamin Lord, Rutland, Vermont, 1770-1843. The only known piece of hollowware made by Lord and the only known piece of hollowware made in the 18th century form.

silver from the inside to produce a raised surface with a shaped decoration. A gadroon or fluted decoration around rims was very popular. Some pieces, such as feet, handles, spouts, and finials, were cast and then joined by silver soldering to the main body. Polishing with a jeweler's rouge erases the markings of such joined work.

You can trace the design of silver easily, as it followed the tastes in furniture. Pieces were made to compliment room settings of furniture, and with such a clue you can reasonably ascribe the period of its manufacture. In the eighteenth century, silversmiths worked in pure forms, with little thought to fancy design or decoration. The Queen Anne period brought with it grace and elegance in curves and a delicate style, which was reflected in all the decorative arts. The mid-century styles of Chippendale influenced the arts with their rococo decoration. This became especially popular after the excavations in Greece and Italy, which created a revival of interest in classical decorative forms.

After the Revolutionary War, the austerity of Hepplewhite brought a return to dignity, expressed through straight lines and less embellishment. What is known now, as the Federal style was quite popular well into the 1830s, after which machines began to erode the quality of silver work. The gaudy productions of the Empire and Victorian periods were in keeping with the furniture of that time, and have only recently been accepted on a wide scale for collecting. Until now, no silver collector would have allowed any nineteenth century silver made after 1830 into his collection. Recent studies into the decorative arts have revealed that much silver was still handmade after 1830, and regardless of style, it represents the craftsmanship of the times. Rather than being made by individual small shops as in the past, large factories were set up to take care of the growing demand for the product at the time of America's great industrial growth.

Pewter

Historical Overview

Pewter is made by casting, hammering, or lathe spinning on a mold. Generally, ornamentation is simple, consisting mostly of rims, molding, or engraving. However, some continental pewter (especially that of the Renaissance period in France and Germany) has intricate ornamentation.

Ecclesiastical pewter was common in churches unable to afford the more expensive silver. Pictured are two communion cups, flagon, and salver. Many sets were sold at auction when affluent church members donated the silver replacements. Value: $1,500

Early on, pewter was used in the Far East, and Roman pieces are known to exist. England was a major center of production from the Middle Ages, and, until China replaced it, pewter was the chief tableware. America imported much English pewter in colonial times and, starting in 1700, began producing its own in large quantities.

Pewter is composed primarily of tin, with the basic formula being 90% tin plus 10% antimony, copper, or other alloys. Lead can be added to give it weight. This is a good clue to Continental pewter, since American and English pewter are lighter in comparison. It is felt that the lead content helped to promote the poisoning of food and caused illness in may of its users. Fortunately, American makers used little or no lead in their production.

Since pewter is soft the pieces would not survive, and they would be taken to a local pewterer, who melted them down in order to recast into new pieces. As payment for his services he retained part of the metal, using it for his own new production. This practice helped diminish the available supply

of eighteenth-century pewter, since so much of it was melted down. The Revolutionary War also helped to create this shortage, as much plate was melted down for bullets. Pewter cannot withstand high temperatures, and any piece coming in contact with excessive heat will be damaged or destroyed instantly. A lot of the early production must have been lost in this manner.

Following the lead of the silversmiths, the pewterers were conscientious in marking their handmade pieces. Those pieces, which were cast in molds, were less likely to be marked. Other makers would not mark pieces, hoping to mislead the public into thinking that they were buying imported pewter, which was considered to be of finer quality.

In the eighteenth century, a shortage of tin plagued American pewter makers. They were entirely dependent on exports as there was no established source in America at the time. Plenty of English pewter was shipped in to take care of the demand and this in effect helped provide the material for some American production.

American Pewterers

Almost every community had its resident pewterer. The pewterer might have been no more than a reworker of metal who had equipped himself with molds into which melted down scrap could be poured. Craftsmen who worked with the hammer and primitive lathes were in the minority, and it is this handwork, which brings top dollar today.

Roswell Gleason—Roswell Gleason worked as a pewterer from 1822-1871 in Dorchester, Massachusetts. His plant used both the old pewter metal as well as the newer Britannia metal in turning out many pieces, which are high on collecting lists today. He is regarded as a top craftsman in the field, as his designs were pure in form and the execution of them was impeccable.

Early in his career, he utilized the popular eagle mark as a touch on his work, but later used "R. Gleason," impressed on the bottom. Any piece with both the eagle mark and his name is worth more than the name alone. Also, he used the Massachusetts coat of arms on some pieces and these are highly desired. Some pieces have his first name spelled out in full, but there is no premium for this.

Gleason is known to have made coffee and tea pots and related items; candleholders, communion sets, coffee urns, water pitchers with covers, mugs, syrup jugs, and even cuspidors. The latter, though very rare, will not command much money because of the lack of desirability for such a piece. In his book *American Pewter* (Bonanza), J.B. Kerfoot illustrates an unusual tankard that boasts a top which screws on instead of being hinged. Kerfoot opines that it may have been a communion piece in which a priest might carry consecrated wine safely to the home of an ill person. If one were to begin collecting pewter (Britannia) of the nineteenth century, he would be well advised to begin with the quality pieces of Gleason.

Zachariah Stevens and His Apprentices— About 1820, Zachariah Stevens moved from England to Maine where he set up shop as a tin knocker in the small town of Stevens Plains, which was eventually named after him. This is just north of Portland and the name has since been changed to Westbrook.

From his shop came some of the most desired pieces of painted tin (his wife and daughters did the decorating). Stevens trained Freeman and Allen Porter, both of whom became pewterers who went on their own and worked together, Freeman (1835-1860s) and Allen (1830-1840) made some of the most collectible examples of pewter in all forms. The pieces are well marked. (If one finds F. Porter on silver, this is the mark of Franklin Porter who worked in New York City c. 1820s). Another apprentice to Stevens was Rufus Dunham (1837-1861) of Westbrook who founded R. Dunham and Sons of Portland (1861-1882). Dunham pieces are also well marked.

Another to seek is Israel Trask (1807-1856) of Beverly, Massachusetts. (All of the above worked in Britannia metal). It would take an entire book to write about the early pewter workers like the Will family in Philadelphia, the Boadmans and Danforths in Connecticut, etc. One should study books on them if interested in collecting eighteenth-century pieces.

Collecting Guidelines

The availability of eighteenth-century American pewter is quite limited. Serious collectors have been buying it for years and, along with museums and historical societies, they have locked up most of it from the general trade channels. An estate will occasionally come up for sale with such early pieces, and prices seem to skyrocket every year as the demand exceeds the supply. There are books providing identification of makers by name and touchmark listed in the bibliography, so there is no great mystery in identifying pewter. You must be careful of fake touches as these will crop up from time to time, but they are the great minority, so do not worry too much about it. Pewter has not been considered a valuable commodity until recently, so there has been little reason to doctor it. Until now, most pewter had gone to serious buyers who would recognize any alteration and there has been little incentive for fakery. Now that that public acceptance has broadened for the product, it is only natural to assume that some unscrupulous people will attempt to take advantage of those with limited knowledge, so the danger is now more present than ever. You should only rely on competent dealers for advice. When an estate is settled, you may also buy with relative safety, as the collector put his stamp of approval on the price just by owning it. If an auctioneer suspects that later work had been done on an item, he will gladly give you the benefit of this advice if you ask him during the pre-sale inspection.

Elegant coffeepot by William Will of Philadelphia, 1764-1798. Many feel him to be America's finest pewterer. He served as salt commissioner for George Washington in the Revolution.

Tankard by Henry Will, Albany and New York City, 1761-1793. There were several members of the Will family who were prominent pewterers. Value: $12,500

Teapot by William Will, Philadelphia, 1764-1798. The pear shape was popular in this period.

Woodenware in kitchens gave way to pewter early in the eighteenth century, both in America and abroad, but a century later, pewter suffered a decline in the face of competition from the expanding ceramics and glass industries. Its final ignominy came after the 1850s at the hands of the silver platers who used Britannia bodies for their wares, covering up the metal, which was once so important to the well being and economy of the world. Collectors who recognize the forms are having these pieces stripped of their blackened and fading silverplate, restoring them to greater interest and value. Much of the early Reed and Barton silverware made in Taunton, Massachusetts, during this period could be plated Britannia.

Handmade Pewter

Casting pewter in a mold would often leave pits and hollows in the metal. These would be filled with a soldering iron using scrap pewter metal or solder. The piece would then be placed in a lathe and "skimmed" by holding a sharp tool against it, shaving off any rough spots and raised imperfections. A spiral mark would quite often be left from this process and it will still be visible. Pieces which were completely hand hammered are most desired, and this work can usually be noted at the booge, where the hammer marks will be most visible.

An early porringer can often be identified by the method in which the handle has been attached. The body would be formed, and then a mold for the handle would be held against it in proper position. The body would be hung over an anvil or other support during this process, and a wet rag or burlap would be used to prevent contact between the piece and the support. When hot pewter was poured into the handle mold, it would melt and fuse with the body, but the body would also soften enough to absorb an imprint where the handle was attached. This "crosshatching," as it is called, indicates the manner in which a piece was made.

Machine-Made Pewter

Mechanization began creeping slowly into industry in the mid-1790s, when Josiah Wedgwood introduced machinery, which speeded up his production in ceramics. But it was not until after the War of 1812 that such progress made any great impact in America. The approximate date used for the beginning of the industrial age is 1830, which coincides with the deterioration of all decorative art, pewter being no exception. By this time, a harder metal called Brittania was in general use. Developed in England during the eighteenth century, the Brittania formula does not seem to have come into general use in America until after 1820. By 1830, most work was in Brittannia, and by 1840, most was machine made. Some work was done by molding, and other work was turned out individually on lathes powered by steam or water. Wooden forms were created in the sizes of dishes or bowls, and these would be fastened in a lathe with a sheet of Brittannia held against them. As the mold and metal were spun, the artisan would hold a steel tool against the metal, molding it to the wooden shape. The piece would then be removed and finished at the workbench, where rims could be worked, and feet, handles, spouts, and the like could be added by soldering. Some very collectible work was done during this period and though not as valuable as the earlier production, it has found great favor with collectors who must settle for second best. Actually, much desirable production was done as late as the 1880s, especially in the newer parts of the country, where artisans worked with less sophisticated tools for a longer period.

Marks

In the British Isles, it was a requirement that all pewter be marked by the maker. The letter X could be added to signify a superior metal. So long as the mark is visible, the marking books help in identifying provenance, maker, and age. Since American pewter of the eighteenth century has ascended to such high prices, there is growing interest for that made overseas. Fortunately, American and British pieces do not contain lead, much of which was used in Continental and Scandinavian pewter, making it heavier. Some feel it is not advisable to eat from dishes with lead content. One good clue in collection is that if the word pewter appears stamped on the bottom of a piece, it is not considered collectible. This stamp indicates a factory mark used from the late nineteenth century to the present. It is the handmade product which has value.

There is much unmarked pewter which could be American and it is being bought by those who hope for a magic formula, which will someday unlock the secret of its origin. Some appears with an eagle touch, which would seem American, but is yet unidentified as to the maker.

Design and Style

Some collectors feel that the rolled edge of a plate or dish could signify country of origin; if it is rolled on the top, it's English; if rolled on the underside, American. There is little to support this theory as it is generally accepted that most American pewterers were trained in England and practiced those techniques here. Tom Williams, perhaps the best-known dealer/collector in the country, told me that if a dish has a hammered booge (a curve raised wall at the bottom of plates and dishes), this is a indication of English work.

Measurements are not much of a clue to country of origin, though no one can authenticate an American charger which measures more than sixteen inches in diameter (known English pieces are larger). You should refer to any flat piece less than nine inches in diameter as a plate, and any nine inches or greater in diameter as a dish. The latter may also be referred to as trenchers or chargers, as these are old English names for serving dishes.

After about 1820, Britannia metal, a harder form of pewter, was in general use in this country and England. Mid 19th century coffeepots like this one were spun on a lathe with handles, spouts, and covers added. Value: $250

Little engraving or chasing was done on pewter in this country. Some European work was decorated in this manner. It is noticeably absent on church communion service, as most of these must have been presentation pieces. However, unlike silver, pewter presentation pieces were rarely marked.

Oriental pewter has been imported for a long time, but it is of poor quality with a heavy lead content. Some work which is mistaken for pewter might even be made of white metal which colors to resemble it greatly. The weight of the piece is a clue to its contents—you must learn to "feel" pewter as well as look at it.

Forms in pewter are important. Items with interesting shapes make ideal shelf and decorative pieces, and are most in demand. Tankards, chargers, whale oil lamps, porringers, sets of measures, posset cups, salts, tea caddies, tea and coffee pots, candle holders, and tureens are ideal items. Rare items like wine funnels and pumps, brandy warmers, barber's basins, chamber pots, and medical items may be in short supply, but are also in short demand. Some enthusiasts like to collect church pewter, such as the beakers, salvers, and flagons used for communion, but these are rare since most churches have disposed of theirs by now.

Pewter should be more decorative than functional, so it is those pieces with beauty of design and great handcraftsmanship which command the highest interest and prices. Proportions and workmanship are vital, but the most important feature is identification with a maker. Some experts feel that Americans pursue this too much as a prerequisite to collecting, and that the piece should stand on its own merit, regardless of maker. This is high idealism and the collecting fraternity is not yet ready for it, so unless you have money to burn, do not get too involved with unmarked pewter.

Cleaning

If pewter is black and scaly with age, do not attempt to clean it yourself. This work should be done by those equipped for it. Good cleaning requires dipping or scouring with such materials as hydrochloric acid, and this can be dangerous work. It must be done under ideal conditions in a well-ventilated area. The acid must be neutralized at the proper moment—so that not too much metal is lost, and so that the touchmarks remain distinct. You find that pieces such as the large chargers are oil impregnated, which makes cleaning quite difficult. It is best to steer away from pewter in this condition. Avoid pewter which has been highly polished, as most collectors want it to retain a soft patina. It has been argued that the metal was originally shiny and that restoring it in this manner should not hurt it. Maybe this is true, but you must recognize that others may not share this opinion, and that the majority of buyers want pewter to have an aged look, if possible. You may have difficulty in selling the shiny product, and therefore, it is not a good investment.

Brass, Iron, and Tin

Historical Overview

Brass, bronze, copper, iron, and tin are metals which have always been used for functional and decorative objects. They are less exotic than gold or silver and do not command anywhere near the same prices. Prices for most items made of these metals have not increased in the same ratio as for many of the other decorative arts, because it is impossible to document them. Craftspeople have never stopped handmaking pieces with these metals and most did not mark them. Therefore, there is no way to determine provenance. For example, brass pushup candleholders, which appeared in the eighteenth century, are still being made. One that is only forty years old will have acquired quite a good patina. Also, there are some shops that will antique them for you with acid, which takes only a few moments. To call some pieces old and some reproductions is not quite correct. How aged must a piece be before it is considered old? And age is not the only factor in determining value.

Brass

Brass is an alloy of copper and zinc. The proportions of each in the mixture determine the hardness of the metal. Brass has been known since ancient times, so there is a history of brass work with which to compare contemporary pieces. As mentioned, the values of brass items pale in comparison to the prices being paid for furniture, glass, silver, ceramics, and the like. A simple redware decorated dish can command up to a thousand dollars, but there are very few pieces of brass that can equal that, no matter how exotic they are.

Most of the eighteenth-century brass you find will have originated in England. There was very little American manufactured which can be documented, and we know that very little was made because of the shortage of materials. Some good Continental brass has arrived, and more is being imported today than ever before. The Mediterranean countries are a good source of brass, as a lot is being discarded by housewives there who are turning to Teflon and stainless steel for cooking. They are tired of polishing brass, and they are quite happy to relinquish this role to the American housewife, who will in time realize that it can be a chore. Dealers tell me that more brass is sold to men than women—men will take it home as a gift, but will rarely participate in cleaning it. The abundance of the product along with the shortage of help to take care of it is a contributing factor to the lack of interest in brass as a collectible. You must survey your needs and your desire to clean it before buying.

Iron

Iron was the metal most readily available to the American colonists, as huge bogs were discovered

Brass fireplace fender with reticulated decoration. I have never seen an old example that was not made in England. Value: $450

right in New England. Bog iron was found in the area around Plymouth and throughout what is now called the greater Boston area. Saugus was the home of the first iron works (dating back to 1636) and the location has been fully restored to its original condition for all to visit. The original pounding hammer was found beneath many layers of earth and has been re-installed to pound iron today. Bog iron is found in marshes or even at the bottom of lakes and ponds. The Saugus marshes and locations in Braintree and Needham yield much iron. The ponds in Gilmanton, New Hampshire, were rich in pure ore. Salisbury, New York, was the site of early ironmaking, as were many locations in Pennsylvania. Ore was mined in those states, and right after the Revolution, coal was used to melt it. The Pennsylvania Historical and Museum Commission has restored some ironmaking locations including those at Hopewell Village, near Reading, and the Cornwall Furnace, near Hershey.

In the 1800s, machines came into their own and coal became readily available to all who wanted it. This resulted in a tremendous expansion of America's iron and steelmaking facilities. The center of the business shifted toward the Pittsburgh area as both iron and coal were available there in great quantity. Birmingham, Alabama became a center for steelmaking and supplied the South during the Civil War. I would need several volumes to discuss everything that was made in iron and steel since then. Much of it, right through the Art Deco period, is being collected today.

Tin

Until recently, tin languished in the role of inexpensive commodity as far as collecting was concerned. Even the Historical Society of Early American Decoration, Inc., founded in the memory of Esther Stevens Brazer, gave little impetus to collecting tin for a long time. Decorating tin is now

Hopewell Forge is in Pennsylvania—where wood heaters were made and shipped throughout the country. Many have fancy molding.

Lighting devices of many kinds were wrought of iron. Shown are 18th century rush and candleholders and a fat lamp.

Esther Brazer at the Bump Tavern in Cooperstown New York, which is part of the Farmer's Museum complex.

Early American decoration may be divided into the following classifications; stenciling on tin and wood, country painting, gold leaf painting, lace edge painting, freehand bronze, glass panels, and Chippendale painting. The Esther Stevens Brazer Guild had established specific categories of craftsmanship for the execution of techniques found in each. Chapters of the aforementioned Society are set up in all the New England states (with the exception of Rhode Island), and in New York, New Jersey, Maryland, Illinois, and Pennsylvania.

Collecting Guidelines

Brass

Brass bells are popular, though most do not command much money. A special bell-metal was formed with the introduction of tin to the mixture and most bells are made of this. Paul Revere is noted for his bells, and if you find one bearing his stamp of manufacture, you are indeed fortunate. However, ordinary school, dinner, and farm bells are relatively inexpensive. Sleigh bells of brass or bell metal are most in demand. Some are chrome plated, so you should use a magnet to check the metal if you are not sure.

a great and rewarding pastime and more attention is being given to this poor man's metal than ever before. Decorators are looking for interesting shapes and forms on which to paint their designs, causing an upsurge in prices. You can see the patterns and research material accumulated by

Provenance of decoration tin document boxes can often be determined by the style of decoration. One must get books to identify them.

Full-bodied weathervane figures are more desirable than those cut out of sheet metals. This 19th century brass cow was found appropriately on a barn in Vermont. Value: $3,500

Much ecclesiastical brass was turned out in the shape of candlesticks, candelabra, and even entire altars. Some is sold surreptitiously on the open market, but much is sold legitimately. A transfer to a new church structure will often attract donations of new church artifacts, and old may be sold to benefit the treasury. However, some pastors in Europe have recently been liquidating church brass to dealers in order to raise funds for operation. Over the years, many churches have received numerous donations of objects, which have fallen into disuse or disrepair and rather than continue storing them, will clandestinely dispose of them. Since a great disturbance was raised over this procedure several years ago, most of it has come to a halt.

Brass candlesticks are quite common, including those dating back to the eighteenth century. There are some from as far back as the sixteenth century that have come to America in recent years. Most were made in England, though you will find Flemish design in some early pieces. The early ones may have a spike or pricket on which the candle could be

One of a pair of brass whale oil lamps, Newburyport, Connecticut, c. 1840s. Examples in brass are rare and the dolphin handles are unique. Value of pair: $1,200

imbedded for support. However, these went out of favor with the appearance of the socket modified by the pushup stem beneath, which allowed one to advance the candle upward to make full use of all of it and made for easier cleaning. The dripless candle was unknown in the early days; so all holders had a drip pan to catch the residue, which could then be recast into a new candle. The bases of candlesticks are no clue to their age—they can be found in square, round, oval, octagonal, and hexagonal shapes, and perhaps in many others as well. Some collectors have stated that a good candlestick would have been made in two sections with a screw assembly to tighten them together. This work was often done in the seventeenth century, and the holder would certainly show their age to confirm this.

You must be careful not to confuse these with holders from the Orient, which were made in great abundance in this manner in the 19th century and into the present one. You should accept this screw base as a sign of recent rather than old manufacture 99 percent of the time. When whale oil became popular about 1820, candlesticks were pressed into service to hold oil lamps which featured a candle-size peg at their base so that they might be inserted into a candleholder. These are called "peg lamps" and may sometimes be found in brass, though glass was used most often.

Brass was used for inlaying furniture, with spectacular results. This art reached its pinnacle in France and Italy. Andre Boulle (1642-1732) worked under the patronage of Louis XIV, and succeeded in turning out work which is the epitome of this form. There was a revival of this work in the early nineteenth century, but none is known to have been done in America. Ormolu mounts of brass were popular at this time, and were used as decoration at corners, feet, and handles. This style was most popular in France and Italy, but some work was also done in England.

Bronze

Since bronze is a close cousin to brass, I might note that there is tremendous interest in the decorative arts which use this metal. Notable are the bronze figures, most of which were done in France and even Russia. The signed bronzes are most popular and valuable. Subject interest is paramount and those with animals in action are quite desirable. Those with solitary figure standing are least desired. The bronzes which depict motion of man or beast are among the best. You must be sure of the metal before investing, as many famous renditions have been reproduced in various other alloys such as spelter, which is a cheap metal with a high zinc content, or even white metal, which is about the cheapest iron-based substitute you can find. White metal contains iron, tin, albata, electrum, argentine, and other metals of lesser nature. A class of bronzes done during the Renaissance in Italy is quite desirable, but it is unlikely that you will find any here. Also, these bronzes have been reproduced over the years, making attribution very difficult. Little or no serious bronze work was done in this country. The bronzes to which the Tiffany name is attached were most often done in France or Russia.

Some of the bronze work being done today is commanding huge prices if done by recognized artists. Some of those done a hundred years ago in France may languish in value because of a lack of desirability. Some collectors are happier buying the work of known contemporary makers than investing in the older pieces, which have no history.

Butterfield & Butterfield.

Contemporary bronze by Malvina Hoffman, Bacchanale Russe, 1917, height 40". Motion is desired in bronzes. Sold by Butterfields in Los Angeles, April 6, 1992 for $33,000.

Nude figure tin bronze, atop a marble base; art deco, c. 1920s. There is no mark as to maker, but its design and quality mark it as a major piece. Most likely European. Value: $4,250

Copper

Copper also has a close kinship to brass. Being a soft metal, it is easily formed, has good color, and can withstand the heat of cooking and other abuse. About all that can be said for brass can be said for this metal. However, there are some exceptions. Horse ornaments, bells, doorknockers, fireplace equipment, warming pans, and candleholders are scarce in copper. It was used a great deal in the making of cooking utensils, which were then tinned on the interior so food would not come in contact with the copper. Brass must have seemed more like gold, hence its greater popularity. Actually, copper could have been used to make just about anything in metal. There were specific uses for it, especially in weathervanes, copper and shot pouches, canteens, daggers, knives and ale warmers. Less spectacularly, it was used as sheathing for wooden vessels as early as the mid-eighteenth century. Along with brass and bronze, it was used as a base for cloisonné, champleve, and enameling.

Copper was not favored as it turns green with age and attrition, and therefore, requires more care than brass or other metals. Food could not be cooked or stored in it, nor did it have the strength of other metals for use in heavy tools. It was used in coinage, and perhaps here one will find its greatest value.

Great weathervane figure in copper, 19th century, with a steam pumper, horses, and firemen.

Brass locks and keys are popular, no matter what country they come from. The door locks are used in restorations, and the padlocks are used as decorative items. Locks for furniture did not become popular until the middle of the eighteenth century. Some of these locks are stamped with the names of the makers, which will heighten interest, if not value.

You will find skillets, shoehorns, tobacco boxes, sundials, spirit measures, spoons, trivets, and weights and measures in brass. You must judge these on their interesting qualities and condition. Repairs to brass are quite visible and must be done in good taste and not offensive. Warming pans sell reasonably, but are of interest. They are judged by their pleasing proportions, condition, and above all by the beautiful or unique pierced design in the cover. Almost all warming pans found in America came from England, though some must be from other countries. There was little or no manufacture of these pans in America. Handles have often been replaced, so you must judge the condition of it at the time of buying.

Reproductions—The problem of reproduction is present, as there are workers today still turning out products which have an eighteenth and early nineteenth century look. Banging a piece up a bit, charring it over a fire, and allowing the iron handles and fittings to rust a little can create an aura of age that can fool the neophyte. You have only to visit a country like Holland to see the tremendous amount of this work going on. The once popular coal hods with Delft handles are now a drag on the market; the sale of the new has hurt the old.

There are several good makers of weathervanes and lighting devices whose works age rapidly in the outdoors. Some are antiqued with chemicals to give them a good aged look, and once they have been used for several years it is difficult to separate them from the truly old, especially if the pieces were cast in sand molds. The roughness can fool you, so you must know from whom you are buying before investing much money.

There is a lot of trinket collecting in brass. Snuff boxes, military buttons, telescopes and binoculars, sextants and octants, ship's clocks, cuspidors, horse-related items (hames, stirrups, brass handled buggy whips), early belt buckles, cigar cutters, stencils, and drinking mugs are popular. Powder and shot holders from the Revolutionary War have value. Whale oil lamps are rarest of all, as most were made of glass, tin, or pewter. Those with interesting shapes and proportion are most desired. Look for signed fireplace equipment, as some makers were diligent in this.

Perhaps the most reproduced forms in brass are the chamber candleholders and candle chandeliers. The former are still being turned out all over the world, with many coming from the Orient. You must understand that 90 percent of the world's population is still lighted by candle or oil and that these chamber holders are very much a part of present day culture. Chandeliers are being made for historical societies and others who are restoring old homes to their original elegance. The early ones were mostly from England, so the reproductions have the same look and are quite well done. You would have to examine them closely to tell the difference. Candelabra were popular, though few early ones are found today. You will do just as well by locating contemporary reproductions as they are faithfully done and in good taste. I might note that at the Peterhof Palace of Elizabeth, Empress of Russia, near St. Petersburg, a hundred people were employed each evening just to light the candles, replace them, and put them out at dawn.

Brass inkwell from England, late 19th century. A great collectible as these were made in many metals, ceramics, and glass. With a double cover, this type was used for travel. Value: $75-$100

Door knockers in brass are quite popular. They are reproduced in great quantities today, and as they age, it becomes difficult to tell when they were made. Present-day sand casting leaves rough marks and impressions similar to those found on the old. Knockers gained popularity in England in the eighteenth century and were brought to America to become part of the popular culture. The eagle, lion, horse, and dog were popular motifs. Rams, flowers, dolphins, and even clenched fists were also included.

Iron

Since iron was readily available, it was used for just about everything where a strong metal was needed. Kitchen pots, pans, and utensils; carpentry and husbandry tools, weapons, horse equipment, lighting devices, door locks, hardware of all kinds, and nails and spikes were all products of pre-1800 manufacture. These items are collectible from the eighteenth century on.

Iron lighting devises have soared in value recently. Both floor and table models of old rush holders and candleholders are of importance. There is one glaring problem, however, and that is in determining the age of iron artifacts. I have seen excellent reproductions aged in a hurry via salt and manure piles—a year or two of this unorthodox treatment can fill iron with pits, rust, and lines which can fool experienced eyes. When someone tells me a piece of iron is old and that he knows this merely by examination, I am quite suspect about his qualifications as an appraiser. I feel that too much money is being paid for "eighteenth century" iron, as I knew a blacksmith (now deceased) who could duplicate it in a year. Hang on to your money before investing great sums in old iron. You may be joining the ever-growing club of losers. Buy only that iron which has documentation if you are spending a great sum.

Lynn Poirier, former director of the Mercer Museum in Doylestown, Pennsylvania has researched old lighting devices in the huge collection there. It is her opinion, after examining old records, inventories, accounts of blacksmith shops, etc., that no rush lighting devices were made in America. She has found no evidence that they were a native product, rather that they must have come from overseas. One must be careful in the use of the term "Early American lighting devices."

Likewise, iron kettles, tin trays, bun baskets, coffee pots, tea caddies, etc., are still coming from

Fireplace back plates often were made with the name of the maker molded on them. This is a rarity with the name of Henry William Stiegel of Pennsylvania, who was noted for glass, which he made. He married an ironmaster's daughter and took over the foundry—a location in which he later made glass.

foundries, cast in the same forms which have been used for centuries and decorated in the manner of the old. Antique weathervanes, some andirons and other fireplace equipment, bed warmers, apple butter kettles, whale oil lamps, buckets, and similar items will often rise in value if the provenance is documented.

One must be careful when buying old iron objects, such as rush candleholders, betty lamps, cruizies, Hessian andirons, L&H hinges, kettle cranes, etc., as they are still being made today.

Tin

Tin is an important base for decoration as many country items were made from it. There were many noted early decorators such as the Butlers in upstate New York and Zachariah Stevens in what is now Westbrook, Maine. Their work, along with that of many unrecorded others, has enabled students to classify the decorations as originating in specific regions. Tin items with existing old decorations have climbed quite high in value. Those pieces that are not decorated but are just old items used about the kitchen and home are climbing in value as artists compete with each other for unusual pieces to decorate. This is a very rewarding area of collecting. You can take classes in decorating techniques, either painting or stenciling, and make yourself a good income by buying, decorating, and selling old tin items.

Tin candle molds are made in many sizes. Usually, they are priced by the number of molds. These have been reproduced, for many years. Value: $50-$60

The late Peter Ompir from Sheffield, Massachusetts and Mona Rowell of Pepperell, Massachusetts have already created a legion of fans who have bought and are buying everything decorated by these two artisans. Tin is very prominent in their work.

Areas of Collecting Interest

Bottle Tickets

Bottle tickets were beverage labels used in eighteenth and nineteenth century England and America before modern packaging techniques. They ranged in design from early rectangles, shields, and crescents to elaborate nineteenth-century labels bearing foxes, grapes, leaves, and cupids. They were made primarily of silver, but one can find them in ivory, mother-of-pearl, and Battersea and Staffordshire enamels. They can appear as boar tusks mounted to represent hunting bugles and some are even set on tiger claws.

The names on the labels provide an intriguing look at the drinking habits of our affluent ancestors. Whiskey, port, brandy, and sherry were the most popular, but occasionally one will find such exotic names as Vidonia, Sillery, Pommery, and Vin de Grave, which are drinks unknown to us today.

The earliest tickets seem to be those which came into use in the middle of the seventeenth century with the introduction of glass bottles. By 1784, an act of parliament in London officially named the labels, "Bottle Tickets" and decreed that they must bear the name of the maker. After the invention of die casting in 1794, the feathered borders and simple designs of the handmade examples developed into more elaborate decoration. By 1810, silversmiths were adding cupids, grapes, lions, shells, monograms, and crests to their work. In the 1830s, cut out initials and names became common in design, and tickets were often attached to the bottle with a silver ring instead of a chain. By 1860, the introduction of clear bottles and the sale of individual bottles, rather than casks or barrels for home consumption, prompted the use of paper labels. The names of American silversmiths have not been found on bottle tickets collected in this country which date before 1850. Tiffany and Gorham made them late in the nineteenth century and into this one.

Brass Beds

Most collectors are not aware that brass beds are really not made entirely of brass. The metal is an alloy of copper and zinc and is quite soft. Bedposts and rails made of it would not support the weight to which they are exposed, so one will find that the framing members are either brass-plated steel or steel posts sheathed in a brass casing. Solid brass will be found where there is ornamental decoration and filigree and often in the ball finials found atop bedposts. Structurally, however, the base metal is steel for strength and support.

If you wish to check your bed, locate a magnet and apply it to the metal. The magnet will be attracted to steel, but not to the solid brass. One should not feel he is cheated—all brass beds are made this way.

Know the rules in brass beds—the fancier the better; the more filigree and decoration, the more desirable. Condition is important, so if the posts are worn and tarnished, most often they need replating, which is expensive. Those kept in best

Example of brass bed headboard and footboard.

condition through the years were lacquered when it was fashionable to do so. This saved on frequency of polishing and protected the metal from pollution and deterioration.

It was not too long ago that brass beds were not in favor. In the 1950s, most were thrown in the dump. A building in New Hampshire has the headboards, footboards, and springs of sixty brass beds in the cement floor to reinforce it. One must note that they are being reproduced and are plentiful in furniture stores. This is bound to eventually depreciate the value of the old ones as the current beds acquire some age.

Fireplace Ovens

The fireplace oven is a product of the early eighteenth century. The English perfected the mass production of sheet tin which was the most inexpensive metal at the time and all kinds of kitchen and household items were made from it. Tin-makers who came to this country carried on the trade

Tin oven which rests in front of a fireplace. Most just have a shelf. This example features a rotisserie as well. Value: $175-$250

and the fireplace oven became almost a necessity. Until that time, baking was done in a brick oven built to one side of the fireplace. A separate fire was built in it and then the coals and ashes were raked out. Baking was done in the heated interior.

The tin fireplace oven did away with this as it could be set quickly before the fire and the reflecting interior would make the heat surround the item in it. These were later refined to hold a revolving spit so various meats could be barbecued with all sides of the meat receiving the heat because of the reflection of the tin.

One will find original ovens made right up to the middle of the nineteenth century. The first iron stove with an oven, as we know them today, was made by the James Stove Company in Troy, New York, patented on April 26, 1815. It was called the Baltimore Cook Stove and was the most popular in use for about twenty-five years. Expensive at the time, it found its way only into the homes of the affluent. It was not until after the Civil War that mass production brought the price down. Hence, the continued use of the tin reflector oven until then.

If you buy such an oven, be sure it is not rusted out. Those with holes have little value. They are being reproduced today, so perhaps you might be content with a new one rather than an old one in poor condition. They age rapidly in front of a hot fire after a few years of use.

Cast-iron still bank of building.

Iron Banks

The nineteenth century brought with it a changing technology, and after the Civil War the inventive genius of America was turned loose. This was one period when factories turned from war production to making goods for consumers, so all sorts of gadgets and tools made their appearance. Many are quite interesting and form the basis for numerous collections today. Notable in this respect are the iron banks, both mechanical and still, which have risen very high in value. Some have reached the five-figure price range, which far exceeds anything made of metal other than silver, pewter, or gold. You must learn what is most desirable for you. Those banks, which are mechanical and scarce, are hot items. All have been cataloged and collectors are always on the lookout for some with which to round out their collections. You should stay abreast of the activity at auctions and shows to inform

Cast-iron still bank of U.S. mailbox.

yourself of values, since they change continually. Early in the 1930s, the *Book of Knowledge* brought out a series of reproductions of mechanical banks and so labeled them on the bottoms. Though not original, they have assumed a good collecting value today. Reproductions are made in Japan at this time, some being quite good and some easily told from the old, the paint jobs being the first clue as to age. It is difficult to duplicate old worn paint. You should never repaint an old bank of any kind, as this will detract from the value. Rust may be cleaned off old banks, but they should not be repainted.

Still banks (those which perform no function other than to accept money in a slot) have assumed importance, since they were made in interesting shapes and some have approached the rare status. Many people are collecting new banks in iron, and as these are often made as special items in limited editions for banking institutions and others—they will have their own importance and increased value in time.

Many iron banks are being made by the John Wright Company of Pennsylvania, and are being done in exact reproduction of earlier banks. As long as a present-day bank is of iron, it can have some value in the future, but you should steer away from plastics, pottery, or other materials. Some of the old tin banks are quite important, and in recent years there have been several new versions which have been made and which have already acquired a good value. Condition is important in judging all banks.

Jewelry

If you want to collect jewelry, you must first learn to identify the metals and gems. This is not as difficult as it sounds, as there are really very few with which you must become familiar. Beyond that, you must appraise a piece in light of its design and condition. Age enhances a piece, but it must be of quality to begin with. Most of the better nineteenth-century jewelry you might find today came from overseas, while quality costume jewelry was made in great quantities in America, particularly in the Attleboro and Fall River areas in Massachusetts. Good costume jewelry is in great demand and relatively inexpensive. The design of costume jewelry is more important than its material content. Earrings, brooches, lockets, and chains are always good sellers. Bar pins and bracelets are plentiful and less in demand, so prices are lower.

Jewelry designs were influenced by the prevailing styles in the decorative arts. The Georgian designs of the eighteenth century were classic and those of the Victorian period of the nineteenth century were rococo with floral inspiration. The designs of the Edwardian era that followed were bold and austere. The Art Nouveau period was reflected in light and airy creations and those of Art Deco are garish by comparison.

Metals

Jewelry is made up of minerals and metals. The more valuable these are, the higher the cost of the jewelry. Gold is rated in carats by weight (1 carat = 200 milligrams). Pure gold is rated at 24 carats (24K). A 14K gold piece or plating is made of 14 parts of gold and 10 parts of alloy. Most good gold jewelry is made with gold of at least 14K. In the better grade 18K is used, but pure 24K gold is rarely used because it is too soft. The carat weight is required to be stamped on all gold items of 10K and above. The term "gold-filled" or "gold-plated" is used to designate a base metal that is covered with a layer of gold of the grade indicated by its carat weight stamp. There is some electroplating in gold, but the thickness is minute and can even be measured in millionths of an inch. Gold wash, which is a method of dipping of another metal to brighten it with a gold finish, may be even thinner.

Silver plate has a greater thickness than gold plate. Silver plate made before World War II is marked accordingly with the plating designations. Other important metals used in jewelry are platinum, palladium, iridium, ruthenium, and rhodium. Although it is a member of this family, osmium is not used in jewelry. These metals are alloyed with others to make expensive pieces, and they are often used in plating to give an expensive finish to lesser metals.

Stones

The diamond is the hardest and brightest of any of the gems. Diamonds are graded, flawless (or perfect); very, very slightly imperfect—VVS; very slightly imperfect—VS; slightly imperfect—SI; and imperfect—I. Diamonds come in tints of yellow or blue. A clear stone is most desired, although some of bluish tint are quite rare and good. Diamond weights are measured in carats and points. A carat contains 100 points.

Pinchbeck

Back in the eighteenth century, Christopher Pinchbeck invented a metal that bears his name. It is a gold substitute so good that royalty had pieces made from it. Some of the crown jewels we see today may be imbedded in this phony metal. Age has given it great patina. Historians tell us that royalty often sold real gems and jewelry to raise money and would have pieces made to resemble them until the originals might be reclaimed.

Here is how he made it: 100 pure parts of copper by weight are melted in a crucible; then 6 parts of magnesia, 3.6 parts of sal ammoniac, 1.8 parts of quicklime, and 9 parts of tartar are added separately and gradually, in the form of a powder. The whole is then stirred about half an hour, then 17 parts of zinc or tin, in small grains, are thrown in and thoroughly mixed. The crucible is not covered and the mixture kept melted for half an hour longer, when it is skimmed and poured out.

Any imitation of gold can be detected by weight. It will dissolve in nitric acid whereas real gold will not.

I do not know whether eighteenth-century pinchbeck is a good investment; we see little in this country. I would expect the jewelry or other items made from it would have value as a functional item of great age and unusual material.

Early diamonds were cut in as few as 24 facets, which accounts for their lack of brilliance when they are compared with modern diamonds cut in 58 facets. Some people buy old diamonds, have them recut to today's standards and feel that they have improved them. The present-day, manmade diamond was created for industry alone, but are used extensively for jewelry.

Emeralds and rubies are next in line in importance as gems. Genuine emerald is one of the gemstones most easily identified by its natural occlusions. A genuine emerald totally without occlusions is practically impossible to acquire. Following behind these are the semiprecious stones such as aquamarine, jade, garnet, lapis lazuli, opal, pearl, topaz, zircon, and turquoise. Good imitations of all of these are made, so you must do business with reliable people, or else learn the game. This field is full of imitations, so be careful.

Amber has been, and is, popular. But you must be sure you are buying the real thing. Amber is petrified pitch, which has lain for millions of years at the bottom of the sea, notably the Finnish gulf, and it often contains bits of insects, bark, and other impurities. Most buyers feel that this enhances its value, and they look for deeper-toned pieces filled with the relics of a long gone age. Amber comes in shades all the way from white to black, but the most popular color is a rich amber brown; followed by the opaque amber; then the cloudy buttercup yellow; and finally the golden transparent yellow. Amber shares the distinction of being a gem of vegetable origin with the diamond alone. It was used in the earliest known jewelry, and the ancients thought it had curative powers because you can generate electricity on its surface by rubbing it rapidly. Some of the world's best rosaries are made of amber and collectors vie to locate these, some of which date all the way back to the fifteenth century.

Fine amber jewelry is obtainable today in Eastern Europe at a fraction of its cost in the west and most tourists avail themselves of some of it. The Beriovska stores, which are maintained for the sale of such items to tourists in exchange for foreign currency, are the best places in which to buy. Amber has been copied in glass, but you can tell the imitations quite quickly, as the true amber is warm to the touch. If you are still in doubt, do what the dealers do—heat the end of a needle or pin, and apply it to a relatively hidden surface, such as the inside of a hole where a bead is strung. If the piece is amber, smoke and the odor of pine will rise from it.

Be sure that you ask for "natural amber" and that you are not sold "real amber." Natural amber is that which is found in its natural state and cut into stones from which jewelry is made. The chips from such cutting and carving, along with other bits and pieces not big enough to be used in fine jewelry, are melted down and poured into molds to form amber stones. This material is called real amber; it is not a synthetic substitute, but the melting process deprives it of its natural luster and shine and destroys the depth and brilliance one can expect from the natural stones.

Strass

A paste known as strass was invented in the eighteenth century. It can be turned into gems that rival the finest diamonds in brilliance. Much phony jewelry has been turned out in strass, and you have to be an expert to detect it today.

Collecting Guidelines

When buying what most call costume jewelry, be on the lookout for certain gemstones that have risen in value. For years, boxes of gaudy pieces have been liquidated at auctions with little thought to whether there were precious gems or metals in them. A new market has been created in semiprecious stones by dealers in South America, notably Rio de Janeiro.

While in the United States little attention has been given to aquamarine. In South America some jewelers have convinced buyers they should part with up to $1,000 per carat for a three-carat stone or better. Most people cannot identify real amethyst and will pay very little for it. Yet I have seen pendants of this stone, surrounded by 14K gold and a few diamond chips, selling for between $2,000 and $3,000.

Citrine is another little-known gemstone, yet it goes for as much as $500 a carat. Rubellite, which is really red tourmaline, is a stone most people cannot identify; yet I saw one pendant in a gold frame that sold for $2,500.

Topaz, tourmaline, garnet, and other semiprecious stones have become very popular in Brazil, and one can only guess when the hysteria for these stones will hit here, but it must be coming if Americans are willing to spend these prices now. We have visited the shops of H. Stern, Roditi, Maximino, Jimmy's and many others in Rio quite a few times over the past ten years and have anticipated this trend. Rio is the center of this activity, although gemstones are featured all through Brazil.

Here are some rules that may help. Aquamarine is the most popular in Brazil. It shades from a light bluish green to deep blue, which is the rarest. The deeper the blue, the better.

When buying diamonds, look for the four Cs: cutting, clarity, color, and carat weight. It must be crystal clear and absent of any color in the body. It must be free of interior and exterior blemishes.

Rubellite runs from pink to dark red—the rarest stones look like rubies. Most have feathers or silky inclusions. Perfectly clear stones are extremely rare.

This is true also of the emerald. Rare is the emerald without an occlusion. I have examined 3 1/2 carat stones in Cartagena, Columbia, the center for them, and noted occlusions, which really are a guarantee that the piece is not glass. Some emeralds are worth more than diamonds. Grass green is the best color—and a true gem will not change color under a bright light.

Tourmaline stones come in many colors and shades, or even a mixture. Many are mistaken for emeralds, so beware.

Topaz ranges from fine golden to brown in color. Some are oxblood in color, yet some are cognac shade. There is a classification of precious topaz to separate this stone from the less expensive citrine. Precious topaz is orange/pink/brown in color and is rare, even in Brazil. Those who wore it years ago felt it would cure insanity and insomnia, and that it averted sudden death.

Amethyst was known to the ancient Egyptians and in other Mediterranean countries. Buyers feel the best comes from Brazil. It can have a violet hue in several shades. The ancients wore the stone to protect themselves from intoxication. The rich royal purple is the most desired color.

In opals, look for the milk white, fiery stone. Some are tinted with colors; others are called black opals because of their dark color. Brazilian opals are rich in reds and yellows, giving them a fine, fiery look.

Ruby is one of the four precious gemstones, emerald, diamond, and sapphire being the other three. The name "ruby" comes from the Latin word "ruber," which means red. The stone that resembles the blood of a pigeon (an orange-yellow) is most desired. The prized star rubies reveal a star after cutting. Rubies were said to preserve the body and health of the wearer, and to remove evil thoughts.

The name "sapphire" is derived from the Greek word meaning blue, although sapphires are known to come in blue, violet, yellow, or green shades. A star may appear after cutting, as with the ruby. Sapphire is known as the gemstone of the soul.

Garnet is found in several colors, though most regard it a cousin to the ruby in color. Garnet in a violet shade is called rhodolite. The stones will change color under light, which makes them attractive, but they are not yet really expensive.

Blue topaz is a stone commanding some attention. It looks so much like aquamarine that few can tell the difference. It is a good substitute at much less cost.

American Indian Jewelry

A few years ago, there was a flush of interest in American Indian jewelry, but it has worn off somewhat. Buyers have become disillusioned because of imitations and lack of knowledge as to what they are buying.

According to the Arts and Crafts Association (an organization formed in 1974 to promote the public image and ethics of the American Indian arts and crafts industry) in Gallup, New Mexico, questionable business firms are producing pieces with imitation, treated, or plasticized turquoise and attempting to pass them off as genuine. They caution buyers to beware of bargain sales, where such jewelry is offered at low prices. Sometimes sellers in shops or at auctions have been found to mix genuine pieces with the bogus. Also of concern is the theft of good jewelry, which has occurred throughout the country, with such items being disposed of at auctions and in shops. Dealers and auctioneers have begun exchanging bulletins to warn of such losses. New Mexico alone generates about $250 million in the American Indian crafts business each year, so you can see why the American Indians and the state are very concerned.

Years ago at a "ghost town" in Colorado, I saw a American Indian hammering out jewelry. I then went into the gift shop next door and purchased a bracelet with turquoise. Back east, a friend showed me the mark of an Attleboro, Massachusetts, maker under the rim. Watch out.

If you are planning to buy such jewelry, make sure you receive a valid bill of sale guaranteeing what you buy. The Indian Arts and Crafts council in Washington has published a Source Directory, which lists more than 150 legitimate makers. For a free copy, write to the Council at Room 4004, U.S.S. Department of the Interior, Washington, D.C., 20240.

Lithographed Tin

Until the 1870s, all printing had to be done in black and white. If coloring was needed, it would be added later by hand. New machinery was invented at that time to print in color in what is termed chromolithography (some use the shortened term "chromo" to designate a printed colored picture). It was not long before it was discovered that this printing could be done on all sorts of materials, so the creation of the colorful commercial containers, called "advertiques" today, became a reality.

In 1909, 15,822 establishments were engaged in the manufacture of tobacco products in the United States and if only a fraction of them used tin containers, this would be enough for a specialized collector today. Some companies used many types of tins for different products (biscuits, tea, coffee, lozenges, powder), which adds to the total. There are good books on collecting lithographed tin and one will learn that it is best to concentrate on a category or two and build a better group of items relating to a particular product.

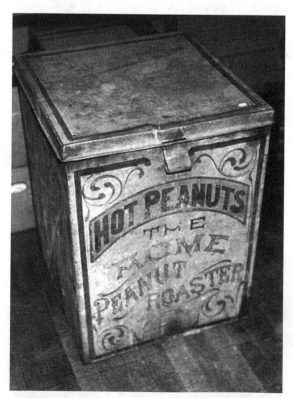

Food, coffee, and tea tins are collected for their interesting lithography. Condition is most important. Value: $350

Original condition is important. Age, color and condition of color must be judged. Do not attempt to repaint or retouch the pieces. Old pieces will be found dull and dingy; clean them with mild detergent in water, then use furniture spray wax to polish and preserve them as well as bring out the old colors. Rust on a piece harms value, so lightly steel wool the rust, then protect with the spray wax. Interesting shapes should be sought. One tobacco can was made to resemble a milk can, others looked like purses, and many looked like people, such as the roly-poly tobacco tins. A relatively small investment can yield a large return.

Ship Models

Visitors to President Franklin Roosevelt's home at Hyde Park, New York, are always attracted to the ship models he collected. Ship models can also be found in abundance at marine museums. Most of these were never made to be sailed, but rather were created as presentation pieces at launchings, as advertising displays for shipping lines and travel agents, and just as decorative items for the office or home. Many were made by home craftspeople who treated this work as a hobby. Unfortunately, many junk models have been turned out over the years to appeal to the tourist trade in this and foreign countries. Doing appraisals, I have seen these in many homes. At times the owners, who treasured them as family items supposedly made by a long gone grandfather or other member of the family, have been devastated to learn that a particular model is not valuable. As with all antiques, each must be seen to be valued.

Sailing vessels seem to be the favorites among models, although every branch of marine activity has been represented. The marine museum at Greenwich, England, has a superb collection of fighting vessels used in that country's many wars. In this country, naturally, models representing American ships are most desired. Collectors like models that show great activity, with figures on board doing something, much as in a genre painting. The more accurate and more true-to-life it is in detail, the greater the interest. The decks should have all the items that would normally be found aboard a ship of its type, and all models should be made true to scale. Best is the model with lifeboats aboard as well as a carved wood figure on the prow.

METALWORK GALLERY

Much pewter was shipped from the Orient, mainly from China. Items such as this late 19th century tea caddy and teapot turn up at auctions and shows. Value: $225

Pewter by Johann Christopher Heyne, Lancaster, PA, 1754-1780. At left is a covered chalice, teapot, and bowl. Heyne was one of this country's finest pewterers.

Matched set of Irish haystack measures, which date back to the early 19th century. These are being reproduced. Value: $2,500

There are many store scales, which were made on both sides of the Atlantic. Small examples are decorative and still useable. Value: $250

Silver coffeepot, made c. 1760 by Zachariah Brigden of Boston. In this period, the form might be called a chocolate pot. The spouts were moved to the top about this time. Value: $18,500

Collectors of militaria-like old powder cans which still retain their old lithographed or paper labels. Value: $75-$85

Iron kettle trivet. They are still used today to keep foods warm. Value: $150-$225

Andirons are difficult to date, as they are still made in the forms and metals that were used years ago. This pair with ball tops could have been made anytime.

Parlor stove in iron. Many of these might have been found in railroad stations, burning coal. They are popular in homes, today. Value: $350

Fancy iron heaters are in demand. Witness this double-column example. It would have burned coal. The added iron resulted in greater radiation of heat. Value: $600-$750

Form of this iron wood heater indicates it is Shaker. Sad irons were placed on the side shelf, where they could be kept warm. Value: $2,200

Fancy molding heightens value of iron heaters. This example was made in Utica, New York in 1845.

Copper and brass fuel pot, used to refill burners under chafing dishes, samovars, and food warmers, without having to put out the flame. Value: $85

Copper still, the type used out in the backwoods. We have sold several to liquor stores who used them for display. Value: $750

Art deco period, c. 1920s, sterling mesh bag with attached purse, carried outside the main purse. Value: $250-$350

Marked old tin is very collectable. This measure is molded with the name of the Dover Stamping Company, whose business originated in Dover, New Hampshire and later moved to Boston. Value: $75

Sugar used to be marketed in loaves. Cutters, such as this were used to break off pieces, as needed. Then, it would be powdered. These 18th century cutting tongs were made in England. Value: $75

There are many forms of hog scrapers, used to remove the bristles after dipping the animal in hot water. The example on left, led to the creation of candleholders, which resemble it. Value: $75-$125

There are collectors of mortars and pestles. One does not usually find them in iron. Value: $150-$225

Biscuit, donut, and cookie cutters of all types are out there. They are still being made, today. Value: $2-$10 ea.

One will find many styles of kettle cranes. One this fancy must have been made overseas. Value: $450

There are different types of enamelware. This neat chocolate set commemorates the age of the Great Clippers, New York, London, etc. It is not overly old, but is well decorated with a clipper ship. Value: $175

Bank collecting has been with us a long time; both the mechanicals and the stills. Many are being reproduced.

Unless very unusual, tin weathervane figures do not
have the value of the brass and copper. These fish came
off the roof of a barn in Maine. The bullet holes attest to
their age and original condition. Value: $750-$1,000

Shelburne Museum, Vermont.

Rare coin-operated metal egg dispenser.

The rooster was most popular as a weathervane
figure. This example, complete with directionals
and arrow, is a very good example. Value: $3,500

One will see these advertised as Victorian birdcages. They are still being made today in Tunisia. We bought one there for $6.

Usually, horse weathervane figures will be found in copper or brass. This is an excellent example in tin, with a sulky rider. These are being made in brass and copper, today, in Taiwan. Value: $3,500

GLOSSARY

Bell Metal: A mixture of tin, copper, and zinc used to make bells.

Brass: A mixture of copper and zinc.

Britannia (Metal): Soft metal made of tin, copper, antimony and other alloys.

Bronze: A mixture of brass, tin, and other alloys.

Champleve: Enameling in hollowed-out surfaces.

Church Plate: An English term for church silver.

Coin: 875 parts silver, 125 parts alloy.

Copper: Malleable reddish/brown metal with a specific gravity of 8.96.

Cruizie: A hanging lamp which most often burns fat.

Enamel: A protective or decorative coating baked on metal, glass, or ceramics.

Gold: A malleable metal found in yellow, white, and various tints with specific gravity of 19.32.

Iron: A strong ductile metal with a specific gravity of 7.874.

Pewter: A mixture of 90 percent tin and 10 percent antimony. Some formulas include lead or other alloys.

Porringer: A shallow bowl with a handle.

Quadruple Plate: A metal which is dipped and plated with silver four times.

Rush Holder: An iron stand which holds waxed pieces of rush, burned for light.

Sheffield: The name of a city in Yorkshire County, England, famous for cutlery since the eighteenth century, where Sheffield plate (the bonding of two thin sheets of silver to a body less expensive metal) originated.

Silver: A malleable white metal with specific gravity of 10.50.

Spangle: Sparking metal or plastic discs, often sewn on garments.

Spelter: A metal made mostly of zinc. Used in inexpensive statuary, etc.

Steel: An alloy of iron and carbon. Additional alloys are added according to specific use and formulas.

Sterling: 925 parts of silver and 75 parts of alloy. This mixture may vary slightly in different countries.

Tin: A metal obtained from cassiterite. Used for plating and as an alloy.

Zinc: A mixture of brass and copper, plus alloys. Used for rust proofing other metals.

Chapter Five

DECORATIVE ART

Folk

Introduction

It has only been in the last years that there has been any great appreciation of what we term "folk art." Folk art encompasses what can be considered the work of relatively untrained hands—items created by people who saw a need for a product and simply made it, or perhaps even invented a tool or kitchen aid to do a particular job in the days when one could not go to the local discount store and buy one. Some items are functional and some are decorative, but collectors today look at them in light of the latter, as most have aged and acquired a patina that endears them to the aesthete. Folk art items were made in all materials, but mostly materials that were easily available around a farm or average home. Though some bear the style of pieces made by city craftsmen for the carriage trade, most do not incorporate the quality which is turned out in the hands of those trained and skilled in their endeavor.

Some people refer to folk art items as "primitives," which is not necessarily an accurate description. Eric de Jonge, the former director of curators at the William Penn Museum in Harrisburg, Pennsylvania, has described this type of work variously as naive art and uninhibited art. There is a market distinction between the work done by untrained hands and the work done by an uncivilized people. The term "primitive" could be more accurately applied to the workmanship done at the earliest stages of civilization when man first gathered crude tools and materials with which to work. This term should represent the beginnings of any art movement and the work done during this period. "Folk art" is a better definition of work done by a civilized people who were simply untrained in the particular field of creation or decoration in which they engaged. There are many natural artists who have a flair for quality—in form, proportion, workmanship, and beauty—and are able to express it with little or no training. These self-taught artists need not necessarily be lumped together with those whose early civilizations gave them little preparation or incentive to do this work. The term "primitive" is used loosely to indicate some early work done in this country and though it is not totally objectionable, neither is it totally accurate.

Calligraphy

Fraktur

The Pennsylvania German Fraktur is an excellent exercise in calligraphy and early examples are quite important and valuable today. Fraktur is a

Left: Pennsylvania German folk art picture depicting field bird. Right: Pennsylvania folk art watercolor of woman dated 1828.

piece of very decorative calligraphy done in a traditional Pennsylvania German style. Practically every family had a member who was responsible for making up the certificates that documented important events, such as birth and death. Most were done in colorful fashion with floral or other decoration adding a touch of beauty. In other sections of America artists worked in this fashion as well, but the Frakturs are more plentiful than other genres and might be easier to find.

After the mechanical printing presses took over (about 1830-1840) handwork waned, and the printed certificate took its place—gone was this native bit of talent, which is so highly prized now. Good collections can be seen in Pennsylvania at the Ephrata Cloister, the Farm Museum at Landis Valley near Lancaster, and the William Penn Memorial Museum in Harrisburg.

Carving

American

There is no area in America in which such work was not done, so you have the entire country in which to collect. The greatest concentration of items has been found in the areas of New England and Pennsylvania, as both were quite prolific in industry, and both had substantial populations. The traditions of the British Isles are quite evident in the New England work, and those of the Germans, Dutch, and Swiss in Pennsylvania. The influence of the Dutch, and later the French, is felt in work from New York State.

Wood—This is a material which has always been plentiful, is easily worked, and can be carved or decorated in many ways. Many kitchen items such as dishes, bowls, butter molds, tableware, rolling pins, funnels, boxes and baskets, dough boxes, pails and buckets, sugar tubs, dippers, spatulas, washboards, and dish strainers were turned out in abundance.

For the farm chores, the man of the house turned his talents to the production of milk pails, churns, stools, watering troughs, fruit baskets, apple driers, herb driers, winnowing sieves, eel traps, bean flailers, kegs for rum and cider, water kegs, feed pails for horses, etc. The well-equipped home also needed a large (spinning) and small (flax) wheel on which to turn out the needed fibers for clothing. The more fortunate lady had a full-sized loom to make cloth, but others were content

Painted, hand-carved wooden mermaid.

Butter stamp, leaf, machine carved.

Butter print, semi-circle thistle, machine carved.

Butter print, tulip design.

with lap looms. Some carvers turned out swizzle sticks, which were used to stir a mixture of ale and beer. Along the coast you will find decoys carved to assist in the hunt. Wooden weathervane figures are common wherever metal was at a premium. Small boxes of all kinds are quite popular; those with carving or painting decorations are most desirable, as they reflect the industry of the man with his knife or other carving tools, and of the lady, who carefully added the flowers, leaves, and pictorial decoration to the effort with her brush and quill.

Some of the greatest work in carving was done for sailing vessels. Huge figureheads fastened to the prow were a must on every ship. Many of these were rather exotic ladies or important historical figures of the times. Since it is our national symbol, eagle carving was practiced just about everywhere, and those who did this work are well recorded. Charles Bellamy, a native of Kittery, Maine, maintained studios both there and in nearby Portsmouth, New Hampshire. His doorway eagles are much desired today, although his work ranged all the way to the huge twelve-foot bird he carved for a vessel made at the Portsmouth Navy Yard. The ship is long gone, but the eagle survives at the marine museum in Newport News, Virginia. Bellmay's work is well recorded and the greatest collection of it is probably at the Shelburne Museum in Shelburne, Vermont.

Another noted carver was Wilhelm Schimmel, whose rather primitive eagles are in great demand in his native Pennsylvania, as well as elsewhere. Schimmel was what is described as an "intinerant" artist, who often did his work in return for meals and lodging. His eagles feature a rare kind of bold cutting; you will know one almost instantly once you have seen some others with which to compare your example.

Bellamy wooden eagle.

Collecting Tip

Carved wooden work must be in good condition. Age takes its toll, and those pieces, which have not survived well, may have little or no value. Old wood that has been repainted has been hurt, as far as collectors are concerned. It is better to leave the faded decoration than try to renew it. Evidence of new saw or chisel marks should make a buyer suspicious. Above all, the pieces must be interesting and reflect an attempt for quality on the part of the maker. Signed pieces, which are infrequent, can have greater value if you can document the maker and the time and place where he worked. Assembling information about one maker can enhance the value of all his work, so long as it is of good quality.

In recent years, a large amount of woodcarving that falls into the folk art category has been imported, especially from Europe and Africa. These items are finding favor here, as their American counterparts have risen greatly in price, and in some cases can rarely be located for sale.

Bone/Ivory/Stone—Another form of carving is done on bone or ivory. If the work is done on materials that come from sea creatures, it is called scrimshaw—if the materials are from land animals, it is usually referred to as engraving or sgraffito work.

Powder horns, knife handles, and sword scabbards and handles were extensively decorated in this manner. Using a pointed tool, the workman incised the lines in the decoration he wanted, then rubbed ink, powder, or other colorings into the crevices, making them stand out in relief against the white substance of the bone or ivory. Actually, bone and ivory work seems to predate the work done on marine materials, as horn carving was popular during the eighteenth century. Items of Revolutionary War vintage are especially good, and work on war-related items continued well through the Civil War. Many soldiers filled their

Scrimshaw, musk ox, carved from walrus tusk, c. 1780.

idle time by making gifts for family and friends, as well as by decorating their own possessions.

The term "scrimshaw" is believed to have originated from the Dutch word *Scrimshander,* which is a reference to a lazy fellow. In reality, the men who did this work were quite talented. It is believed that they actually competed with each other to turn out the best works of art. Such objects were not necessarily made aboard ship. Most of the work we collect is from the first three-quarters of the nineteenth century (after the American merchant marine enlarged to take care of our world trade). Much is

Carousel Figures

One of our prime examples of American folk art is fast disappearing as we witness the sale of circus carousels. Some carved figures have sold for six-digit prices. As each carousel is dismantled and sold piece by piece, the prices just seem to go up, with the demand far exceeding the supply. The names of Stein and Goldstein, Gustav and William Dentzel, Herschell-Spillman, Philadelphia Toboggan Company, and others are well known to collectors.

Animals and birds, some real and some mythical, have been the inspiration for many figures. The different forms are most interesting—for example, flying, standing, and jumping horses, kangaroos, deer, goats, griffins, sheep, lions, roosters, and many more.

Some variations of the animals are quite desirable. The most elaborately carved animals were featured on the outer ring, where they were seen more easily, and the lesser animals positioned on the inner rings. Some warlike figures featured armor. Generally, every carousel features an animal with a shield or other device with the maker's name carved on it.

The figures were carved of wood, most often in sections, which were glued together for strength. Early carousels were operated by steam; some that ended up in Tahiti were fueled by coconut shells in the absence of wood or coal. The steam calliope, most often played by an employee, came into being to provide music. This gave way to the electric models, with an automatic calliope.

Old carousel horses are getting more difficult to buy as the carousels are being restored for continued use. One with the maker's nameplate is quite good. This is the mark of Stein and Goldstein, New York.

The outer horses are most desired, as they were seen by the crowds; hence, they featured fancier design and carving.

made from teeth from sperm whales, whalebone only or lower jaw of the sperm whale, baleen (the tough straining fiber masses in the mouth of the sperm whale), woods available on ships from all over the world, as well as mother-of-pearl, abalone shell, and coconut shell. Whale's teeth might be found as long as 10-1/2", hollow, and about two inches wide at the base, tapering to a point.

The artisans began by scraping the teeth or bone with a knife or sandpaper, and then scratch carving it with a steel needle. A whaling ship held up to thirty men, and quite often remained at sea for two years. One can only guess at the amount of scrimshaw that returned with them.

When ships are portrayed, you should notice how the flag is flying, as it should be in the direction of the wind, and the men on board should be portrayed in some activity. If a picture is done, it should have a frame around it. English scrimshaw can be judged by the length of the teeth—they are often up to ten and one half inches long—and by the English flag. Also, the English carved more strongly than the Americans. Scenes from *Godey's Ladies' Book* were often reproduced.

If possible, you should collect teeth in pairs, and they should point in opposite directions, being matched from opposite sides of the jaw. Some teeth feature pictures in frames in

Baleen

Baleen is a very hard substance found at the rear of the mouth of a whale. It forms a strainer that filters out unwanted items as the huge mammal moves through the ocean. Some refer to baleen as "bone hairs," though it does not resemble human hair. Rather, much of it is flat and can be up to several inches in width. Naturally, baleen is rare, and one must screen much of it to get enough strands of uniform size to make baskets, ship models, etc. Baskets with fine weave are most valuable, and items of this type are being made today and are valued at almost the price of the old, as the material is scarce. Once the killing of whales is stopped all over the world, no baleen will be available at all. Baleen was used by sailors around the world as a material to work on while at sea. One item, which is a rarity, is the sailor's valentine made of shells, coral, baleen, bone, and other items from the sea. These are a form of statuary most often kept under glass, as they are great dust catchers.

Scrimshaw, wale's tooth, eagle design.

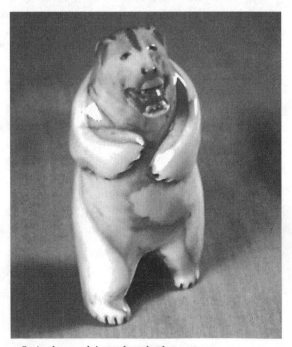

Scrimshaw wale's tooth, polar bear.

Scrimshaw Eskimo and dog sled, carved ivory.

daguerreotype fashion, others may be inlaid or painted. Patriotic teeth and those that commemorate the death of famous people such as Presidents, with angels, tombstones, and the like, are important. One tooth pictures a barber giving a haircut to William Henry Harrison—the other side reveals that it was cut too short and that the President caught cold and died. Other collectible teeth are those with harbor scenes of ships or even the sailor's home in the background. Memorial or mourning teeth might feature a lady leaning on a tombstone with space left for the name of the sailor and when he died. Others feature women and children weeping. Teeth carved in relief, such as one found showing a man kissing a girl's foot, are important. You may also find architectural scenes of buildings done from prints. Very rare and valuable is the "Susan's Tooth," which features a picture of the ship *Susan* and was done by a man who lived on Nantucket Island around 1820-1830. Only about a dozen have been found. You might look for the signed work of William Parry of New Bedford, who was active in the 1930s and whose work is perhaps the best among his contemporaries.

Many items were made from bone or ivory and then decorated, such as small carved boxes, sewing baskets and implements, jagging wheels, crimpers, bodkins, sewing needles, candleholders, swifts, dolls and beds, rolling pins, chess figures, chessboards, napkin rings, canes, shoehorns, doorknobs, magazine racks, dippers, water kegs, billy clubs, bird cages, and even rope bed tighteners.

Since there is an embargo on killing whales, it is only natural that even the reproductions of this work being done today will eventually rise in value. Research I did in 1975 revealed more than

a thousand people still doing scrimshaw in Maine, New Hampshire, Massachusetts, and Rhode Island. Old whale teeth turn up by the basket full at marine auctions, and these are still being used. Most new work, however, lacks the dexterity in penmanship as well as the determination, follow-through, and bold strokes that characterize the old.

The Endangered Species Act of 1973 placed limitations on carrying teeth, tusk, and bone matter from marine animals across state borders. You might check with people from whom you buy about these restrictions.

The work of the Alaskan Eskimos, even contemporary work, is assuming new importance. Eskimo carvers are skilled with ivory, bone, and stone, creating vibrant human and animal forms, which radiate a strong sense of life. It is believed that the Eskimos originally carved for religious reasons or for tribal chiefs, who gave gifts to other leaders. The carvers attempted to portray their immediate lifestyle and that of people about them, often working with a soft stone, which is abundant in the Arctic. They created works around the shapes of the chunks as they were broken from the ground. The forms of nature inspired much of their work.

The changes in Eskimo lifestyle are noticeable in the work they do today. Although there are many regions of the Canadian and Alaskan Arctic where life is similar to what it has been for centuries, in other areas civilization has brought with it a different approach to artistic endeavors. There are purists who say the twentieth-century Eskimo carver has gone commercial, changing from ethnological inspiration to the inspiration of the dollar. The Eskimos have created cooperatives to market their work through a central agency, which does smack of commercialism, but you must remember that life near the North Pole is difficult and dollars are hard to come by. If we are to condemn them for commercialism, we might as well condemn Toulouse-Lautrec, Wilhelm Schimmel, or John James Audubon, whose work often went for groceries and spirits to replenish their souls.

Eskimo work is also referred to as "Inuit," which means "the people." If you wish to collect Inuit artifacts, go to Lapland, Iceland, Greenland, or Canada. Other than that, make the acquaintance of someone in the military who is to be stationed at the Dew Line or some other remote hardship post.

Ivory vs. Ivorine

One must be alert when collecting carved ivory. It is organic, and therefore, perishable if exposed to abnormal conditions. Check the size of any ivory object. The largest piece can be no wider than an elephant or rhinoceros tusk—six or eight inches at the widest point. I have seen plant stands with tops over a foot in diameter, which people have bought as ivory. This is rather wide for a tusk.

Decoration is done by scratch carving teeth or bones from any sea animal or teeth, tusks, and bone of land animals. Unfortunately, companies are selling kits of vinyl teeth for carving at home, and, once decorated, can fool unsuspecting people.

Another problem lies in the use of Ivorine. After ivory is carved, the shavings and other bits and pieces can be melted down with a chemical—this mass can then be molded into familiar forms. When solid, the pieces are identified as real ivory and rightly so, but the item has not been hand carved. How does one tell ivory from Ivorine? Anything that is cut or carved has sharp edges. It is impossible to mold a sharp line in ivory, glass, or any other substance. The melted ivory should be called "Ivorine," its proper name.

Also, bone carvings are limited by the size of the animal. Each bone has a marrow center that must be discarded, leaving a thinner shell, which is used. Bone and ivory will color a little with age, the former more than the latter.

Highly carved elephant tusk.

Carved ivory figurine with revolving face.

Ivory bird and fisherman.

Give him your shopping list and the amounts you wish to pay. Contemporary work is very collectible at its present prices. There are galleries in America that carry carving and other work, but those with the widest variety, according to our travels, are in Canada. The Canadians have assembled the best collections of Eskimo art, from both their country and Alaska, and have sent exhibitions of it throughout the United States and Europe.

Russia

If you collect carvings and know people going to Russia, ask them to obtain some of the artistic soft stone and bone carvings from the Ural Mountain area. The first record of stonework is from the eighteenth century, when deposits were discovered on the mountain banks of the Irgina and Sylva rivers. The stone is found in many colors and is excellent for artistic carving. Peasants of the Perm region began to make Easter eggs, picture frames, flower-petal-shaped ashtrays, and even platters of white gypsum and selenite. They imitated the forms of porcelain articles and wood carvings. When the decorative arts declined in Russia in the late nineteenth and early twentieth centuries, this work all but halted. There was a revival in this art form in the 1930s, however, and today the Russian government encourages this carving as it brings in hard currency from other nations and is a highly-desired Russian export. The animals carved in the soft stone are beautifully done and on a par with the best you can find anywhere.

Bone carving in Russia has a more ancient history, as it dates back to the tenth century. Bone carvers of the Moscow Palata were quite famous in the seventeenth century. In the eighteenth and nineteenth centuries, the Kholmogory craftsmen in Archangel province began turning out intricate pieces, such as bone caskets and little cases and boxes, and doing much fret-work and adornment with carvings of men, flowers, and animals. The pieces were often colored to heighten their beauty. In the second half of the nineteenth century, craftsmen from Tobolsk turned out miniature sculpture done on mammoth bone, drawing on animals and birds for their inspiration. Some of these were brought to this country by immigrants, and some are being shipped here toady by dealers who are picking them up all over Europe and Asia. These little-known collectibles are sleepers in American collecting today.

Weather Vanes

Early weather vanes are often classified in the folk art category. The weathervane was the farmer's trusted friend in predicting the weather. A south wind in the summer meant fair; if the wind shifted to the east, it brought rain. West winds meant fair all year around. If the wind blew cold from the north when a storm cleared, it meant the storm had backed up and would come again. A northeast wind brought a storm that usually lasted three days, and a southeast wind brought one of lesser duration.

Not many wooden weather vanes have survived, but those in tin, copper, and brass show the ingenuity of their makers. You may find the figure of a horse, man, fish, driver and sulky, locomotive, feather, building, bird, deer, other animal, or just about anything that could have excited the maker's imagination.

Perhaps the most popular and common figure is that of a running horse. Legend has it that a pacer named Smuggler raced in the 1870s. In 1874, he was entered in a trotting race and had to wear toe weights to correct his stride. He won the then-big $10,000 purse. He was immortalized as a weathervane figure by Harris and Company in Boston between 1874 and 1881. Another model was made by W.A. Snow Company in Boston between 1883 and 1940.

Tin weathervane, arrow style.

If I were to calculate the rarest of the vanes, I would list these—sulky and driver, fire engine, locomotive, centaur, and oddities such as the minister in a long coat riding a high wheel bicycle. Geese are rare, roosters are common. Plows were popular, along with horses, dogs, sheep, and cows. Some vanes were even gilded for fancy homes.

It would be difficult to grade the designs as to quality, since the figure alone is not sufficient for judgment. The size, condition, and material from which the weathervane is made are important, as well as its age. Those which were used for target practice by hunters and contain bullet holes are not as desirable as those in pristine condition. Some are dimensional, with filled-out bodies rather than just sheets of material, and these are more desirable. One of the most impressive of these is a huge ram, which once graced the Amoskeag Mills in Manchester, New Hampshire, and is now displayed at the Currier Gallery of Art in that city.

When old weather vanes are taken down, they are often injured since the iron rod on which most are mounted is cut. The rod usually comes down

Copper weathervane, horse and directional letters.

Copper angel weathervane, original paint.

Example of an early American weathervane.

through the ceiling of the cupola and is imbedded in the floor to give the weathervane strength and stability. Rather than disturb the roof, removers will often cut the rod just above it, and this does not help in its resale.

Fine reproductions are being done today, and these are quite acceptable for use on an old building. The price of the old weather vanes has risen so much, that perhaps a new one is a much wiser investment at this time. After all, most people cannot tell old from new when they have the item in their hands. If it is perched on your roof, forty or fifty feet away, perhaps you will never know.

Paintings

Introduction

Let us trace briefly the history of oil paintings and their care today. Western painting was influenced by the Greeks and Romans, who used tempera, a simple recipe containing either a whole egg or just the yolk mixed with gelatin made from parchment skin. The first mention of oil colors appears in a thirteenth-century German manuscript, but these were not very good, as a proper solvent had not been developed. Alchemy soon brought forth turpentine, and varnish was created from resin boiled in linseed, poppy, or walnut oil. Painting was done on wood or parchment, and gold leaf often applied by a jeweler. Early painting was featured on horse ornaments and carriages. Portrait painting soon became quite popular, followed by landscapes.

Conservators and scholars can tell much about a painting by thorough examination. Photographs, x-ray, infrared, and ultraviolet lights are employed to check layers of painting, signatures, ground color, and canvas to determine age and authenticity. Experts can discover repairs, addition of new paint, loss of old paint, and even sketches beneath the paint from which the artist worked. Total examination involves measurements, as no picture is supposed to be reproduced in the exact measurement of the original and most of these are well catalogued. The expert can judge the age of the canvas, frame, ground layer, and picture layer of paint, along with the surface coating used for protection.

Butterfield & Butterfield.

SCOUTING THE WAGON TRAIL, Olaf Carl Seltzer, 1877-1957. Many artists came from Europe to paint our West. Value: $35,000-$50,000

He can tell old oil since it becomes translucent with age. You must be familiar with an artist in order to compare a picture with his known works. You should be versed in the language and literature of the country of origin, as a great deal is related by the time span and subject matter of a painting.

Paintings deteriorate slowly; they are usually brittle and fragile. It is best not to touch a damaged area with your fingers, apply a self-adhesive tape to a tear, or try to protect the surface with a blanket or wrinkled papers, which can exert pressure on the painting surface. Dust is detrimental to canvas, and the reverse of a painting should be protected with a stiff board or paper, which is *not* in contact with the surface itself. Paintings suffer from extremes of dryness and humidity; a uniform 45% relative humidity is best. Paintings should not be hung in sunlight or over radiators or fireplaces.

Above all, do not attempt to clean a painting at home. Old remedies, such as rubbing bread or a sliced onion over the surface to clean, are taboo. Do not use a detergent or any soap in attempting to clean canvas. Special solutions are employed by conservators, and these range in varying strengths and solubilities. Each solution must be tested on the painting before use to make sure it will not lift the original paint with the dirt. The canvas is cleaned bit by bit with a small cotton swab in order to make sure there is no change in pigment strength or vulnerability to the solution being used. This is an art practiced by professionals, so leave the cleaning to them. At home, an occasional light dusting or gentle wiping with clear water on a damp rag is permissible once the painting has been restored properly and a protective varnish coating applied.

You must also realize that the professional has the proper materials if any repairs to tears in the canvas are required. The paint formulas used by the original artist have been catalogued so that the expert can match them exactly for touch-ups and restorations. This is important if the work is to be done properly. If the painting is worth saving, have a professional save it for you.

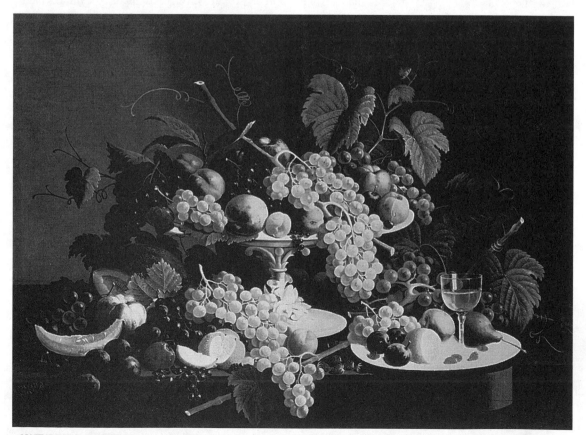

NATURE'S BOUNTY, oil on canvas by Severin Roesen, American, 1853. Still lifes of fruit and/or flowers are difficult to paint because of the restrictions of light.

American Oils

In the eighteenth and nineteenth centuries many itinerant artists worked decorating walls and furniture, as well as painting portraits of members of a family. It has been said that some artists prepared bodies on canvas during the winter months and during the good weather traveled to homes, painting heads for the bodies. Eric de Jonge, chief curator at the William Penn Museum, questions this notion, saying that no unfinished body pictures have ever turned up to confirm this tale. He feels that no woman, especially, would want to be painted in any finery other than her own.

In family portraits, it was not uncommon for a new baby to be added to an old picture as the artist made his rounds from year to year. Many old portraits such as these are unsigned, but there is new interest in them. Their value is measured by the ability of the artist, the interest he conveys, and the condition of the work. Years ago many such pictures were thrown away and the frames adapted for other use. This practice has driven the price up on the remaining pictures. Of special interest are groups of people engaged in some activity, such as a battle, party, band concert, or some other facet of life, whether peaceful or brutal. Some pictures are painted on materials common as a mattress cover, but do not worry about this as it may enhance the value.

White Mountain and Hudson River Schools

The eighteenth century produced little or no American landscape work. The settlers were surrounded by the beauty of the outdoors, and did not need to capture it to bring into their homes. Without photography, portrait painting flourished as a means of preserving the images of family and friends. Early in the nineteenth century, as America's cities grew and the great outdoors became more remote, landscape work flourished. The industrial age brought with it teeming cities, tenements, and pollution from smokestacks. Even the factory worker attempted to bring some of the outdoors into his home via a painting or even a print.

Thomas Cole, Alvin Fisher, and other artists went to the top of Mount Washington to paint as early as 1825—beginning what is now referred to as the White Mountain School of painters. Their New Hampshire landscapes created a great impression, and soon artists were seeking out other places of beauty to capture on canvas. The Hudson River area gave birth to a school of painters who did fine landscape work, and it was not long before many painters headed west to capture the mountains and scenery there. These were schools of realism in that the artist attempted to portray a scene faithfully with no attempt to alter it. This is a phototechnique that has gradually been challenged by succeeding generations. Such artists worked well into this century, and are well documented in the books listed in the bibliography. A good rule is that if an artist does not appear in the books, he has not arrived as far as collecting is concerned. These two schools of painters are highly desired today, and prices are rising on their work every year. You would do well to invest in works by known American artists of this period who are recorded, as they represent perhaps the finest investment in antiques today.

Modern Art

Unfortunately, there has been, in my opinion, little painting of great renown done since the Depression, which spawned a group of artists who lived mostly in major cities, some existing on funds from the WPA. This program granted them survival and freedom to work, but much of what they turned out was revolutionary with a Bolshevik tint. Communism was being preached everywhere as the solution to America's economic problems, and art naturally reflected this. Some depression art is being collected today and touted as great art, but in my opinion, you should be very careful before you invest in it.

The period that followed World War II brought with it perhaps the greatest era of mediocrity in the history of art. We have been subjected to rather amateur work in most of the arts: painting, sculpting, ceramics, and even music. There are those who have found a formula for becoming rich by thrusting upon the public the most devious and garish work in an attempt to be so different that they stand apart from everything else. These practitioners have succeeded in luring supporters to their work, whether it is good, bad, or indifferent. The most tragic consequence has been that museums and galleries are lending their space to exhibit this work regardless of quality. Some analyze this as the "Art Institute syndrome," in that the museums do want to be left behind again as they were in the exhibition of Impressionism, and therefore, will exhibit just about anything today. It is a situation, which will

ROOM OF FLOWERS, Childe Hassam, American, painted in 1890. The artist lived in Boston and is well known as one of our American impressionists. Value: $110,000-$120,000

reverse itself in time, since new young artists are coming along who will have nothing to do with such mediocrity. A new school of realism is already at work throughout the country and the small exhibitions at crafts festivals and fairs reflect this.

On examination, you must concede that to achieve the workmanship necessary to the realist, Barbizon, and Impressionist schools, one must be an accomplished painter, since these are the most challenging and difficult styles to do well. Those who indulge in the action school (which is nothing more than what appears to be paint thrown at a canvas) and those who paint geometric forms are just exhibiting to us their inability to really do anything with brush and canvas. Those who attempt to interpret a mess of gobbledygook as projecting a message are being rather demagogic in relation to good art. Creating good art makes demands on the ability, time, and patience of the artist. Those works that can be splashed out in five or ten minutes in kindergarten fashion certainly do not meet this test. All the explaining in the world cannot compensate for this, any more than all the talking in the world can improve the quality of a piece of furniture ground out by machine in Grand Rapids, Michigan, in the 1920s. When you invest in modern art, you must judge the work on its quality—good taste, good design, and good workmanship. The minute you stray away from this, you are gambling. Those who gambled on Picasso years ago have made out quite well, but he is an exception—how well can you pick the exceptions today?

At a talk with college students, the noted cartoonist Al Capp was asked, "I look at a Picasso painting and I think it is garbage. How can I learn to appreciate art?" Capp replied, "You understand it well, it is garbage." Which prompted a further question, "Who determines that a Picasso painting is worth five hundred thousand dollars?" Capp's answer was, "The dealer who just paid one hundred thousand for it." The price of art is relative to those who appreciate it and also depends on who

Hudson River landscape in the style of Thomas Chambers, c. 1830s. The Barbizon technique in oils was being developed in this country at this time. Dark foreground, lighted middle ground, and silhouetted or luminescent background. Value: $2,500-$3,000

Marine Paintings

Marine paintings are what the name implies—scenes of ships at sail, in a harbor, or docked. America had many fine marine artists from the eighteenth century all the way to the twentieth. Works by accomplished artists will have value, as is the case with most art. Condition is important and the scene portrayed has a bearing on the value. The better artists are listed in the books citied in the bibliography and those of the earlier period usually command better prices. Scenes of ships should include men in action on board, and the introduction of whales, sea gulls, or other marine life is important. Flags, preferably American, should fly. Size is quite important, since most collectors like large marine paintings because of their panoramic quality.

Many English and French marine paintings turn up in this country which are quite well done. Again, those by famous artists are of importance in America. The next most important school of marine painters flourished in Chinese ports during the last century. Artists often painted the sailing vessels that dropped anchor and sold the finished products to the captains. Some of these were probably exported to America as part of the active America-China trade. The background of an oriental city with an American ship in the foreground makes for quite an interesting painting and you are well rewarded in collecting them.

Oil on canvas by Antonio Jacobsen, 1850-1921; American Marines of this type are always in demand. Value: $6,500-$7,500

owns it. In the hands of a well-known person, some oils are valuable, but if you own them, you may have long trying days to dispose of them at any price.

European Styles and Influences

Investment in European paintings by unknown artists is hazardous, as years ago (as well as today) paintings were turned out almost on a mass-production basis. If the artists are not regarded highly enough to receive acclaim in their native countries, they do not represent a good investment. Many travelers buy such oils on trips, hoping they have uncovered an artist who someday may be famous. You should buy these unknown Europeans for enjoyment alone, and invest in the American painting for enjoyment as well as future reward.

Barbizon School

When landscapes came into fashion early in the nineteenth century, a group of artists began painting scenes in places such as the Black Forest near Dusseldorf in Germany. The French picked this up in their forests at Fontainebleu, and both efforts resulted in what is termed the Barbizon School of painting. It is characterized by dark foregrounds which frame the lighted middle ground, which is the central theme of the picture, then a luminescent or silhouetted background, which creates a three-dimensional effect. This school served as an inspiration to many American painters who came to Europe to study. Corot, Daubigny, Millet, and Rousseau are among those who painted during this period.

Impressionism

Impressionism followed the Barbizon School and was pioneered by Monet, Renoir, Cezanne, and others. These artists created their atmospheric impressions of nature by breaking up the line of light and substance to give a rather dreamy quality to their work. Impressionism was not readily accepted either in Europe or in America, and it was not until the Art Institute of Chicago hung some Impressionist works in the 1890s that any measure of apperception was shown. At the time, the institute was the target of many critics who felt the work was quite inferior, and today it still tries to protect its reputation for being first in the exhibition of new works in order to live up to its late nineteenth-century success. Impressionism is quite popular today, with the work of some artists selling in the millions.

Cubism

Picasso revolted against Impressionism with a form generally referred to as Cubism. This is a technique of breaking down and taking apart forms of nature. It has a geometric quality which reshapes known forms to the idea of the artist and is not bound by any rules of conformity to accept forms. There have been few successful practitioners of Cubism, with Picasso remaining as the leader and the best known. Though other styles have succeeded it, some work in Cubism is still being done.

Surrealism and the Ashcan School

The twenties brought the Ashcan School, which was nothing more than a realistic portrayal of life in the city. The street or alley scene usually contained the inevitable waste receptacle, which gave this school its name. Much of this is good art and the supply is quite limited. Though it was not appreciated very much at the time, values on this school have risen a great deal today.

A new idea was also brewing at the same time; surrealism, or super reality. Its goal is to liberate man's unconscious personality from the chains of reason and inhibition; its best-known exponent is Salvador Dali. Surrealism could well be called a partner to abstractionism, and uses shapes, forms, and colors that have no counterparts in nature. Though this school has its investors and aficionados, it has not yet taken the country by storm, and only time will tell if it can repeat the successes of early styles, which had to wait years before being appreciated.

Expressionism

There has been one constant in all the painting styles which were instituted thousands of years ago, and that is the work of the expressionists. Expressionism is a revelation of the artist's personal emotions which may be traced throughout his or her lifetime. This style, more than any other, conveys feelings on a canvas through the use of brush and paint. In 1975, the Tate Gallery in London staged a retrospective of the works of John Constable. Moving from picture to picture, one could see the changing emotions of the artist. He painted three canvases of his father's farm in Dedham. Each with a different perspective. The

Currier and Ives print of American Forces under Gen'l Scott, Landing At Vera Cruz depicts activity during the Mexican War.

gallery indicted that the best version is at the Currier Gallery of Art in Manchester, New Hampshire.

El Greco, who made his fame and fortune in Spain, was very religious. All of his figures, whether human, animal, or imaginary are elongated toward heaven in search of the Divinity. El Greco's work is easily identified because of this personal expression.

Van Gogh's work clearly reflects his tormented passion as he painted before, during, and after his period of madness. When you see a complete showing of his work, such as the one staged in the 1960s at the Guggenheim Museum in New York, you can trace his emotions quite easily as you view successive canvases.

Prints

Engraving

The first plates from which prints were made were wood engravings, which produce what are now called wood-block prints. This work had been done in Europe for many years, but the first recorded American artist in this medium was John Foster of Boston, who did a likeness of the Reverend Richard Mather.

Where the artist wants a white space, he carves out the wood, leaving the remaining surface to receive the ink. Printing is done by rolling the paper over the inked block. This crude work, an early form of the art of reproduction likenesses, has great appeal. Many newspapers and periodicals relied on woodcuts for printing pictures right into the nineteenth century.

Line engravings were made in eighteenth century America by cutting or incising a design or picture on a soft copper plate with a sharp tool. Paul Revere made many of these; including his famous "Boston Massacre." This type of cutting is known as "intaglio" work. In "relief" work, the engraving is left raised above the plate. Intaglio and relief work are done by putting ink into the cut lines, wiping the plate clean, and then rolling damp paper against the surface on a press and forcing it into the lines, where it picks up the ink. The work was later done on steel plates, as copper was quite soft and could not make as many impressions as the harder metal. This technique was developed about 1820, so steel engravings may all be dated after that time.

Stipple engraving is done by impressing a design in dots rather than lines. An artist coats a plate with wax, and then stipples through it to the metal beneath. An acid which does not penetrate the wax is then spread over the plate, eating out holes in the metal at the points where the stippling was done. After the wax has been removed, the design is printed from the acid-etched plate.

Mezzotints were first made in the early part of the seventeenth century. A copper plate is roughened by crisscrossing it with lines, using a sharp tool. This roughness is smoothed out and shaded in areas to create the picture in reverse. After being inked, these plates are used for printing and several colors can be employed at one time. Shading to give better dimension to the work is possible with this technique. The English and French did excellent eighteenth century mezzotint work, which is very collectible today.

Etching is done in much the same manner as line engravings in relief, in that acid is used to score unprotected areas on the plate's surface. It was refined so that an artist might repeat the acid baths in certain areas to effect shading. In drypoint etching, no acid is used, and a pointed tool is employed to do the entire job, requiring the hand of a master.

Aquatint was developed at the end of the eighteenth century. It is a refined form of etching in which masses are printed more easily. A finely powdered resin is spread over the plate and solidified by heat. After the design is traced through it, acid is applied and reapplied to create the design and shading.

Lithography

Lithography is a process in which a greasy crayon is used to trace a design on a very porous stone. The stone is then soaked in water, and it absorbs the moisture in its clear areas. Ink is rolled on the surface and it clings to the crayon areas and is repelled by the wet stone. A sheet of paper is rolled on the stone, picking up the design from the remaining ink. Most colored lithographs were painted by artists after the printing. There is a revival in this form of work today, and some fine artists are quickly being recognized for their work.

This work by contemporary artists is not to be confused with the reprints of old work being turned out on sophisticated presses today. The offset method of printing has made faithful reproduction of old work possible, and you must be careful to examine prints to determine their age and authenticity. Also, beware of the practice of turning out prints by contemporary artists, numbering them in a short series, and then selling the complete series in different areas of the country. Buyers have been deluded into thinking they are getting limited edition originals. Most are dressed up in expensive frames, which enhance their appearance. Although the prints cost only a few cents to make, their frame dressings and a gullible public have resulted in quite a profitable business for the fakers.

Areas of Collecting Interest

Frederic Remington

Paintings of the Old West are very much in demand these days. One name that stands above most is Fredric Remington. Born in Canton, New York, in 1861, he migrated west, where he proceeded to capture the American scene in paintings, sketches, and bronzes. In 1990, one of his paintings sold for almost $4.5 million.

Most people cannot afford the luxury of such a painting, but there is one area of Remington collecting that is still open to most. Early is his career; he worked for *Harper's Weekly,* creating woodblocks of western scenes. This is the only place such work appears, as the originals and woodblocks have literally disappeared. Several museums as diverse as the Remington Art Memorial in Ogdensburg, New York, and the Bowdoin College Museum of Art in Brunswick, Maine, display collections from time to time. You can find an example in the book *Fredric Remington: Artist of the Old West,* by Harold McCracken (Lippincott). Though this book is no longer in print, perhaps your local library has a copy. These prints in *Harper's Weekly* date as early as 1886. Some are signed, some not. In 1890, 119 of his works appeared in the publication.

During this period in the latter 1880s, several Remington watercolors appeared in exhibitions in New York City, guaranteeing him a future as an artist. Some of the early *Harper's* prints sell in the three figures, so they are worth collecting. Often boxfuls of papers are sold at auction. Any from 1886 on are worth inspecting and possibly buying.

Historical Paintings

Paintings that depict the history of our country are much in demand. Many artists traveled from coast to coast to record the scene as they saw it in the nineteenth century. Along with photographers, they have made it possible for us to see our country as it was. Some of these paintings were reproduced as prints so that they might be made available to even those with meager means.

It is only recently that illustrative artists have come into their own. General opinion was that they painted quickly, only for money. Of course, they were commissioned to do their work under publishing deadlines. Many turned out fine work.

At the time of our centennial in the 1870s, many paintings with patriotic themes appeared and were quite popular. They still are today. They represent perhaps some of the best investment in art, as the big galleries have all but ignored the illustrative artists, so prices have not yet risen too high.

Original paintings or sketches by book illustrators appear at auction from time to time. If you can locate a copy of the book for which the work was done, you have a very interesting combination. Collect historical painting, etchings, and prints. They are much better than those with nebulous themes.

Japanese Woodblock Prints

A wide range of Japanese woodblock prints appear on the market and in auctions. They depict scenery of that country as well as portraits of the people in it. The most fascinating I have seen are those that portray Japan's modern wars, late in the last century and early into this one.

All in color, many in triptych, they portray battles on land and sea and present a view of the development of Japan as an industrial and militant nation. This art documents events in a manner that photography could never capture. Many of the artists are better known for their prints of life in the Meiji Period, 1868-1912. They excelled in their use of color. The stark coldness of winter battle and experiences are expressed with dramatic detail.

The golden age of Japanese woodblock printing generally is judged to be the eighteenth and early nineteenth centuries. The artist-designer, publisher, wood engraver, and printer together created masterful prints using the sophisticated techniques of embossing, color gradation, and overprinting. Probably few Japanese artists actually went to the battlefronts. Rather, their information came from photos or published accounts. They must have appealed to the pride of the Japanese as more than 100,000 impressions were made of some prints. Throughout history, the Japanese have enjoyed anything that conveys the bravery and loyalty of the military class (samurai).

Nantucket Baskets

The island of Nantucket is full of history and folklore. It is also the source of a very popular collectible—the Nantucket basket. The design for it was basically copied from that of the American Indians who lived there for centuries. The baskets are also called Nantucket Lightship baskets, as many were made on the South Shoal Nantucket

Portrait of Revolutionary War officer.

Nantucket pocketbook with ivory fittings. The famed Nantucket baskets were made at first aboard the lightship stationed there, then the craft continued ashore. The item pictured is one of the type being made there now.

Lightship between 1854 and 1890. They are unique in that they show the influence of the coopers, with bottoms, staves (vertical splints), and hoops (tops) in the manner of the whale oil barrels. Most were made by men aboard ship during lax hours, or around an iron stove ashore during the bad winter weather.

Nantucket baskets vary in size from quite small to about a peck capacity. In early baskets, two boards might make up the bottom; later ones had a single board with grooved channels to receive the splint. Staves were mostly of ash, oak, or hickory. Often, they were split of cordwood brought from the mainland. The weaving strands are cane or rattan. Most handles are eared so they can swing; very few are rigid. Some may be brass-eared. Nails are mostly copper, but later baskets have brass or iron nails. The baskets are characterized by their extremely tight weave, strength, and durability. Tops of Nantucket handbags most often feature a carved ivory or bone, or exotic wood panel, attached or embedded for decoration. A nest of eight baskets in different sizes today sells in the four figures.

There are contemporary makers whose output is spoken for many months in advance; in fact, some of the new sells for more than the old. Be aware, however, that they are being imitated, and quite well, by artisans in China who are sending them to us via Hong Kong. Look for labels or get other certification that yours is a real Nantucket basket. Unless you know how to tell them apart, you may be purchasing an import.

American Indian and Eskimo Artifacts

American Indian artifacts have soared in value, although most are not really very old. In fact, newer pieces are commanding more attention, especially those made in this century, because they are in better condition.

New England is not a good place in which to collect, as few items have survived. Most American Indians had left the area by the time of the Revolutionary War, so New Englanders must content themselves with broken shards of pottery, glass, arrowheads, and some metal items found in burial grounds years ago. None of the cloth, baskets, or decorated bone and ivory have survived in this area. Pennsylvanians have been able to come up with some later objects, but it is in the Far West that most collecting can be done. When American Indians migrated from the East to escape the oncoming settlers, they took everything with them, often even the bones of their ancestors, which were dug up, bagged, and reburied at their new home site.

The Hershey Museum in Hershey, Pennsylvania, features a large collection of American Indian artifacts. The Mount Kearsage Indian Museum in Warner, New Hampshire, also has exceptional artifacts, which its owners have collected over a period of many years.

Poster Art

Posters are known to have been made during the time of the early Egyptians and Romans. About 1840, posters gained popularity in France when they were used to advertise books. The female figure was added about 1880, and a whole new area of advertising was born. The advent of color lithography made it possible to reproduce huge paintings in billboard size, often in sections. Circuses, theaters, and businesses of all kinds seized on this method of attracting a crowd to their offerings and products. Noted artists whose work is sought today, such as R. Atkinson Fox, Maxfield

Navajo rug.

Wood ceremonial mask, c. 1830.

Pueblo pot, earthcolors.

Fringed pillow cover.

Parrish, and Henry Herrick, were among those who centered their work for commercial purposes and illustrated everything from newspapers and books to large posters and billboards. By 1895, poster art was well accepted; its popularity continues undiminished to this day.

Collectors are centering their activity on the older work which pictures the nostalgic years behind us. Some collect in categories, such as circuses, movie stars, theaters, etc; others acquire what they can just for decoration. The most desired posters seem to be those from France, particularly those by noted artists such as Manet and Toulouse-Lautrec.

The rules for collecting are quite simple. Subject matter is important—it must be of interest. Condition must be good. Many posters are water-stained from being framed with glass against them or foxed (discolored) from being backed with wooden boards (the pitch from the old boards will stain them). Rips and tears are a no-no. Color must be bold. Known artists are collectible.

Theorem Painting

Most old homes out in the country contain at least one painting on velvet, a product of the first half of the nineteenth century. Most are still lifes of fruit or flowers. Historians tell us artists traced a stencil on the cloth, then painted the design with watercolors directly on the cloth. Some feel this was a type of seminary art, learned by young girls along with household duties such as spinning and weaving. Yet there is evidence that many such paintings were done by housewives as an extra-curricular activity. None that I have seen has been attributed to a known painter.

Velvet is quite fragile; so many theorems have not aged well. Putting them into frames with glass against them and wooden pine boards behind has contributed to the attrition of many. Changing temperature in a home creates condensation on the underside of the glass, staining the cloth and removing the color.

Metals

GOLD

United States	**England**	**Europe**
24K pure	24K pure	1000 pure
22K 2 alloy	18K 6 alloy	800, Germany, Italy, Holland
18K 6 alloy	15K 9 alloy	
14K 10 alloy	13K 9 alloy	
10K 14 alloy	13K 11 alloy	

SILVER

United States, England, France	**Europe**
1000 pure	1000 pure
925 75 parts alloy, sterling	
900 100 parts alloy, France, sterling	
875 125 parts alloy, coin silver	

SHEFFIELD silver bonded to inferior metal by heat and rolling
SILVERPLATE silver bonded to inferior metal, electrically
EP electroplate
EPNS electroplated nickel silver
EPBM electro plated Britannia metal
SC silverplated on copper

PEWTER
90% tin 10% antimony
After 1820, Britannia pewter would withstand heat better, added—alloy metals
Under 9" diameter—plate
9" diameter and over—dish, charger, trencher

English Hallmarks on Silver 1794-1892

initials of maker

touch mark

head of reigning monarch

lion passant sterling mark

date letter

Brass is a mixture of copper and zinc. Bronze and bell metal are brass alloyed with other metals—formula dependent on foundry.

DECORATIVE ART GALLERY

THE COURSER AT SEA, oil on canvas, Joseph Lee, 1827-1880. Sold by Butterfields, Los Angeles, Dec. 13, 1994, for $50,600. Look for marine paintings with the American Flag, men, and activity on deck.

APPROACHING STORM NEAR NEWPORT, Martin Johnson Heade, American, c. 1860s. Heade is noted for landscapes and seascapes.

Many ship paintings are signed T. Bailey. Thomas Bailey painted in Newburyport, Massachusetts. Of Jewish decent, he changed his name to make a living in a Yankee community much better. He instructed art and many feel paintings attributed to him were done by his students and marketed with his signature. In the 1970s, there were at least 5 painters in the Boston area, still signing paintings, T. Bailey.

RETRIEVING, Edward Henry Potthast, 1857-1927. American artist well known for his beach scenes. Value: $17,500-$20,000

DOCK SCENE, Gloucester, MA, Childe Hassam. This area has inspired many painters who like harbor scenes. It sold November 30, 1989, at a Sotheby's auction for $770,000.

Worcester Art Museum.

REINE LEFEBVRE HOLDING A NUDE BABY, Mary Cassatt, American, 1844-1926, oil on canvas. Cassatt is one of the few American women painters who achieved international recognition.

GROUP AT NIAGARA FALLS, daguerreotype attributed to Platt D. Babbitt, c. 1855. Babbitt was one of the first tourist photographers who would snap pictures of groups and sell them on the spot.

Unmarked print of the view of Boston Harbor from Dorchester Heights, as it looked at the time of the Revolution. When George Washington took command of the Colonial armies, it was from this fort and two others that he harassed the British until they evacuated the city.

Early tintypes fall into collecting categories. Ordinary portraits have limited value. This, of George Armstrong Custer of Custer's last stand fame, is one that most collectors would like to have.

Daguerreotypes of public buildings are quite rare. This of the Capitol in Washington, was found on a flea market table.

VIEW ON THE ARNO, Thomas Cole, American born in England, 1801-1848. Oil on canvas painted 1837. Cole painted extensively in Europe as well as in this country.

PULLING DOWN THE STATUE OF GEORGE III, by Johannes B. Oertel. The event took place on July 9, 1776. New York Historical Society.

THE LAST OF THE MOHICANS, Thomas Cole, 1827, with scene from James Fenimore Coopers' novel, showing Coar kneeling before Tamenund. Oil on canvas.

Mourning pictures and prints were popular in the 19th century. There are variations seen throughout the country, inspired by the ethnic origins of the inhabitants.

Joseph Davis, an itinerant painter, worked in Southeastern NH, in the second quarter of the 19th century. His work is well documented as to the identity of his subjects and is characterized by fanciful floor and table coverings.

FOURTH OF JULY PARADE, Dorothy Davis, Yarmouthport, Cape Cod, Massachusetts, 1775. Davis is well known for painting on old breadboards, which gives her work a nostalgic look. The antiques shop proprietor witnesses the parade from her open door. Value: $2,500-$3,000

ELECTION RETURNS, TO THE POLLS, Thomas Waterman Wood, 1823-1903. Watercolor, 1867.

Trade advertisements are nostalgic.

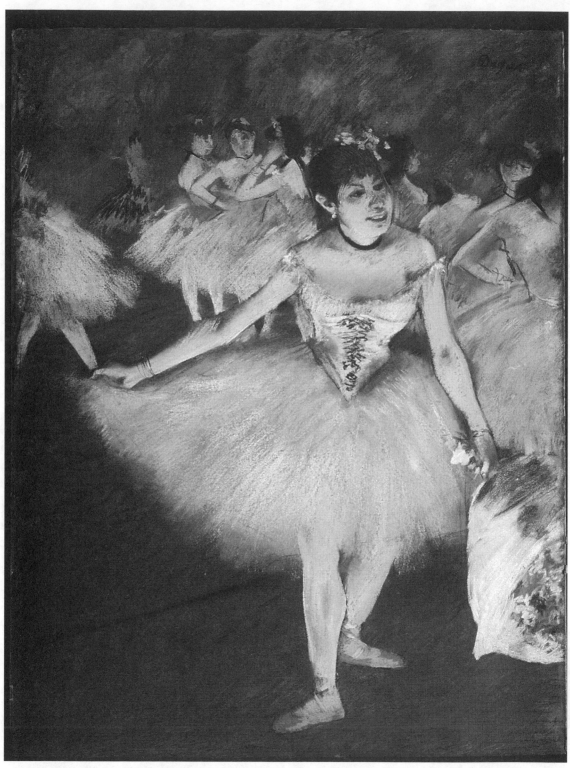

SUR LA SCENE, Edgar Degas, c. 1881. Pastel on Paper. The artist is well known for picturing ballet dancers.

Chapter Six

TEXTILES

Wall Hangings

Samplers

A sampler is a wall decoration created by embroidering hand-woven cloth. Most samplers were done on linen until the middle of the nineteenth century, when the less expensive cotton took over. Samplers tested a young girl's ability to sew an alphabet and figures, and to create an interesting and pleasing design. Those of the eighteenth century are the most desired, because of their age and primitive quality. They were not originally made to

Samplers were made by almost every young lady back in the 18th and 19th centuries. They are judged by interest in design and condition. Pictured is one of the best type. Value: $4,000-$6,000

be framed, but in the early part of the nineteenth century it became fashionable to hang them as interesting works of art. They were more appreciated by the descendants of those who made them. In the second quarter of the nineteenth century, less attention was paid to the letters and figures and more to scenic decoration, such as farm buildings, trees, flowers, and animals. These pictorial samplers are judged not only on quality of work, but also on design. These were the work of the younger girls, with the older girls turning their attention to embroidered pictures.

The nineteenth century saw the arrival of "Berlin Work," named after a light wool used to make clothing and gloves. Designs were woven to a base cloth in artistic fashion, and a three-dimensional effect could be achieved because the thread could be raised at the whim of the artist. Most designs were made on canvas, but some were done on the combed or worsted wools of the day. Patterns were copied from publications such as *Godey's Ladies Book* and some were copied from the paisleys done in Scotland at the time.

Stevengraphs

Another product of the Victorian era is the Stevengraph, a silk picture framed as a wall hanging. The jacquard loom was invented in France in 1810 and made weaving pictures into any fabric possible. Soon manufacturers everywhere were using it. The loom was computer-operated in that pierced cards were used to direct the pattern being woven. French silk was permitted free entry to England at the time of the Cobden Treaty in 1860 and this harmed the economy of the English mills. Coventry was a center of this work, and the enterprising

Thomas Stevens of Coventry created bookmarks that caught the public fancy. He later turned to the production of pictures in silk. Even those made by the other firms that followed are given the generic name Stevengraph. The first of these was made about 1879, and was introduced at an exhibition in York. Even postcards were made with woven silk panels and these are collectors' items. Condition is most important in determining value today; many are water-stained and/or faded. Some were unmounted, but those with aged frames are best.

Rugs

Early American

Early rugs are one of the most expressive forms of American folk art. When you consider that practically every young lady was taught to spin, weave, and sew, you would think there should be an abundance of floor coverings as millions must have been made since the Pilgrims landed. However, collectors do not find it easy to locate outstanding examples since, as with most art, few fit this description. While thousands of artisans plied every trade, only a few set themselves apart as true artists whose work is of great quality. Though many girls were proficient with tools such as looms, wheels, and winders, not all could be classified as true artists in their work—they made necessities for the home, perhaps with little or no talent for good design and decoration.

Hooked rugs made of wool on a foundation of homespun linen between 1775 and 1840 are direct and original in design. Folk rugs were given an added brilliance with the introduction of Turkey red dye in 1829. Chenille, the rarest product of hand manufacture, is made by threading a half inch strip of cloth lengthwise, gathering and rolling it to appear like a furry caterpillar, and then stitching it on to a closely woven fabric.

Naturalistic floral medallions, with scroll borders and corner spandrels, appear frequently in rugs made in the latter part of the nineteenth century. These were first popularized by Edward Sands Frost of Biddeford, Maine, a tin peddler, whose stenciled burlap designs tolled the knell of the bold original patterns of the earlier period. While peddling tinware, Frost had noted many housewives at work at their rug frames, and vowed he could create better designs than the housewives had available. He traced and cut out tin stencils using his shears, reproduced them on burlap, and began peddling these along with his other products. His designs soon caught on and he created a full line, many of which are reproduced for visitors at Greenfield Village at the Henry Ford Museum in Dearborn, Michigan. Frost's pattern Number Two features the initials of a bride and groom worked into the border, about four feet apart. On the facing border is a place for the minister to stand, and all step into position for the wedding vows.

Large rugs were used as bed coverings at first, since they were considered too fine to suffer abuse on the floor. Their quality of warmth and the greater availability of materials soon resulted in their common use as floor coverings. Until that time, it had been popular to paint floors in colorful designs. Later on, canvas might be painted to spread as a covering, and this may have been the forerunner of the gaily printed Linoleums. Braided rugs are in keeping with early homes, as are oriental rugs.

Oriental

Oriental rugs represent a complete study in themselves, as they are judged by pattern and workmanship. They were popular in wealthy homes, and many were carried here in the China-American trade. Rugs from the Near East gradually assumed greater importance to buyers in America, and the rugs from old Persia, now Iran, are among the best to collect. Rug weaving by hand is tiresome work, and a large rug will often consume up to five years in the making, with several people working at it. It is said that the art of making them may die out since young people are not eager to take on such a chore. I wonder at the abundance of these rugs coming into America at this time, which are often sold in major cities at auction in order to dispose of them. Can it be possible that some machinery has been smuggled into the hills to help out in production? If this is a dying art, how can so many be offered at auction brand new?

The Peoples Republic of China is responsible for some exceedingly fine rugs that are finding their way out to the open market via Hong Kong. The workmanship is superb, and prices for these rugs are on par with the best from Iran and in some cases exceed them. There has been a continual output of "oriental" rugs from Belgium; during the

One must do a lot of learning to get involved in the collecting of Oriental rugs. Pictured is a carpet from India, dated to the 17th century.

1950s thousands must have been sold here at low prices. Dealers purchased the 9 x 12 size at three for $100 and pitched them out at auctions for $50 apiece. Although beautiful in design and color, they are quite thin and wrinkle easily on the floor. Those from the Orient and Middle East are much heavier and of better quality. (See *Oriental Rugs* under Areas of Collecting Interest for more information, page 310)

Quilts

Quilts are common, as most old homes have a trunk or two full of them. The quality of each piece must be judged on the originality of the design, quality of work, color, and condition. If it is documented with the year and possibly the name of the maker or owner woven into it, a quilt will assume much more importance. Pennsylvania, Ohio, and New York take top marks for the production of quilts in the nineteenth century, as the designs are colorful, reflecting the German-Dutch heritage of many of their settlers. New England can be credited with much fine work, but there was less attention given to dating and naming these.

Construction Techniques

A quilt is made up of three parts—the top that carries a main design, the filler, and the back. In the old days, cotton and wool were favorite fillers, but many synthetics are used today. Quilts were not always fancy looking; many of the earliest were called *white-on-white*, the design being impressed as the upper cover was stitched to the backing. When the stitches are spaced apart to form ridges that outline a design, it is called *trapunto* work. A

pieced quilt is made by stitching different pieces, often of different colors and patterns, together to form a design. *Appliqué quilts* are made by sewing different pieces to the top cover, forming the design in this manner. *Crazy quilts* were made in the Victorian era and were so called because they consisted of such random pieces as parade ribbons, flags of all countries, advertising flags, and even neckties. These are judged in the same manner as the earlier ones and should be preserved as interesting bits of Americana.

One of the most desired pieces is a Baltimore quilt, so named because of the city in which they were made. These were made by girls facing marriage, and most are really great works of art. Some have sold well into the four figures because of their superb quality and beauty. It would seem that the young ladies vied to outdo their friends and that such competition resulted in greatness.

It is thought that the *patchwork quilt* was a creation of the New World, where cloth was at a premium. The economy of the times is reflected in the quilts: Clothing and other cloth items eventually appeared as patches in quilts. In the eighteenth and nineteenth centuries, young girls were expected to have at least thirteen quilt tops—twelve for everyday and one special top to show their most elegant work before becoming engaged. When betrothed, a young woman would invite friends to a quilting bee, and after setting up the bridal top on a frame, all would join in quilting it.

Quilt designs have names, and patterns for quilts were circulated for all to use. Most were made from scrap material and old discarded clothing. Cooperative quilts were made by members of churches or organizations. Each member contributed a square of work, often signed, and these were later sewn together to make the finished product. Some quilts relate the history of a group or an event. For example, the English regimental quilt at the Shelburne Museum in Shelburne, Vermont, depicts scenes from the many countries in which this regiment served, along with views of its permanent station in the British Isles. Others were made with materials from France, which might be separate squares with pictures of U.S. Presidents or other famous people printed in the fabric. Some were made from cloth with designs already worked in it on Jacquard looms. Exotic fabrics such as silk and embroidered cottons found their way here from India and were used to good advantage.

Quilt wrought by Arlette Hathaway Howard, 1840-1990, in various fabrics.

Appliquéd and embroidered Hudson River Quilt, made between 1969 and 1972. Sold by Sotheby's on January 27, 1990 for $23,100.

Designs were printed in many of the women's magazines of the day, but most quilts were the result of the material available and the individual taste of the maker. Some designs are geometric, others floral, and some even approach pure abstract art. Making a quilt is rather like painting with cloth, and it is in this light that each is judged today.

It is felt by some historians that, during the middle of the last century, the quilters in Baltimore raised this work to the level of an art form. Tradition tells us that most young ladies were expected to make at least thirteen quilts before becoming really proficient in creating one of these categories. These final efforts are among the best ever made in this country and are sought by collectors. Perhaps one of the best examples one might see is at Claverton Manor in Bath, England, the site of the American Museum in Britain.

Today quilt makers are still at work, working in traditional as well as contemporary designs. Whether their work will be revered as much as those of the last century must be left to the judgment of time. The outstanding place to see and buy contemporary quilts is the annual Mennonite auction held in Harrisburg, Pennsylvania. The women of this religious group spend the year making up to 300 quilts, which are sold to raise money for relief purposes throughout the world. The quality is very good, and because of this, the auction attracts about ten thousand people, which must make it the largest in the world.

Areas of Collecting Interest

Clothing

In the past two centuries, there have been three basic skirt forms: The hoop, the bustle, and the sheath. The latter is the only style to survive. In the last century a poet immortalized the plight of a suitor, saying, "He must stand and bellow in thundertones, across half an acre of skirts and bones, as if hailing a ship on the ocean." With the demise of the hoop and bustle, the fashion world lost some colorful and graceful styling in feminine apparel.

At the time of the Revolution the bustle was in, but shortly thereafter, there was a return to the simple sheath. Examples of sheaths were found during excavations in the Mediterranean area. About 1820, the hoop was introduced, and grew wider

and wider until it reached its maximum width before the Civil War. After the war, in a time of conservatism and restraint, it lost its popularity. Women fought for suffrage and for liberation from the old ways, including dress.

However, the wealthy preferred a fancier look and the bustle returned in the late 1860s. It was once termed the "upholstered" look because every inch of fabric was secured by hundreds of tuckings. Never has a period known more opulent materials, color combinations or lavish use of trimmings. Homemakers and working girls, however, had to content themselves with what they could turn out on their sewing machines or, toward the

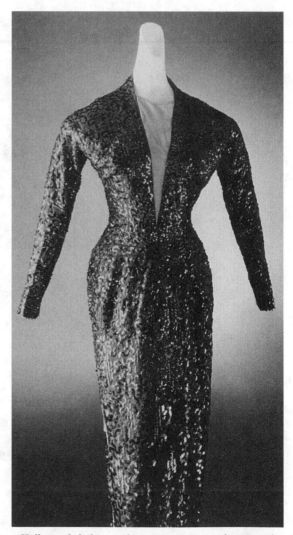

Hollywood clothing and accessories are another area of collecting. Pictured is a red sequined evening dress worn by Marilyn Monroe in Gentlemen Prefer Blondes.

Collectible Coverlets

A coverlet is a woven bed cover made on a loom. Our earliest collectible coverlet is called a linsey-woolsey. Those eighteenth-century examples that have survived are treasured today. There is still a question as to whether they are all wool, or part linen, as the name implies. Late research suggests they are named for the town of Linsey in England where they were reportedly first made. Identified by their wool-like quality, linsey-woolsies are really two layers of homespun stitched together, often in design. Each layer is a different color, with a lighter side for summer and a darker for winter. The cloth was dyed with readily available materials, such as onionskins, beets, bark, and ochres. They are subject to damage by moths, so most reveal a hole or two, but some were protected in cedar chests over the years and have found their way to some historic home or restoration. In later years, coverlets were decorated with embroidery, and some are works of art. The Shelburne Museum features a sample quilt on which the maker worked the alphabet and numerals in several different fashions, along with floral motifs and other decorations. A person ordering a coverlet from this maker would be able to choose a design and a type of lettering and numbering. Such sample quilts are rare.

Redwork coverlet with eagle, c. 1861.

end of the century, what was available from a Sears Roebuck or Montgomery Ward catalog.

With the advent of mail order, styles were kept simple for ease of packaging. Huge textile mills were supplying the world with inexpensive fabrics from which clothing could be made quickly for all members of the family, but most of this lacked high style. It was left to the major stores in the large cities to import the newest fashions from overseas for the wealthy, who would have nothing to do with production fabrics, and so helped keep a modicum of style here.

Around 1879, skirts narrowed, with long, slim trains supported by a bustle-like pad with a tied-back look. The largest bustle size was reached by 1885, then the style gradually faded away early in the twentieth century.

Some of the most desirable clothing was made during the Deco period between 1920 and 1940, when designers were dressing the movie stars in regal attire. Boas and sequins over form-fitting silks made quite an impression, still enjoyed today. At home, the wealthy sought out the services of such independent designers to make their high-style clothing as well. This gave rise to boutiques, run by many who are legends today.

Until our bicentennial, few people saw value in keeping old garments. Actually, not many survived as they were cut up for quilting or rug making, or handed down until worn out and eventually used as rags. Those locked in old trucks were most often sold with the trunk at auction. Few museums paid attention to garments, as they are fragile, take much room to exhibit, and models for them are costly.

At the Smithsonian, however, an exhibit of the inaugural dresses worn by our first ladies stimulated interest. More recently, some museums have added old "costumes" to their collections. Collectors entered the competition to be ready for the bicentennial celebrations, which many felt would create a demand for period clothing.

In the late sixties and early seventies young people began dressing in offbeat clothing as a rebellion against conformity. They haunted auctions and thrift shops, searching out the bizarre as well as practical. Some have told me they did not have money and this was the only clothing they could afford. Whatever the reason, the interest in old clothing has grown and one must compete for the old clothing now.

"Flame" Stitching

If you have an old handbag or chair seat covering with a V-shaped, rather jagged design, it could be very old. This design is known as Irish stitching; in this country, some refer to it as "flame" stitching. In the seventeenth and eighteenth centuries, the most popular work done on canvas used the Irish, tent, cross or queen s stitches. The latter is the most difficult of all and very few examples have survived from that period.

The Irish stitch is vertical on the front and diagonal on the reverse side. It was relatively easy to do as thread went over three or four weft yarns, while in other stitches the thread might pass over only one yarn. With the Irish stitch it was possible to create large areas of cloth suitable for such big jobs as upholstering a chair. Anyone who has a chair with this original flame stitch upholstery has a treasure indeed. The Irish stitch takes several forms: a diamond within a diamond, flowers, or even geometric shapes. Today, some use it in bargello work.

Flame stitching is one of the earliest forms of needlework in which the artisan might sign the work by stitching in a name, year of manufacture, and possibly location—something that was done extensively in the jacquard coverlets of the early nineteenth century in this country. The Irish stitch can be found on panels used in early fire screens, chair seats, and footstools, and also on tablecloths.

Most of the early Irish stitch work found in this country was probably done here. Immigrants from the British Isles brought the tradition with them. One should seek advice on the care of such fabric, as it is highly sought by museums and collectors.

Clothing Accessories

Buttons

Button collecting first took hold in this country during the Depression. The National Button Society of America was organized to promote collection and display of buttons.

There are many classifications of this collectible, with a wide range of types to choose from. Eighteenth-century buttons are rare since not many have survived. The most familiar are the military buttons, which were saved because of an attachment to the history of the American Revolution, which prompted many people to save the uniforms of their ancestors. While the uniforms disappeared due to the ravages of moths or time, the buttons were most often saved as a final remembrance. Much of the clothing of the eighteenth century was held together by sashes, belts, and hooks.

In the early nineteenth century, fashionable women were dressed in the Greek Revival style, and buttons were used sparingly on their draped clothing. Buttons were used mostly by men. It was not until the change of styles after the Civil War that buttons came into general use on clothing for all members of the family. Early buttons were made of copper, porcelain, precious metals such as gold and silver, glass, steel, bone, ivory, and even wood. Decoration was done by enameling, carving, molding, and gilding. Some buttons were silver plated after this technique was developed in the 1840s. Many housewives made buttons from the bones of farm animals by cutting, shaping, and polishing, and these were used frequently on undergarments. You can tell bone from ivory by examining the material with a magnifying glass—bone will have small black specks throughout, whereas ivory is clear. Many "gold" buttons are actually made of pinchbeck, which is a manmade product, so you must judge most of these in this light. The technique of decorating buttons by enameling them originated overseas many years ago and was not practiced much in America, so most enameled buttons we find are probably European.

Metal buttons were chased and engraved with decorations, and some are now called "steel cut," referring to the bright facets left by such work. Hunt clubs often had sporting buttons with hunting scenes on them made up for their members. Some buttons were enameled on metal, and others were done on porcelain. Some buttons were made in concave or convex fashion and joined together at the rims to form a hollow button. Exotic materials such as shell, mother-of-pearl, and tortoise are found, but although these are not common, they do not command much interest.

Housewives often made fabric buttons by sewing material over a shaped disc and then drilling holes to accommodate the thread. Some of the early steel buttons will rust and must be oiled or otherwise protected. Gems were used on royal buttons, but it is unlikely that you will find any of these in America.

Horn was sometimes used for button making; some was simply carved, and another technique involved molding the material by using heat. Most American "pearl-looking" buttons came from Birmingham, England, where they were made in abundance during the middle of the 19th century. This pearl look was later duplicated in plastic, which eventually dominated other materials in button manufacture. Compositions of plastic and other synthetic materials became the rule in button making and fine quality gradually disappeared except in buttons made for the carriage trade.

Other materials of exotic nature used in buttons were vegetables, ivory, nuts, and even seeds. Jet is best known for its use in jewelry, but it was also used for buttons. It is actually a natural material called lignite, which has a coal black quality that was eventually reproduced in a black glass, which can fool the uninitiated. Pressed glass buttons were turned out by major factories, but the quality of most is not great, and they are collected for their curiosity value alone. Paperweight buttons were made to look like the larger weights and are interesting to collect. Then there are the charm string buttons—every string contains at least a thousand small buttons, each different from the others. A girl would collect these buttons until, supposedly, the final one was put on by the man she married. Some doubt that they ever existed, while others feel that the strings were long ago broken up as a practical matter when clothing needed mending.

The decorating motifs and shapes of buttons were influenced by the art forms prevalent in other decorative items, so a true collector can soon learn to classify his collection into different periods. You must keep abreast of the action in button buying and selling, but this can be difficult as there are few specialists in the field because of the low rewards. There are many buttons selling for just a few cents and this brings a much lower return than antiques, which sell for many dollars. You can learn a lot on your own by buying boxes of buttons at auctions and then sorting them out. Those of interesting and/or valuable materials, those with good design and decoration, and those that show some handwork in their making are ones you can consider saving. You will assimilate much knowledge if you deal in buttons and keep buying and selling until you learn what the collectors want, and this will guide you in what you should be collecting if profit is important to you. If buttons are represented, as having come from the garments of famous people, be sure you have documentation before buying. The woods are full of good storytellers.

Parasols

Back in the Victorian era, when walking was the method used by most people to get from place to place, the parasol was considered a definite part of a lady's costume. A woman had to be quite strong to carry one, as many parasols weighed eight or ten pounds.

The oldest and heaviest parasols seem to be in demand today. The handles are the key to desirability. One will find handles in carved bone, walrus tusk, horn, tortoise, precious metals, gem encrusted, bamboo, and many other kinds of wood.

Early in the nineteenth century, parasols were quite small, designed more as protection from the sun. By the 1880s, they were made of a variety of materials and were much larger. Some were made of colorful silk and even striped with red tassels and cords. In the 1880s, an inventor created one whose cloth might be changed to complement whatever costume its owner wore.

Once parasols had to be crammed into trains and automobiles, they were transferred into functional protection against wet weather, streamlined, and reduced in size. Those most favored today collapse and can be placed in a large handbag. Buy the old for decoration, not use, as the old materials have become fragile with age.

Oriental Rugs

More and more people are turning to Oriental rugs not only as a floor covering, but also as an investment. Homer mentions them in his Odyssey as early as 800 B.C., and even the great philosopher Plato is known to have had an outstanding collection. The turbulence in Iran has created pressures on the rug market, as it is not known how dependable the supply will be—hence the growing interest in those already in this country.

There is perhaps no field of collecting in which the majority of buyers know so little about the product; so much education is needed before one ventures out into the world of Oriental rugs. One must identify origin, material, weave, and dyes, and should ask the following questions as well:

Does it lie flat or is it crooked? Has it been washed and repainted to brighten the colors? Are the edges bound? Has it been clipped and possibly made up from several rugs? Do the colors bleed? Does it have jufti knots (knots tied in four rows of warp threads instead of two, which takes less time to weave)? Was it made of dead wool (that taken from a dead animal), which will wear more rapidly? And on and on. The rules in Oriental rug collecting are numerous, and one must be well advised before investing.

Many antique items bought for investment are relatively low in cost, but the investment in a good rug may run into the thousands. This is why reading good literature and doing business with reputable people in the field is most important.

Condition of a rug is also important. Keep animals from soiling your rug. Keep it out of the sun so an end won't fade, and, above all, change the position of your furniture from time to time to even the wear.

Printed Textiles

Printed scenic wallpapers, printed ceramics, and printed cloth all seem to have had their beginnings in the eighteenth century. Textiles were printed from wood blocks, which had been cut to the desired pattern. The durability of the inks is attested by examples in museums today. In the beginning, such printing was used for decoration alone. The cut surfaces of the blocks were inked with the colors desired, then pressed one by one alongside each other to create the picture. An artist was at hand to ink in the borders where the lines might not join as accurately as desired.

Late in the century, the English used this technique to create such mundane objects as handkerchiefs. Some featured noted events of the day, such as the opening of a bridge or the creation of a new building. Early in the nineteenth century, events such as the first railroad to go into operation were memorialized on cloth. Soon, printed squares were sewn together to create coverlets, pillows, and the like.

In our country, printed cloth was soon used to promote patriotism as well as politics. With the machine age came the engraved rollers, which could print the cloth as rapidly as it could be fed through them. In France, copper plate printing was developed early in the century and combined in the roller plates. One will find panels with likenesses of Washington, Lincoln, and other patriots. They can be framed and preserved as excellent wall hangings.

Sampler, Dorothy Kirtlan, aged 9, 1834.

Sampler, Sarah Jane West, December 1837.

Needlepoint sampler,
Leah Barlow,
May 12, 1850.

Sampler, Sally Harmon, aged 4, July 16, 1822.

"Yo-Yo" bed cover and 2 pillow shams, c. 1920.

Stevensgraph woven bookmark.

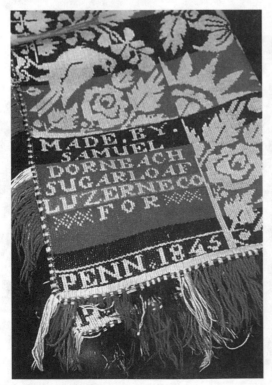

American made coverlet dated 1845.

American quilt c. 1880-1890

Satin fan with painted flowers and mother-of-pearl.

Fans seem to go back to the beginnings of civilization. They reached their zenith in the 19th century, when silk fans from the Orient, as well as Europe, were readily available and fashionable. Value: $250-$300

George and Martha Washington are immortalized in this covert which features their portraits done from copper plate printing in France, c. 1840s.

Fine silk needlework, about 10" x 12", worked by a seminarian in Maine. Sold in 1975 for $1,000 in Portland.

Historic Deerfield.

Smithsonian Institution.

Years ago, all young ladies were taught needlework. This framed example from the 17th century could have been made from patterned linen.

Quilt made from banners from the 1848 presidential campaign when James Polk and George Dallas were proposed as Democratic candidates.

Linen pocket early 18th century. Forerunner of the pocketbook, handbag, or reticule purse.

Navajo Germantown woman's wool chief's-style blanket. Value: $6,000-$9,000

THE CRYSTAL BALL

When I entered this business in 1950—it was easy to collect. Nobody wanted anything made after 1830—about the time machines took over. We did not have to learn anything about Victorian, Eastlake, Mission, Art Deco, Art Noveau, etc. Nor was there interest in Depression or carnival glass or Fiestaware, as everyone was still using it. We sold Tiffany vases for two to five dollars; Rookwood vases with Indian pictures on them went for the same price. Now, these are in the thousands. The leaded shades were broken up to melt the frames for the lead. Oak was cut up to feed our auction gallery stoves as nobody would bid on it. Those were the good old days.

One might be horrified at these revelations, but I am sure you have heard them before. Who knew we should save the crumby looking Pairpoint lamps, or round oak tables, or the Eastlake Texas highboys? We enlarged my gallery building and buried 60 brass bed headboards, footboards and springs in the cement floor for reinforcement. The rails went into the foundation walls. Yet, many ask what we should be collecting now for the future. Collecting has taken off and those of us involved are getting a better handle on what might be good to collect based on our past experiences and mistakes. Remember, the more documented history there is for a piece the better.

Contemporary furniture has a future, but it is already quite high in price. It can only go higher, if made by a recognized craftsman. Glassblowers, potters, silversmiths, jewelry designers, and others are making pieces that compete with the old for dollar value—so one must seek out those who are doing the good work. In the collectibles' field, items made of Bakelite, old golf equipment, home run balls hit by famous players, autographs of sports and entertainment figures, commemorative china and glass items made at the turn of the century, c. 1900 are nowhere near at their height now, photography collecting is in its infancy—there is still much out there in tintypes, ambrotypes, and glass plate negatives to find and process. War items now command premium prices, especially if they are related to noted warriors in our several conflicts. A more esoteric collectible is the hound-handled pitcher, mostly in Rockinghamware—made both here and overseas. The various hounds help identify the makers.

I advise staying away from any item which can be reproduced easily—many by machine. This has harmed values in art, depression, and carnival glass. Copper luster pitchers have declined since the 1950s because of reproduction.

Another good area of collecting involves books on antiques and collectibles. Most are published in small editions and never printed again. There is so much in them that one might miss, if they are not available. I use information from some which were published late in the nineteenth century—some issued by museums. My favorite texts are the 1829 and 1869 sets of encyclopedias, leather bound, which tell us exactly what was happening at those times.

Some publishers are reproducing original catalogs printed by companies in the nineteenth century. Such treasures—as they picture by line drawings and photos what the items are and how much they cost originally. Book collecting is high on the list for the future.

Toys are appreciated by almost everyone. Some collect the new in various categories, planning to save them for years, before liquidation. Left in the original boxes and never played with, they are bound to rise in value. Look at what has happened to the toys of the 1950s and 1960s.

In conclusion, there is no set place where money should be invested for the future. Do what gives you pleasure. Do not worry about future values—just enjoy what you have, so long as you do not incur heavy financial investments that are a burden. You should buy everything as if you plan to sell it someday, but there is nothing wrong about buying good items and enjoying them as well.

GM

Wood-handled kitchen utensils are being collected and used. They make a colorful display hanging on the kitchen walls. They are being reproduced.

Leather fire buckets were a necessity in every home. While helping in a fire, the buckets could be mixed up; hence the name of owner on the side. Value: $450 ea.

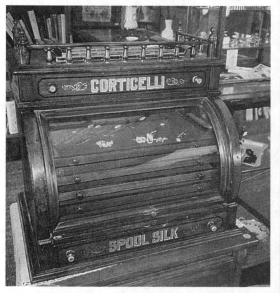

Corticello spool silk cabinet in walnut, dated c. 1870-1890. This was priced in a shop in Wisconsin in 2001, for $495, which I considered a very reasonable price.

Necessities for the early home were a large (spinning) wheel and a yarn winder.

Very popular are these sewing boxes, many made of papier-mâché which came from the Orient. They came filled with the necessities for doing needlework of all types. Value: $450-$600

The last remaining wood from the elm tree in Cambridge, Massachusetts, under which George Washington took command of the colonial troops, was made into 75 oval spandrel frames to commemorate the occasion. These were made by the Old Schwamb Mill, Arlington, Massachusetts, the nation's oldest picture and frame manufactory.

Folding screens are made of many materials, silk, leather, wood, embroidery, etc. This is a fine hand-printed silk screen, most likely from the Orient. Seen at a museum in Capetown, South Africa.

Player pianos were common in the 20th century household. Public places like restaurants and bars had the versions which required a coin to operate them. One still sees them out West in restored towns. Value: $3,500-5,000

Many artists paint tin, mostly at home. They haunt auctions and shops for old trays, teapots, and the like. This tray was painted by Mona Rowell of Townsend, Massachusetts, an instructor in the art. Value: $600-$700

Butterfield & Butterfield.

Most large sculptured pieces are expensive to collect. Witness this carved white marble figure of a fisher boy, c. 1900 which sold at Butterfields in Los Angeles, 3/30/93 for $16,100.

Chalkware rooster and hen, late 19th century. Sold for $2,500 at Sotheby's 5/25/97. Items like these are most likely made of plaster.

Historic pocketknife with ivory hands inscribed, "Gary Owens Boys, Home of the Brave Fighting 7th," 1862. Marked Taylor, Sheffield. This was found at Camden Passage Market in London. 4-1/2". Value: $350

Carved wood Czar's plate, which reads, Eat Bread And Salt And Talk Straight In Face. When a ruler came into town in Russia, he or she was greeted with one of these with bread and salt on it, some of which must be eaten before entering the town. The citizenry then expected the truth from the monarch. One will find these in porcelain and silver offered in the richer communities. Bought in Moscow during 1970. Value: $350-$500

Carved wood butter mold bought in Vienna. It would form just about a pound. Value: $150

Food chopper invented by Charles Starret of Newburyport, Massachusetts, 1865. These still work quite well.

Quite unique is this record player built into a lamp stand. This is hand crank, 78-RPM. Value: $450-$600

Plate warmers were a necessity during the cold weather. They sat next to the fireplace. All I have seen were made in England, but it is felt that any well-appointed home in this country had one. Value: $800-$1,200

One of the variations in music boxes is this double disc version by Symphonion. This is quite a rare example with two discs.

For some reason wooden bit braces still sell well. I understand it is because these are the only drill devices which can hold the old spiral drill bits, many of which are made of quality steel.

These are whaling tools which were used for the grappling of whales and the cutting of blubber.

Wooden planes are plentiful. Best ones are marked by maker, generally imprinted on the end of the bodies. Many are still used.

Wooden ironers which one will find in Northern Europe and Scandinavia. Some were made in Pennsylvania. These were filmed at Christianfeld, a Moravian settlement in Denmark.

Cutters and choppers of all kinds were made to prepare vegetables and meats for the table. This is an elaborate two-handled example. Value: $150-$250

Coffee grinder made by Enterprise in Philadelphia—a fixture in most grocery stores in the late 19th and early 20th centuries. They were made in three sizes. Value: $450-$600

There are collectors of horse-drawn vehicles, many of which are sold at auctions which feature them, exclusively. Those seen in movies are much desired, such as this Brougham which was featured in "Journey To The Center Of The Earth."

Classic and antique automobiles have been collected since the 1930s. Witness this classic Bugatti from Italy made in the 1930s.

Pre-Columbian figures are made primarily of clay and have aged over the years. Often, they are whimsical, and many, examples of which can be seen in the arts museum in Lima, Peru, are quite erotic. They are being reproduced and aged, so get a certificate of authenticity if you purchase one. Value: $1,200

Tobacconist counter sign, something that maybe will never be made again. Value: $800-$1,000

Most carved wooden African art has come into this country in the hands of tourists. Most is not of high quality as it is made by untrained artisans who work at this trade to obtain money on which to live.

These are nameplates from fire trucks of the early 20th century. Value: $50-$200

Fire trucks of any period are collectable. Look for original paint and figures, hoses, reels, ladders, etc., that belong on the truck.

Sotheby's.

An early Marklin tinplate clockwork paddleboat, St. Paul. Sold by Sotheby's 6/22/91 for $15,400.

There are collectors of toys as well as fire wagons who would compete for a piece such as this. Must be complete with horses and driver as well as assistant at rear. Value: $2,250

Whirly-gigs have been around for centuries. One will see excellent examples on tours overseas. These were popular during the depression, when out of work wooden workers loaded their lawns with examples to sell for a few dollars. Value: $250

Dancing Minstrel, made in Rochester, New York. He would rest atop a 78-RPM record as it is spun and dance to the music, c. 1920s. Value: $250

The Acrobats, by C.M. Crandall and Company, Montrose, Pennsylvania, c. 1870s. The acrobats could be interlocked in many different poses. Value: $850

Unusual Santa ornament, showing him arriving in a rocket ship. Old and unusual ornaments like this have sailed up in price. Value: $250

Bisque head doll made by Simon and Halbig, Thuringia, Germany. Many are just marked S&H. One of the better dolls to collect. Value: $600

Rare Bru circle dot poured bisque head bebe doll, French, c. 1870s. Value: $1,200-$1,500

Santa is a favored figure to collect. This figure is in celluloid. He sold at an auction in the 1970s for $300.

Rockers were put on many devices. We see them here on a child's rocking horse with seat back, as well as on the butter churn beneath. Value of horse: $350; churn: $250

Often, parents or grandparents would make toys for children. This folk art crow, which clacks his beak up and down while moving, is a good example. Value: $75-$85

Early 20th century, wooden rocking horse, handcrafted by Relko of England. Sold at Butterfields in San Francisco, 12/4/90 for $1,320.

Butterfield & Butterfield.

Cast iron boat, with four-man varsity crew, 1898. A lot of action from the rowers as the boat is pulled along. Value: $6,000-$8,000

Popeye On A Motorcycle, made by Hubley, c. 1932, in iron. The famed sailor first appeared in a 1929 comic strip. Value: $600

Some examples which date back to the 1920s and 1930s. They were practical, as mice were a problem in many homes and could not gnaw tin. Value: $35-$50

Medicine bottles announce cures for just about anything. Bottles keep turning up with original labels.

Color printing was made possible about 1870. Artists were employed to create pictures, which would help sell a product. Value: $450

There is great interest in old movie posters. Those featuring the most famous names often command the highest prices.

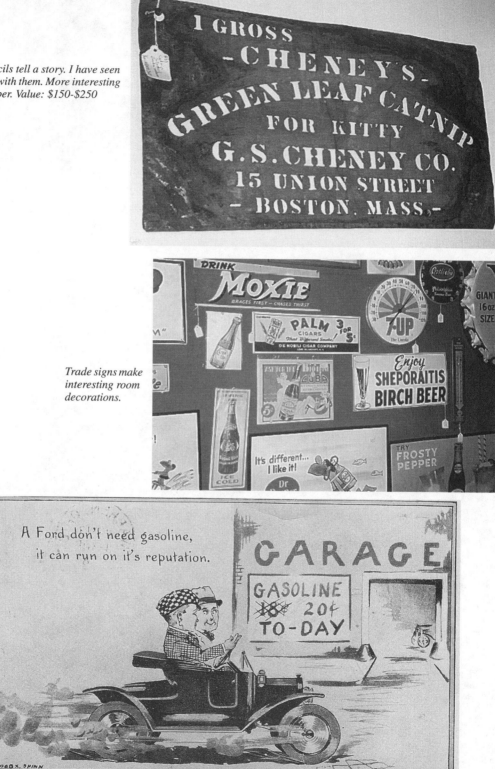

Copper stencils tell a story. I have seen a wall filled with them. More interesting than wallpaper. Value: $150-$250

Trade signs make interesting room decorations.

There are many postcards to collect. This is a reminder of what gasoline once cost. Value: $10

Another type of music box was this, with a gentleman who whistles while leaning on a lamppost.

The Conquistadores left many stirrups in South and Central America. Most are brass. This example in carved wood is in excellent condition. Bought in Peru during 1992 for $500.

Wooden wheel bicycles made their appearance at about the middle of the 19th century. This, with two wheels at the rear offered great stability. Value: $2,500-$3,000

Carnival item, "Strength Tester," with Uncle Sam. Value: $800

Most early gatepost eagles are hand carved from wood. One will find excellent examples in folk carving. Value: $1,800-$2,200

Wooden flag. One sold in 2000 for nearly $7,000. A prime example of folk art.

Rogers statuary, John Alden and Priscilla, marked, 22-1/2" h x 16" w.

Granite utensil rack, 5 pieces, c. 1910.

Pairpoint swan paperweight.

"Moxie" advertising ashtray supported by figure of man.

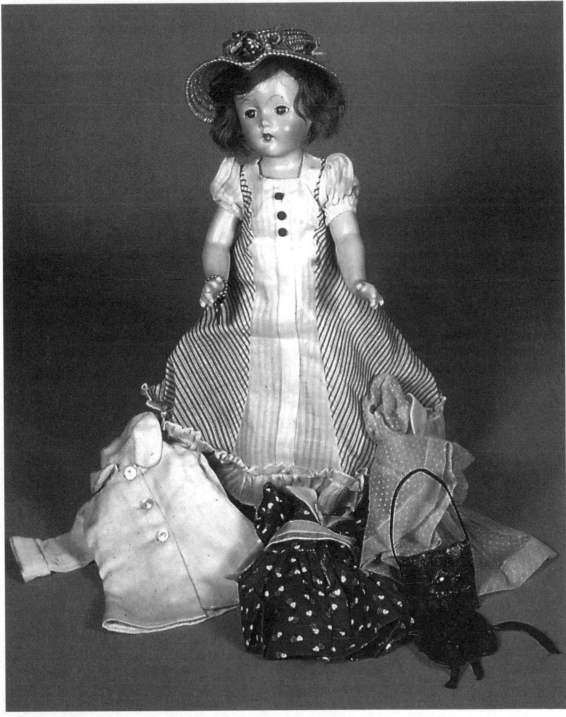

Effanbee "Suzanne" doll with bracelet and four outfits in case.

Early American wood box made in Philadelphia, Pennsylvania, paper cover to simulate leather.

Engine and two passenger cars, c. 1915, Ives RR Line.

Kelva cigar humidor, floral motif.

Woodenware wringer, patented June 3, 1870.

Coffee mill, Imperial #1 Mill,"
patented June 5, 1894.

BIBLIOGRAPHY

Furniture

Beckerdite, Luke. *American Furniture.* University Press of New England.

Boger, Louise Ade. *The Complete Guide to Furniture Styles.* Scribner's.

Butler, Joseph T. *Field Guide to American Antique Furniture.* New York: Facts on File, 1985.

Jacques & Hay, *19th Century Toronto Furniture Makers.* Boston Mills Press.

Jobe, Brock. *Portsmouth Furniture.* University Press of New England.

Kaye, Myra. *Fake, Fraud, or Genuine? Identifying Authentic American Antique Furniture.* Boston: Little, Brown, and Company, 1987.

Montgomery, Charles F. *American Furniture: The Federal Period.* New York: Viking Press, 1966.

Naeve, Milo, N. *Identifying American Furniture: A Pictorial Guide to Styles and Terms, Colonial to Contemporary.* Nashville, TN: American Association for State and Local History, 1989.

Rubira, Jose Claret. *Encyclopedia of English Furniture Designs.* Sterling Publishing.

Santore, Charles. *The Windsor Style in America.* 2 vols. Philadelphia, PA: Running Press: 1981.

Smith, Nancy A. *Old Furniture: Understanding The Craftsman's Art.* Boston: Dover, 1992.

------------. *Furniture of the Depression Era: Furniture & Accessories of the 1920s, 1930s, and 1940s.* Paducah, KY: Collector Books, 1987.

Ward, Gerald W.R. *American Case Furniture.* New Haven, CT: Yale University Art Gallery, 1988.

Watson, Aldren. *Country Furniture.* Crowell.

Glass

Barlow, Ray, and Joan Kaiser. *The Glass Industry in Sandwich. 4 Vols.* PO Box 1180, Sandwich, MA 02563: Barlow-Kaiser Publishing Co., 1987.

Boggess, Bill and Louise. *American Brilliant Cut Glass.* New York: Crown.

Florence, Gene. *The Collector's Encyclopedia of Depression Glass. 10th ed.* Paducah, KY: Collector Books, 1992.

Heacock, William. T*he Encyclopedia of Victorian Colored Pattern Glass. 9 vols.* Marietta, OH: Antique Publications.

Hollister, Paul. *The Encyclopedia of Glass Paperweights.* Paperweight Press, 1969.

Innes, Lowell. *Pittsburgh Glass, 1797-1891.* Houghton Mifflin Co., 1976.

King, Thomas B. *Glass in Canada.* Erin Ontario, Canada: Boston Mills Press.

Lee, Ruth Webb. *Victorian Glass.* Charles Tuttle Co.

Luckey, Carl F., and Mary Burris. *Depression Era Glassware, Identification & Value Guide. 2nd ed.* Florence, AL: Books Americana, 1986.

McKearin, George and Helen. *American Glass.* Crown. 1975.

Thuro, Catherine M.V. *Oil Lamps 3: Victorian Kerosene Lighting, 1860-1900.* Collector Books.

Wilson, Kenneth M. *New England Glass & Glassmaking.* Crowell

Ceramics

Arman, David and Linda. *Historical Staffordshire: An Illustrated Checklist*. Canville, VA: Arman Enterprises, Inc., 1977.

Barber, Edwin Atlee. *Marks of American Potters*. Southampton, NY: Cracker Barrel Press.

Chaffers, William. *Marks and Monograms on European and Oriental Pottery and Porcelain. 14th ed.* Los Angeles, CA: Borden Publishing Co.

Evans, Paul. *Art Pottery of the United States. 2nd ed.* New York: Feingold & Lewis, 1987.

Gates, William C., Jr., and Dana Omerod. "The East Liverpool, Ohio, Pottery District." *Historical Archaeology* (The Society for Historical Archaeology) 16 (1982) nos. 1-3.

Gaston, Mary Frank. *Haviland: Collectables & Objects of Art*. Paducah, KY: Collector Books, 1984.

Hamer, Frank. *The Potter's Dictionary of Materials & Techniques*. Watson Guptil Publications.

Kovel, Ralph and Terry. *Kovel's New Dictionary of Marks*. New York: Crown, 1986.

----------. *Kovel's Guide to American Art Pottery*. New York: Crown, 1974.

Oates, Joan Collett. *Phoenix Bird Chinaware. 4 vols*. Published by author, 1984.

Van Patten, Joan F. *The Collector's Encyclopedia of Nippon Porcelain. Collector Books Series, nos. 1-3*. Paducah, KY: Collector Books.

Williams, Petra, and Marguerite R. Weber. *Staffordshire, Romantic Transfer Patterns. 2 vols*. Jeffersontown, KY: Fountain House East.

Metalwork

Silver

Belden, Louise Conwoy. *Marks of American Silversmiths*. Charlottesville, VA: University of Virginia Press, 1980.

Bradbury, Frederick. *History of Old Sheffield Plate*. Sheffield, England: J.W. Northland Ltd., 1968.

Fallon, John P. *Marks of London Goldsmiths & Silversmiths, c. 1697-1837*. Charles Tuttle Co., 1988.

Forbes, Dr. H.A. Crosby, Johns Devereux Kernan, and Ruth S. Wilkins. *Chinese Export Silver*, Salem, MA: Peabody Museum of Salem.

Kovel, Ralph and Terry. *American Silver, Pewter & Silverplate*. New York: Crown, 1974.

McClinton, Katharine Morrison. *Collecting American 19th Century Silver*. Scribner's.

Rainwater, Dorothy. *Encyclopedia of American Silver Manufacturers. 3rd ed.* West Chester, PA: Schiffer Publishing, 1986.

Wyler, Seymour B. *The Book of Old Silver: English, American, Foreign*. Crown, 1937.

Pewter

Cotterell, Howard. *Olde Pewter, Its Makers & Marks*. Charles E. Tuttle, Co.

Jacobs, Carl. *Guide to American Pewter*. McBride Co., 1957.

Kerfoot, J.B. *American Pewter*. Bonzana, 1924.

Laughlin, Ledlie. *Pewter in America*. Barre, MA: Barre Publishers.

Montgomery, Charles F. *A History of American Pewter*. Weathervane Books.

Decorative Art

Ehrmann, *Art Price Annual.* ADEC.
Falk, Peter Hastings. *Dictionary of Signatures and Monograms of American Artists.* Sound View Press.
Fielding, Mantel. *Dictionary of American Painters, Sculptors and Engravers.*
Hislop, Duncan. *Art Sales Index.* Surrey England.
Howat, John K. *The Hudson River and Its Painters.* Apollo.
Johnson J., and A Greutzner. *Dictionary of British Artists, 1880-1940: An Antique Collector's Club Research Project Listing 41,000 Artists.* Antique Collector's Club, 1976.
McKittrick, Rosemary and Michael. *McKittrick's Art Price Guide.* Dealers Choice, 1990.
Theran, Susan, *Fine Art, Identification and Price Guide.* Avon Books.
---------. *The Official Price Guide to Fine Art. 1st ed.* New York: House of Collectibles, 1987.

Textiles

Dolan, Maryanne. *Vintage Clothing, 1880 to 1960: Identification and Value Guide. 2nd ed.* Florence, AL: Books Americana, 1987.

Collectibles

Barlow, Ronald S. *The Antique Tool Collector's Guide to Value. 3rd ed.* Windmill Publishing Co., 1991.
Cunningham, Jo. *The Collector's Encyclopedia of American Dinnerware.* Paducah, KY: Collector Books, 1982, revised 1992.
Docks, L.R. *American Premium Record Guide: Identification and Value Guide 1915-1965, 78s, 45s and LPs. 6th ed.* Krause Publications, 2001.
Foulke, Jan. *10th Blue Book of Dolls & Values.* Cumberland, MD: Hobby House Press, Inc., 1991.
Franklin, Linda Campbell. *Identification and Value Guide: 300 Years of Kitchen Collectibles. 3rd ed.* Krause Publications, 1997.
Hake, Ted, and Russ King. *Price Guide to Collectible Pin-Back Buttons, 1896-1986.* Hake's Americana & Collectible Press, 1986.
Horsham, Michael. *The Art of the Shakers.* The Apple Press, 1989.
Klug, Ray. *Antique Advertising Encyclopedia. 2 vols.* West Chester, PA: Schiffer Publishing, Ltd., 1978.
Kovel, Ralph and Terry. *The Kovel's Bottle Price List, 8th ed.* New York: Crown Publishing, Inc., 1987.
Lemke, Bob and Dan Albaugh. *Sports Collectors Digest Baseball Card Price Guide. 2nd ed.* Krause Publications, 1988.
O'Brien, Richard. *Collecting Toys: A Collectors Identification and Value Guide. 5th ed.* New York: House of Collectibles, 1990.
Overstreet, Robert M. *The Overstreet Comic Book Price Guide, 22nd ed.* New York: Avon Books, 1992.
Sargent, Jim. *Sargent's American Premium Guide to Pocket Knives.* Charles E. Tuttle Co.
Schiffer, Peter, Nancy, and Herbert. *The Brass Book.* Exton, PA: Schiffer Publishing Ltd., 1978.
Schugart, Cooksey, and Tom Engle. *The Official Price Guide to Watches. 8th ed.* New York: House of Collections, 1988.
Sprigg, June and David Larkin. *Shaker Life, Work, and Art.* Stewart, Tabori, & Chang, 1987.

Book Publisher's Addresses

Krause Publications, 700 E. State St., Iola, WI 54990-0001
Dover Publications, 31 E. Second St., Minneola, NY 11501
Collector Books, PO Box 3009, Paducah, KY 42002-3009
Schiffer Publishing Co., Ltd, 1649 Morstein Road, West Chester, PA 19380
University Press of NE, 23 S. Main St., Hanover, NH 03755-2048
Windmill Publishing Co., 2147 Windmill View Road, El Cajon, CA 92020
Boston Mills Press, 132 Main St., Erin, Ontario, N0B 1T0

Metal still bank of antlered stag.

INDEX

PHOTO CREDIT

The following list of pages contains photos that are copyrighted by Krause Publications and may not be reproduced without prior consent. All other photos belong to the author, unless other credit is given next to the photo.

Page: 9, 12, 13, 14 (top right), 17, 49, 75, 77, 123, 137 (top left), 142, 152 (bottom left), 160, 178, 180 (bottom right), 184, 185, 190 (top left and right), 192, 193, 197, 200 (right), 201, 207, 213 (top left, right column), 218, 219, 220, 245, 247 (top left), 248, 266, 267, 268, 269 (top), 270, 271, 272, 273, 274, 284, 287, 307, 311, 312, 313, 314 (top right), 337, 338, 339, 340, 341, 345.

Cover:
All items on front cover, spine, and the textile photo on the back cover.

Expand Your Collectibles Knowledge Even Further

Assign Values To All Of Your Finds